"Creech's examination of the biblical, historica[l] of pastoral ministry adds a distinctly Baptist vo[ice] explores the *who* of pastoral ministry as well a[s] prophet, priest, and servant. Along the way, he addresses with care and skill an issue on which Baptists differ: the ordination of women as pastors. Creech's study will challenge readers to think through their philosophy of ministry, and the book deserves a place on any course syllabus used in preparing pastors for Christian ministry."

—**Adam Harwood**, Baptist Center for Theology & Ministry, New Orleans Baptist Theological Seminary

"New pastors need seasoned pastors who will walk alongside them as they navigate the contours of pastoral ministry. These experienced pastors provide vital mentoring in the classroom and in the congregation. Creech is just such a person. In this book, he unearths a treasure of Baptist theology and practice for those yearning to make sense of what it means to be a pastor. Creech highlights three pastoral tasks: preaching, pastoral care, and leadership. Each chapter demonstrates how these tasks are rooted in Scripture, how they have been rehearsed throughout history by Baptist pastors, and how we can reflect theologically about these tasks. By engaging the work of theologians like James McClendon and pastors like Martin Luther King Jr., Creech reminds us that the heritage Baptists inherit is as diverse as it is deep. Those longing for a biblical alternative to the 'pastor as CEO' model of pastoral work will find a refreshing vision, rooted in a rich heritage, for faithful pastoral ministry."

—**Emmanuel C. Roldan**, senior pastor, Primera Iglesia Bautista, Waco, Texas

"Creech has written a stellar text on Baptist theology. He writes as a Baptist pastor and professor who loves the tradition that formed him and who both affirms and thoughtfully stands apart from it. The book fills a huge void in Baptist literature and is written in a scholarly yet highly accessible manner. He grounds the work theologically, traces its development historically, and offers his own theological reflection as a loving critic. I commend this work to you."

—**Jim Herrington**, former executive director of Union Baptist Association, Houston, Texas; coach and consultant with The Leader's Journey

"Finally, we have a Baptist perspective to add to the pastoral theology guild. Creech brilliantly explores fundamental and perennial pastoral undertakings from his experience in Baptist life. Readers will be both informed and inspired by Creech's work. While proudly providing the reader a Baptist-shaped lens to peer into pastoral theology, those from other faith traditions who dare to read this book will not feel excluded. Creech invites adherents from all faith traditions to constructively critique, cultivate, and commend their way of thinking about and performing pastoral ministry."

—**Delvin Atchison**, senior pastor, Westside Baptist Church, Lewisville, Texas

PASTORAL THEOLOGY
in the BAPTIST TRADITION

PASTORAL THEOLOGY
in the BAPTIST TRADITION

DISTINCTIVES AND DIRECTIONS
FOR THE CONTEMPORARY CHURCH

R. ROBERT CREECH

Baker Academic
a division of Baker Publishing Group
Grand Rapids, Michigan

© 2021 by R. Robert Creech

Published by Baker Academic
a division of Baker Publishing Group
PO Box 6287, Grand Rapids, MI 49516-6287
www.bakeracademic.com

Printed in the United States of America

Library of Congress Cataloging-in-Publication Data
Names: Creech, R. Robert (Richard Robert), author.
Title: Pastoral theology in the Baptist tradition : distinctives and directions for the contemporary church / R. Robert Creech.
Description: Grand Rapids, MI : Baker Academic, a division of Baker Publishing Group, 2021. | Includes index.
Identifiers: LCCN 2021009316 | ISBN 9781540962584 (paperback) | ISBN 9781540964533 (casebound) | ISBN 9781493432639 (ebook)
Subjects: LCSH: Pastoral theology—Baptists.
Classification: LCC BV4011.3 .C7385 2021 | DDC 253/.36—dc23
LC record available at https://lccn.loc.gov/2021009316

Baker Publishing Group publications use paper produced from sustainable forestry practices and post-consumer waste whenever possible.

21 22 23 24 25 26 27   7 6 5 4 3 2 1

To my pastors:

Rev. Lee Roy Pearson
Glenn Rose Baptist Church
Houston, Texas

Rev. Jay B. Perkins
Hibbard Memorial Baptist Church
Houston, Texas

Dr. Daniel Vestal
Southcliff Baptist Church
Fort Worth, Texas

Rev. Hal Farnsworth
First Baptist Church
Groesbeck, Texas

Dr. Jerry Lemon
Garden Oaks Baptist Church
Houston, Texas

Dr. Mike Clements
First Baptist Church
Floresville, Texas

Rev. Josh Carney
University Baptist Church
Waco, Texas

Dr. Eric Howell
DaySpring Baptist Church
Waco, Texas

Rev. John Garland
San Antonio Mennonite Church
San Antonio, Texas

The Man Born to Farming

The grower of trees, the gardener, the man born to farming,
whose hands reach into the ground and sprout,
to him the soil is a divine drug. He enters into death
yearly, and comes back rejoicing. He has seen the light lie down
in the dung heap, and rise again in the corn.
His thought passes along the row ends like a mole.
What miraculous seed has he swallowed
that the unending sentence of his love flows out of his mouth
like a vine clinging in the sunlight, and like water
descending in the dark?

Wendell Berry

Contents

PART FOUR   Leadership: Pastor as Servant

Acknowledgments

All who consider themselves fully independent should write a book to divest themselves of that illusion. Ascribing a project like this to an author seems unwise when so many other hands and minds have shaped it. I am delighted to recognize those whose contributions to this work have made it possible for me to foolishly attach my name.

Baylor University's George W. Truett Seminary graciously granted me a study leave in the fall of 2020 to devote time to this project. I am thankful to Baylor University for approving and funding the sabbatical and to our seminary's dean, Todd Still, and associate dean, Dennis Tucker, for arranging to cover my responsibilities while I was away. I appreciate supportive colleagues who have been available for conversations and email exchanges to share their thinking. No matter which chapter I was working on, it seemed that one of the expert Baptist voices in the field was someone with an office down the hall. Their names often appear in the footnotes.

I am grateful for graduate assistants who helped me assemble research in the early days of the project: August Higgins (now PhD), Ryan McCoy, Nathan Gibbs, and David Jentzsch. Unseen assistants at Baylor University Libraries filled my online requests and put volumes in the mail or scanned needed articles, supplying my needs from a distance during a global pandemic. The university library system supports our faculty in a way that continues to impress me even after a dozen years.

Thanks to pastors Becky Jackson, Doug Jackson, and Grover Pinson for reading the manuscript in its draft form and offering suggestions and corrections. The editors and staff at Baker Academic have once more been immensely helpful. Robert Hosack offered direction and encouragement in refining the project. Julie Zahm and her staff's careful eyes shepherded the work to publication with their usual attention to accuracy and detail. I value their partnership in this endeavor.

I am indebted to the pastors in my life, to whom I have dedicated this volume, especially Rev. Lee Roy Pearson (1918–2017), who was my pastor for eighteen years as I grew up in Houston, Texas. When I sensed a call to ministry, his was the only example I knew. My memories of his generous and joyful ministry remain formative. I also owe a debt of gratitude to the people of the University Baptist Church in Houston, who in 1987 called an inexperienced thirty-four-year-old university professor to be their pastor and then spent twenty-two years teaching him what that means. These souls are in the background of every chapter of this book.

Finally, I offer profound gratitude to my wife, Melinda, who has shared the journey of pastoral ministry and academic life with me for almost fifty years. During the final six months of this project, she thoughtfully encouraged and protected my writing time as the deadline approached and took care of the fall garden on her own. To say that I owe her is an understatement. I completed final edits on the manuscript in Anchorage, Alaska, where Isaiah Bryan Amber, our fifth grandchild, entered our lives, supplying a blessing at the end of a year of global and national chaos.

Thanks to all who have been part of this venture.

Introduction

In 2017, I taught a pastoral ministry course at Baylor University's George W. Truett Theological Seminary. Our reading list included some excellent, standard pastoral theology works by Will Willimon, Thomas Oden, and Eugene Peterson. We were also reading Richard Lishner's autobiographical work on pastoral ministry, *Open Secrets*. Midway through the semester, Evelyn Ofong, one of the students, observed that the required reading list included two Methodist writers, a Presbyterian, and a Lutheran. Then she asked, "Where is the Baptist voice?" Given that Truett Seminary identifies itself as "an orthodox, evangelical school in the historic Baptist tradition," the question was appropriate. Where *was* the Baptist voice?

I responded somewhat apologetically, "There is none." I did not mean that I had somehow failed to include a Baptist pastoral theology in our reading list. I was confessing that, as far as I knew, such a definitive work in our tradition did not exist.[1]

She retorted, "Then why don't you write one?" Evelyn's question stayed with me, and eventually this project made its way into my research and writing plans.

I am offering a volume of Baptist pastoral theology—the biblical, historical, and theological "why" behind our practices as Baptist pastors. By focusing on a distinctively Baptist pastoral theology, I do not intend to be parochial. Instead, my approach recognizes that we produce our theology in a context. In the words of Baptist theologian James McClendon, theology requires "a

---

1. In the early twentieth century B. H. Carroll, pastor of the First Baptist Church in Waco, Texas, and founder of Southwestern Baptist Theological Seminary, wrote, "There is . . . no Baptist who has covered the entire field of Pastoral Theology." "The Twentieth-Century Pastor; or, Lectures on Pastoral Theology," *Southwestern Journal of Theology* 58, no. 2 (2016): 184. Carroll offered an outline of such a work, still emphasizing the practices of pastoral ministry more than a theological treatment. A hundred years later, Carroll's assessment remains accurate.

community of reference," of which, he argues, "baptists" are a distinctive type.[2] Just as we Baptists benefit from the theological reflection done in United Methodist, Presbyterian, or Lutheran communities, the work of Baptist theologians can contribute to communities beyond our own. That theological work will be done in our specific context and from our given perspective, however.

McClendon's systematic theology project first appeared near the end of the twentieth century as he responded to what he identified as the "poverty" of Baptist theology.[3] Through four hundred years of history, Baptists have not been as theologically fruitful as other tradition streams. He considered why this might be so.[4]

McClendon says that the lack of Baptist constructive theology may be partly because—in the earliest years of the movement on the Continent, in England, and in America—Baptist leaders' intellectual energies were directed toward survival. They wrote apologetic and polemical confessions and

2. McClendon uses a lowercase *b* for baptists to take in a broader group than those who call themselves "Baptists." He includes all churches or movements tracing their lineage to the Radical Reformation. Others refer to this community as the "Free Church" (e.g., Franklin H. Littell, *The Anabaptist View of the Church: A Study in the Origins of Sectarian Protestantism*, 2nd ed. [Boston: Starr King, 1958]) or the "Believers' Church" (e.g., Conference on the Concept of the Believers' Church, "The Concept of the Believers' Church: Addresses from the 1967 Louisville Conference" [Scottdale, PA: Herald Press, 1969]). Roland Bainton calls this group of churches "the Left Wing of the Reformation" in his article by the same name in *Journal of Religion* 21, no. 2 (April 1, 1941): 124–34. The earliest participants in this movement were labeled *Wiedertäufer*, or Anabaptists—the "rebaptizers." They considered themselves simply "brethren," or *Täufer* (i.e., "baptists"). McClendon says "baptist" could include Mennonites, Disciples of Christ, Churches of Christ, Adventists, Russian Evangelicals, African American Baptists (who sometimes use other names besides Baptist), the (Anderson, Indiana) Church of God, Southern Baptists, British Baptists, European Baptists, American Baptists, the Church of the Brethren, the Assemblies of God and other Pentecostal bodies, as well as Quakers, and many of the contemporary evangelical independent churches and Bible churches. Although these may not all share the full "baptist vision" that McClendon outlines, they will find connections with its core. See James William McClendon Jr., *Ethics*, vol. 1 of *Systematic Theology*, 2nd ed. (Nashville: Abingdon, 2002), 19, 33–34. I will employ the uppercase *B* when referring to Baptist groups, congregations, or denominations. If this book is helpful to Baptists, it should prove useful to those other "baptists" as well.

3. McClendon, *Ethics*, 20–26.

4. James Leo Garrett Jr. lists prominent Baptist systematic theologians through the twentieth century. His chronological list includes John Leadley Dagg, Augustus Hopkins Strong, Alvah Hovey, James Madison Pendleton, James Petigru Boyce, William Newton Clarke, Ezekiel Gilman Robinson, Edgar Young Mullins, Walter Rauschenbusch, John Alexis Edgren, Thomas Polhill Stafford, Walter Thomas Conner, Herschel Harold Hobbs, Frank Stagg, Ralph Edward Knudsen, William Wilson Stevens, Dallas M. Roark, Dale Moody, Bruce Milne, J. Morris Ashcraft, Millard J. Erickson, Gordon Lewis, Bruce Demarest, Wayne Grudem, Stanley A. Nelson, A. J. Conyers, James William McClendon, James Leo Garrett Jr., William Boyd Hunt, and Stanley Grenz. "Missions and Baptist Systematic Theologies," *Baptist History and Heritage* 35, no. 2 (2000): 67–71.

provided instructions for the faithful along with some historical narratives. The Calvinist-Arminian clash engaged Baptists as they experienced the tensions of the awakening movements of religious revival. This dispute set the theological agenda for a time. Later, in the nineteenth and twentieth centuries, much Baptist reflective writing attended to the issues about Scripture raised by the Enlightenment, historical criticism, and the modernist-fundamentalist debates. McClendon notes that other problems have attracted Baptists' attention over time, including "revolution, slavery, war, Enlightened thought, the hunger for salvation in alienated lives, global missionary openings and closings, economic hardship and excess accumulation, the roles of the sexes and of the family, and depth psychology."[5] He says, "For baptists in later centuries, these older matrices of faith and practice had no outcome in theological fruitfulness of the sort that others in comparable epochs of church history have enjoyed."[6]

McClendon concludes that "baptists in all their variety and disunity failed to see in their own heritage, their own way of using Scripture, their own communal practices, their own guiding vision, a resource for theology unlike the prevailing tendencies around them."[7] This distrust of their vision, he believes, left Baptists susceptible to ideologies left and right, spiritually impoverishing not only themselves but the wider Christian community as well. McClendon's three-volume *Systematic Theology* was his effort to identify a distinctively "baptist vision" and work with that to discover, describe, and transform Baptist theological convictions and practices systematically.[8]

What has been true of Baptist systematic theologians over four centuries has also been the case for our pastoral theologians. Historically, Baptists have been more active than theologically reflective. We have been doers rather than thinkers. Books and sermons by Baptist writers instructing their readers *how* to do pastoral work abound, but they have little to say about *why* Baptist pastors do what we do or *what we mean* when we act as pastors.

Our ministry takes place in a Baptist context and derives any distinctiveness that it may have from that reality. Over time a list of "Baptist distinctives" has developed, seeking to provide the distinguishing traits of those churches who trace their ancestry in any way back to the Radical Reformation.[9] The list

5. McClendon, *Ethics*, 19.
6. McClendon, *Ethics*, 25.
7. McClendon, *Ethics*, 26.
8. McClendon, *Ethics*, 23.
9. The precise connection between the emergence of English Baptists and their relationship with Dutch Anabaptism is unclear. Some Baptist historians, such as Franklin E. Littell (*The Anabaptist View of the Church* [see note 2 above]) and William R. Estep (*The Anabaptist Story*, 3rd ed. [Grand Rapids: Eerdmans, 1995]), argue for a more direct connection between John

generally includes such marks as biblicism, liberty, discipleship, community, and witness (or evangelism).[10] McClendon identifies a "baptist vision" that he believes comprehends these distinctives—a "governing vision that, once seen, will evidently require them all."[11]

The vision McClendon distills is essentially ecclesiological. It is "a shared awareness of the present Christian community as the primitive Christian community and the eschatological community."[12] He simplifies that vision as a "motto": "The church now is the primitive church and the church on judgment day." In other words, the liberty and obedience that the earliest followers of Jesus displayed is our liberty and obedience until the end of the ages. McClendon converts this vision into a principle of biblical hermeneutics he calls "this is that."[13] On the day of Pentecost, Peter declares "this" (the events occurring in Jerusalem) is "that" spoken of by the prophet Joel (2:16–21). Such a principle, "this is that," expresses the essential Baptist vision regarding the church and its life. Baptists understand ourselves as directly connected, through the Spirit and the Word, to the primitive church of Acts and the eschatological church at the end of the age. McClendon argues, "I claim that this understanding of the vision is sufficiently encompassing and sufficiently distinctive to enable us to interpret baptist practices by it; I claim that this sense of vision adequately incorporates the other four senses reviewed above

---

Smyth's party, the Waterlander Anabaptists, and what became the first Baptist congregation on English soil. Others, such as H. Leon McBeth, are more guarded in their conclusions. McBeth says, "Baptists emerged out of intense reform movements, shaped by such radical dissent as Puritanism, Separatism, and *possibly* Anabaptism." *The Baptist Heritage: Four Centuries of Baptist Witness* (Nashville: Broadman, 1987), 21 (emphasis mine). For a critical examination of the historical sources for the emergence of the Baptists and the relationship of the Smyth congregation to the Mennonites, see James Robert Coggins, *John Smyth's Congregation: English Separatism, Mennonite Influence and the Elect Nation*, Studies in Anabaptist and Mennonite History 32 (Scottdale, PA: Herald Press, 1991), 61–65.

10. Other proposed Baptist distinctives are the autonomy of the local church, the priesthood of the believer, soul competency of the believer, regenerate church membership, believer's baptism by immersion, and a free church in a free state. McClendon traces these to the core baptist vision he offers.

11. McClendon, *Ethics*, 27–28.

12. McClendon, *Ethics*, 30.

13. According to Richard N. Longenecker, this hermeneutical principle, known as *pesher* interpretation, was common in first-century Judaism, especially among the covenanters at Qumran. Jesus frequently employed this approach to Scripture. Longenecker says, "But while there are a number of instances recorded in the Gospels of Jesus' use of literalist and midrashic exegesis, his most characteristic use of Scripture is portrayed as being a *pesher* type of interpretation. The 'this is that' fulfillment motif, which is distinctive of *pesher* exegesis, repeatedly comes to the fore in the words of Jesus." *Biblical Exegesis in the Apostolic Period*, 2nd ed. (Grand Rapids: Eerdmans, 1999), 54. Longenecker demonstrates that same principle in the sermons in Acts and in the New Testament Epistles.

[i.e., liberty, discipleship, community, and witness (or evangelism)]; I claim, in sum, that the vision so understood is a necessary and sufficient organizing principle for a (baptist) theology."[14] His systematic theology project attempts to use that principle to define a baptist theology for the postmodern era.

This volume employs McClendon's "baptist vision" to "discover, describe, and transform" Baptist pastoral theological beliefs and practices. It attends to Baptist voices over the past four centuries as they speak their convictions regarding pastoral ministry. We will listen to sixteenth-century Anabaptists as well as twenty-first-century megachurch pastors. Both Baptist women and men have a place in this project, as do a racially and ethnically diverse array of Baptist pastors, past and present.[15] Both my inadequacies as an untrained historian and my limited exposure to the wider Baptist world will leave my choices open to criticism by scholars whose knowledge of the field is deeper or broader. I encourage those scholars to join the endeavor to articulate a Baptist pastoral theology with corrections or expansions.

"Pastoral theology" deserves to be defined. Derek Tidball, a former British Baptist pastor, describes it as "an elusive and complex discipline," with "no consensus on the essential nature" of the field.[16] Seward Hiltner offers a widely accepted definition of pastoral theology: "Pastoral theology is defined here as that branch or field of theological knowledge and inquiry that brings the shepherding perspective to bear upon all the operations and functions of the church and minister, and then draws conclusions of a theological order from reflection on these observations."[17] Tidball, however, critiques Hiltner's definition for being too functional, focused on what a pastor does. It attends too little to the theological foundations that support the role. He concludes,

14. McClendon, *Ethics*, 33.

15. Unfortunately, the available sources are mostly written by White European and American male pastors and theologians. Our story is broader than that, however. I have surely missed some potential additional sources that would have provided a greater diversity of perspective. One source that remains to be mined is the plethora of sermons available online, either in audio, video, or written form, from nonmajority voices. Additionally, other older Baptist voices, such as Alexander Maclaren's, could speak to the topic if someone were to scour their sermons preserved in various collections. Eileen Campbell-Reed is on target in observing, "It is time for disruption of scholarship as usual. It is time to move beyond studying, teaching, and writing about Baptists uncritically and beholden to privileged white narratives of male actors and big institutions. Southern Baptists need decentering, and Baptists in other locations and with other experiences need to be put at the center of our attentions and conversations about Baptist experience and identity." "New Intersections in Baptist Studies," *Perspectives in Religious Studies* 44, no. 3 (2017): 288.

16. Derek Tidball, *Skillful Shepherds: An Introduction to Pastoral Theology* (Grand Rapids: Ministry Resources Library, 1986), 18, 21.

17. Seward Hiltner, *Preface to Pastoral Theology*, The Ayer Lectures, 1954 (New York: Abingdon, 1958), 20.

"Pastoral theology, then, relates to the interface between theology and Christian doctrine on the one hand, and pastoral experience and care on the other. As such, it is found to be a discipline in tension. It is not theology in the abstract, but theology seen from the shepherding perspective. The shepherding perspective may well inform and question the theology, but more fundamentally the theology will inform and question the work of the shepherd and that relationship must not be reversed."[18]

In this work I understand a Baptist pastoral theology to be an attempt to describe the practice of pastoral ministry informed by the biblical, theological, and historical resources of the Baptist tradition. A Baptist pastoral theology arises from questions such as these: What does the Scripture teach about the subject? How have we Baptists formulated our teaching about the matter over the centuries? What practices have we engaged historically? How do our distinctive doctrines—such as the priesthood of all believers, the autonomy of the local congregation, or the separation of church and state—bear on our understanding of pastoral ministry?

Given the variety of methodologies theologians have used to approach the topic, it is inaccurate to say that we have no Baptist pastoral theologies. Some have treated pastoral theology as a subset of ecclesiology. As they have written about the nature of the church, they have necessarily reflected theologically on the meaning of pastoral ministry.[19] However, much of the literature Baptists have produced focuses on the practice of pastoral ministry and leadership, with a thin foundation biblically, historically, or theologically.[20] In

18. Tidball, *Skillful Shepherds*, 24.

19. Thomas Martin Lindsay, *The Church and the Ministry in the Early Centuries* (London: Hodder & Stoughton, 1903); Burnett Hillman Streeter, *The Primitive Church, Studied with Special Reference to the Origins of the Christian Ministry* (New York: Macmillan, 1929); Kenneth E. Kirk, *The Apostolic Ministry: Essays on the History and Doctrine of Episcopacy* (London: Hodder & Stoughton, 1946). Among Baptists who have taken this perspective, see Franklin M. Segler, *A Theology of Church and Ministry: The Christian Pastor; His Call, His Life, His Work in and through the Church* (Nashville: Broadman, 1960), and Stanley J. Grenz, *The Baptist Congregation: A Guide to Baptist Belief and Practice* (Valley Forge, PA: Judson, 1985).

20. For example, see Deron J. Biles, ed., *Pastoral Ministry: The Ministry of a Shepherd* (Nashville: B&H Academic, 2017); John R. Bisagno, *Pastor's Handbook*, rev. ed. (Nashville: B&H, 2011); Carroll, "Twentieth-Century Pastor" (see note 1 above); H. B. Charles Jr., *On Pastoring: A Short Guide to Living, Leading, and Ministering as a Pastor* (Chicago: Moody, 2016); W. A. Criswell, *Criswell Guidebook for Pastors* (Nashville: B&H, 2000); Brian Croft and H. B. Charles Jr., *The Pastor's Ministry: Biblical Priorities for Faithful Shepherds* (Grand Rapids: Zondervan, 2015); Mark Dever and Jonathan Leeman, eds., *Baptist Foundations: Church Government for an Anti-Institutional Age* (Nashville: B&H Academic, 2015); John W. Frye, *Jesus the Pastor: Leading Others in the Character and Power of Christ* (Grand Rapids: Zondervan, 2010); John Piper, *Brothers, We Are Not Professionals: A Plea to Pastors for Radical Ministry* (Nashville: B&H, 2013); Samuel DeWitt Proctor and Gardner C. Taylor, *We Have This Ministry: The Heart of the Pastor's Vocation* (Valley Forge, PA: Judson, 1996); Jim Savastio and Brian Croft, *The*

the mid-twentieth century Wayne E. Oates and Franklin M. Segler connected pastoral theology more directly to the pastoral care and counseling movement, bringing theology into conversation with the social sciences.[21] Tidball offered a significant work on pastoral theology in 1986, arguing for the analogy of pastor as shepherd as a dominant biblical theme.[22] He also delved into the role of pastor historically, but not from a specifically Baptist perspective. Tidball later explored the implications for pastoral ministry contained in each New Testament book.[23] In 2004, Erick Sawatzky assembled essays reflecting current Mennonite thinking about the nature of pastoral ministry.[24]

I intend this work to fill a gap in pastoral theology literature by grounding pastoral ministry firmly in Scripture and providing the testimony and thinking of Baptist pastors and theologians, including some of those just mentioned. I hope to contribute to the education and training of men and women who serve Baptist congregations, but I trust this work might enrich other faith communities as well. The volume is more descriptive than prescriptive, more biblical and historical than constructive. I have organized each chapter around three foci. First, I attend to the biblical foundation underlying the chapter's topic. Second, I call on voices from the Baptist tradition to take us down historical bypaths related to the theme. Third, I conclude the chapter with my own theological reflection on aspects of the subject, particularly as it connects to contemporary Baptist church life. Space remains for Baptist pastors to do the personal practical theological work of thinking through their own twenty-first-century context as they reflect on and learn to rely on their heritage. I offer questions following each chapter to engage readers in that reflective process. Responding to those questions in writing is one way to define one's personal expression of pastoral theology. Putting one's responses on the table for discussion with others in a classroom or study group could take that effort further.

The book comprises four parts: (1) Becoming a Pastor, (2) Proclamation: Pastor as Prophet; (3) Care: Pastor as Priest, and (4) Leadership: Pastor as

---

Pastor's Soul: The Call and Care of an Undershepherd (Welwyn Garden City, UK: EP Books, 2018); L. R. Scarborough, *My Conception of the Gospel Ministry* (Nashville: Sunday School Board of the Southern Baptist Convention, 1935); J. B. Tidwell, *Concerning Preachers: What All Preachers Should Know* (New York: Fleming H. Revell, 1937); Jim Vogel, ed., *The Pastor: A Guide for God's Faithful Servant* (Schaumburg, IL: Regular Baptist Press, 2013).

21. Wayne E. Oates, *The Christian Pastor*, rev. ed. (Philadelphia: Westminster, 1982); Segler, *Theology of Church and Ministry*.

22. Tidball, *Skillful Shepherds*.

23. Derek Tidball, *Ministry by the Book: New Testament Patterns for Pastoral Leadership* (Downers Grove, IL: IVP Academic, 2008).

24. Erick Sawatzky, *The Heart of the Matter: Pastoral Ministry in Anabaptist Perspective* (Telford, PA: Cascadia, 2004).

Servant. Each part includes chapters exploring aspects of Baptist pastoral practices theologically, listening to Baptist voices over the centuries in biographies, confessions of faith, sermons, and books. My purpose is to examine these resources in light of McClendon's Baptist vision and to discover, describe, and transform our convictions about pastoral ministry in our *Baptist* community of reference.

As a way of acknowledging that I am working within the Baptist pastoral community, I will not refrain from first-person pronouns and my own testimony. I will say "we" when referring to Baptists or to Baptist pastors. This is the community of faith in which I have been formed and to which I belong. I have learned from pastors and scholars whose faith tradition differs from mine, and I will continue to do so. In this project, however, I am unashamedly seeking to discover, describe, and transform the Baptist tradition that has been a spiritual and theological home for me. I am fully aware that no Baptist speaks for all Baptists. This is an effort to describe *a* Baptist pastoral theology, not *the* Baptist pastoral theology.

Many of those I depend on to help tell the story of the development of Baptist pastoral theology lived and worked when people commonly used masculine language to speak of both humanity and God. Also, most of them lived in contexts where only men served as pastors. Consequently, when quoting them I will necessarily be bound by their expressions. When I offer my views, I use language without such gender bias; but when citing our Baptist ancestors, I refrain from correcting them on the basis of their descendants' standards.

PART ONE

BECOMING
A PASTOR

1

Pastoral Identity

The Shepherd and the Flock

Shepherds are they called. Oh, keep and feed the lambs of Christ; leave them not nor disdain them.

—Menno Simons, *The Complete Writings of Menno Simons*

I am the Good Shepherd. The Good Shepherd puts the sheep before himself, sacrifices himself if necessary. A hired man is not a real shepherd.

—Jesus (John 10:11–12 Message)

Mike and I played golf as a twosome one spring morning when a young man asked to join us. We welcomed him, and Mike introduced himself. Then, gesturing toward me, he said, "And this is Robert. He's my pastor." Later I asked him, "If I were your barber, would you have said, 'This is Robert. He's my barber'?" Mike looked puzzled. I learned something about pastoral identity that morning—how I understand myself in the role of pastor and how members of the congregation think about that. I do not just *do* the work of a pastor. I *am* a pastor.

Church members have introduced me as "our pastor" in hospital rooms, in community meetings, and at funerals, weddings, and family gatherings. Never once have they presented me as "our elder" or "our overseer" or "our bishop," although in the New Testament these words more frequently describe church leaders. "Pastor" is different. The term connotes a relationship marked by compassion, care, and concern. The possessive pronoun "my" fits with it, as it does with "my friend," "my father," "my mother," "my daughter," or "my son." These expressions do not indicate ownership but mutuality.

Forming a pastoral identity involves coming to terms with the unique relationship between the pastor and the congregation. What does it mean to be a pastor? What demands and expectations appropriately accompany that office? This chapter explores the biblical terms and guiding metaphors that have shaped a Baptist understanding of this role. We will survey how Baptists have formulated our thinking about church leadership in our confessions of faith over the past four centuries. And finally, we will consider the practical aspects of pastoral identity by reflecting theologically on what it means to be called "pastor."

Biblical Foundations

Titles—Elders, Bishops, and Pastors

The "this is that" principle discussed in the introduction, which has guided Baptists in reading Scripture, informs our thinking about pastoral identity. We look to Scripture to discover examples and models of what it means to "be a pastor." Unfortunately, explicit examples of pastoral ministry are few, and biblical terminology can sometimes be confusing. The noun "pastor" (*poimēn*) as a reference to a church leader occurs only once in the New Testament (Eph. 4:11). More frequently, the church leader is an "elder" (*presbyteros*) or "overseer" (*episkopos*),[1] titles that the early church used interchangeably.

In Acts 20:28, Paul addressed the Ephesian "elders" (*presbyterous*, v. 17), encouraging them to "shepherd" (*poimainein*) the "flock" over which the Holy Spirit had made them "overseers" (*episkopous*). Paul uses these concepts synonymously. *Elders* are the ones who *shepherd* (pastor) and *oversee* the flock. The Holy Spirit has given them this task.

A similar pattern occurs in 1 Peter 5. Peter addresses the "elders" (*presbyterous*) as a "fellow elder" (*sympresbyteros*) and urges them to "shepherd"

---

1. "Elders" as Christian leaders appears in Acts 11:30; 14:23; 15:2, 4, 6, 22, 23; 16:4; 20:17; 21:18; 1 Tim. 5:17, 19; Titus 1:5; James 5:14; 1 Pet. 5:1, 5; 2 John 1; 3 John 1. Additionally, 1 Tim. 4:4 refers to a "council of elders" (*presbyteriou*). "Overseers" appears in Acts 20:28; Phil. 1:1; 1 Tim. 3:2, 7. Translators sometimes use the word "bishop" to render *episkopos* since it derives from an Old English word *biscop* or *bisceop*, meaning "to oversee."

(*poimanate*) the "flock" (*poimnion*) of God, "overseeing" (*episkopountes*) with integrity and modeling the Christ-life for the "flock" (*poimniou*) (5:1–3). In 5:4 he calls Jesus the "chief shepherd" (*archipoimenos*). Earlier, Peter describes Christ as the "shepherd [*poimena*] and guardian [or overseer, *episcopon*] of our souls" (2:25). As in Paul's address to the Ephesian elders, Peter encourages the *elders* in his congregations to *serve as shepherds* (pastors) and to *oversee* the flock.

The conversation between Peter and the resurrected Jesus that John narrates in his Gospel is echoed in 1 Peter 5. Peter had denied Jesus three times (John 18:15–27) as the Lord himself had predicted (13:36–38). Now, restoring Peter to service, Jesus asks Peter three times about his love for him (21:15, 16, 17). Three times Peter affirms his love for Jesus, and three times Jesus gives him a practical way to demonstrate that love: "feed my lambs [*arnia*]" (v. 15), "tend [*poimaine*] my sheep [*probata*]" (v. 16), and "feed my sheep [*probata*]" (v. 17). Jesus gave a *pastoral* (shepherding) commission to an *apostle* who will later describe himself as an *elder* (1 Pet. 5:1).

Additionally, in his Letter to Titus, Paul tells his coworker in Crete to appoint "elders" (*presbyterous*) in every town (1:5–6). Paul then changes terms, referring to these leaders as "bishops" or "overseers" (*episkopoi*) in verse 7 as he continues to delineate their qualifications. The apostle uses the terms "elder" and "overseer" interchangeably in this passage.

These key terms—elder, overseer, and pastor—have formed the basis for a Baptist understanding of the pastoral role. Yet Baptists have, for the most part, settled on the title "pastor" to define the office of congregational leadership.[2]

Models—Prophets, Priests, Apostles, and Scribes

Besides the titles themselves, Baptists have indirectly used a variety of New Testament models to understand pastoral ministry, such as the acts and teachings of Jesus, the stories of the Twelve, the seven leaders selected in Acts 6, and the lives of Paul and his associates. We have often looked to these resources for direction and examples to understand church leadership. These models do not provide specific instructions for pastors or definitions of the pastoral role, but they nevertheless offer guidance for the practice of leadership in the kingdom of God. Baptists regularly turn to such passages to clarify the role of congregational leadership that our pastors occupy.

2. As early as the Anabaptist Schleitheim Confession of 1527, church leaders are called "shepherds" (*Hirten*). William L. Lumpkin, *Baptist Confessions of Faith*, ed. Bill J. Leonard, 2nd rev. ed. (Valley Forge, PA: Judson, 2011), 27.

Other biblical figures have helped form a Baptist understanding of pastoral ministry as well. The call of the Old Testament prophets, the compassion of the Old Testament priests, and the commitment of the New Testament apostles all resonate with our thinking about who our pastors are and what God has called them to do. The critical thing to Baptists has been the line connecting God's people in the Old Testament, the earliest church, and contemporary congregational life.

The hermeneutical move from the contemporary pastor to the images of prophets, priests, apostles, elders, overseers, and shepherds of God's flock is classically Baptist: "this is that." The interpretive principle that leads Baptists to affirm that the church today *is* the church of the apostles and the eschaton connects the leaders of the early Christian movement, their ancestors in ancient Israel, and the church of every age. Baptist pastors have opened the Scripture and have seen themselves and their work reflected in the various leaders of God's people that appear in the sacred narrative. This is that.

The Old Testament *prophets* were not *pastors*, yet their faithfulness to their calling, their bold proclamation, and their willingness to offer sacrificial obedience to God have shaped pastoral identity among Baptists through the years. Because God has called pastors to proclaim the Word of God, the Old Testament prophets have shaped a Baptist understanding of the task of preaching.

Ancient priests stood faithfully between Yahweh and Israel, interceding for them, offering them grace, and leading them in worship. Although Baptists have affirmed that all believers are priests, this priestly work of prayer and care has formed our understanding of pastoral work. Pastoral work was the responsibility of Israel's priests, just as it is for those who serve Baptist congregations (Ezek. 34).

Additionally, the Jewish role of scribe, showing up first in the Old Testament in Ezra's ministry, has contributed to our thinking. The scribe's careful study and exposition of Scripture parallels the pastoral work of research and teaching that is part of most Baptist pastors' weekly activity. Jesus referred to the "scribe . . . trained for the kingdom of heaven" who can bring out of his treasure both old and new truth (Matt. 13:52).[3] This is what we strive to become.

Peter, James, and John play leading roles in Luke's account of the earliest church in Acts. Luke never refers to them as *pastors*. They are *apostles*. Yet their ministry in the Jerusalem community gestures toward pastoral leadership. Paul, who calls himself an *apostle*, not a *pastor*, has frequently provided a

---

3. Derek Tidball describes the role of scribe as a model for ministry in *Ministry by the Book: New Testament Patterns for Pastoral Leadership* (Downers Grove, IL: IVP Academic, 2008), 18–37.

model for interpreting the pastoral role. His epistles describe his ministry and his relationship to his churches, which have served as paradigms for Baptist pastors over the past four hundred years.

Qualifications and Accountability

Despite a lack of biblical specificity about the role, Baptists persist in relying on Scripture for direction and understanding of pastoral ministry. The New Testament provides no clear examples of what pastors do, leaving us to infer pastoral roles from the prophets, priests, scribes, and apostles. However, the New Testament does offer guidance about the character that qualifies one to occupy the position of pastor. Consequently, the effort to ground the pastor's work biblically carries profound ethical implications for Baptist pastoral identity. The role requires both character and skill (1 Tim. 3:1–7; Titus 1:5–9). To lead God's people is to be accountable as stewards (1 Cor. 3:5–9; 4:1–5). To teach God's people is to adhere to a higher standard of behavior (James 3:1). Although Baptist pastors have sometimes failed to live up to these demands, churches continue to appeal to these standards as benchmarks for leadership qualifications and responsibility.

Shepherd Imagery

The most powerful biblical influence shaping our understanding of Baptist ministry is the metaphor of sheep and shepherd.[4] Shepherd imagery prominently appears in the life of Jesus, the Good Shepherd (John 10:11), the Chief Shepherd (1 Pet. 5:4), "the great shepherd of the sheep" (Heb. 13:20). Both Peter and Paul instruct leaders to tend the flock of God (Acts 20:28; 1 Pet. 5:1–2). Shepherd imagery is especially important for understanding pastoral work because Baptists have largely settled on the word "pastor" or "shepherd" to designate our congregational leaders.

This shepherd-sheep imagery appears in the Old Testament, where Yahweh is the Good Shepherd (Ps. 23; Ezek. 34:11–31) and Israel is God's flock (Ps. 100; Ezek. 34:30–31).[5] False prophets and unfaithful priests are wicked shepherds

4. In a how-to approach to pastoral ministry, Deron J. Biles assembled a series of essays on pastoral ministry that thoroughly explore and apply the shepherd imagery; see *Pastoral Ministry: The Ministry of a Shepherd* (Nashville: B&H Academic, 2017). Although Derek Tidball laments that shepherd imagery is outdated (I do not fully agree), he employs that metaphor throughout his introduction to pastoral theology, *Skillful Shepherds: An Introduction to Pastoral Theology* (Grand Rapids: Ministry Resources Library, 1986), 14–15.

5. Blaine McCormick examines Ps. 23 as a model for organizational leadership, drawing implications from Yahweh's relationship with the people of Israel; see *Shepherd Leadership: Wisdom for Leaders from Psalm 23* (San Francisco: Jossey-Bass, 2003).

who destroy the flock and face Yahweh's just judgment (Ezek. 34:1–10; cf. John 10:1, 5, 8, 10, 12–13). Although these shepherds have failed, Yahweh promises to send a shepherd like David to care for the flock (Ezek. 34:23–37). The accusations made against these wicked shepherds help form a description of the work of faithful shepherds. God calls the faithful shepherds to do for Israel what the wicked have failed to do.

The pastoral/shepherding tasks are feeding (Ezek. 34:2; John 21:15, 17), caring (Ezek. 34:4–6; John 21:16), and leading (Ps. 23:2; Ezek. 34:5–6, 11–16). Those who take on these tasks in the congregation are the pastors/shepherds of God's flock (1 Pet. 5:1–2). Although Baptists have sometimes referred to their leaders by using the title "elder" or "bishop," "pastor" is the title most frequently chosen. That choice may be the result of theological intuition rather than a response to a biblical mandate. Regardless, the "this" of Baptist pastoral ministry connects with the "that" of the biblical shepherd imagery.

The shepherd-flock imagery is inherently relational. It implies a relationship intended ultimately for the flock's well-being, not for the shepherd's benefit. Those who use their position for themselves at the flock's expense are the false shepherds whom Ezekiel castigated (Ezek. 34:1–6). Jesus also warned of "hirelings" who were not true shepherds and of thieves who come to kill and destroy the flock (John 10:1, 5, 8, 10, 12–13). Paul alerted leaders in Ephesus to the "savage wolves" that would eventually come to ravage the sheep (Acts 20:29; cf. Matt. 7:15). The shepherd's role is to protect the flock from such assaults, even if it calls for sacrifice (John 10:11).

Baptists' understanding of ecclesiology struggles to clearly describe the relationship between the pastor and the congregation. Baptists' affirmation of the priesthood of all believers sometimes clashes with our concept of a pastor/shepherd's role. If we are all priests, then what is the significance of the pastor? We will take up this paradox when we examine the beliefs and practices that Baptists hold around ordination in chapter 3, the question of pastoral authority in chapter 10, and the doctrine of the laity in chapter 11. For Baptists, "pastor" may better serve in that tension than "elder" or "overseer," given its focus on caring, feeding, and leading for the sake of the flock. Authority is not a concept we associate with the image of a shepherd.

Other traditions have focused on alternative terms for their leaders—ministers, clergy, elders, apostles, bishops, or priests. Although Baptists might at times speak of our leaders as ministers or clergy, we have, as noted, found that the term "pastor" best identifies and defines those who stand in our pulpits, sit with us in counsel, bow with us in prayer, enter our hospital rooms, guide us through crises, and dream with us about a future together.[6]

Historical Bypaths

As the Baptist movement emerged in the sixteenth century and congregations formed, practical questions arose about how these churches would function. Who would be their leaders? What responsibilities and authority would they have? What would they be called? Who would choose them? What qualifications would be required? Responding to their essential vision, they naturally looked to the church in the New Testament to guide them in these matters. For Baptists, the "this" of the church in the sixteenth century and beyond must be the "that" of the Gospels, Acts, and the Epistles.

Early Anabaptists Confess Their Faith

Committed to forming a church based on Scripture, Baptists have identified our leaders with biblical titles from the earliest days of the Radical Reformation, and we have most frequently opted for the title "pastor." Even when other titles appear in confessions of faith, Baptists often equate them with "pastor" or interpret them in terms of the shepherd-sheep metaphor. With a few exceptions, this has remained true across time and cultures.

We Baptists have consistently shied away from "creeds" as authoritative documents demanding one's affirmation and loyalty. Some have even employed the naive motto "No creed but the Bible," as if we encounter the Scripture unmediated by assumptions, traditions, or interpretations in the absence of a creed. But Baptists have not been reticent about publishing "confessions of faith," declaring to the world who we are.[7] Beginning with our earliest

6. The only church leadership title among Baptists that has vied with "pastor" is "preacher," especially in the American South. This title greatly constricts the role of pastor to a single domain of pastoral ministry, identifying the person by what they do, like the title "overseer." "Pastor," however, focuses on a relationship.

7. A somewhat simplistic distinction between a creed and a confession of faith is that a creed addresses faithful insiders. One must affirm the creedal statement in order to belong. A confession of faith, on the other hand, addresses outsiders, declaring to the world who we are and what we believe. One conflict that raged among Southern Baptists in the 1980s and 1990s was the increasingly creedal use of the Baptist Faith and Message (1963, 1998, 2000). The Preamble to the 2000 Baptist Faith and Message for the first time referred to Baptist confessions as "instruments of doctrinal accountability." Tom J. Nettles and L. Rush Bush reflect this change in perspective: "Baptist confessions do not have as their primary purpose the setting forth of 'Baptist' distinctives; their primary purpose is the setting forth of true doctrine. . . . They are expressions, declarations, or affirmations of the Christian faith as

Anabaptist ancestors, confessions of faith have helped Baptists define ourselves and differentiate ourselves from other movements. A brief survey of how Baptists have formulated views on church leadership in our confessions of faith will make clear our effort to connect Baptist practices ("this") with the story and experiences of the earliest church ("that").[8]

The *Eighteen Dissertations concerning the Entire Christian Life and of What It Consists* (printed pamphlet, 1524), written by Balthasar Hübmaier, pastor of Waldshut, is one of the earliest Baptist confessions of faith.[9] Hübmaier offered these propositions to the city and country clergy for debate at their pastoral conference. Whether the discussion ever took place is unclear, but Hübmaier later published the dissertations. He had not yet fully positioned himself as an Anabaptist, but his theses nevertheless represented perspectives that would characterize the Swiss Brethren movement.

Hübmaier, writing as Balthasar Friedberger (Friedberg was his hometown), refers to himself as "doctor and pastor at Waldshut."[10] He describes the work of "nourishing the Christian flock," and he writes of the work he shares with his fellow pastors: "We should nourish, not our bodies alone but also our souls, with food and drink and thus be more useful to our flocks and feed them the Word of God in peace and unity."[11] He explicitly uses these pastoral metaphors, allusions to the work of shepherds and their flocks, to identify the work he and his fellow priests were engaging.

In the eighth dissertation, Hübmaier affirms that each individual must come to faith on one's own, be baptized of one's own accord, and consult the Scriptures directly to determine whether one is "being properly nourished by his pastor."[12] The twelfth thesis refers to the preacher of the Word of God as "a true priest." The congregation is to support and protect those who teach "the Word of God in its purity."[13] Although he is writing to his fellow Roman Catholic clergy, Hübmaier's sense of identity is primarily pastoral, not priestly.

On February 24, 1527, members of the Swiss Brethren met in the little town of Schleitheim to address key issues they faced. A significant document emerged from that gathering: the Schleitheim Confession, seven articles

---

Baptists understand it." *Baptists and the Bible: The Baptist Doctrines of Biblical Inspiration and Religious Authority in Historical Perspective* (Chicago: Moody, 1980), 372.

8. This section relies heavily on the standard work on Baptist confessions of faith by William Lumpkin, *Baptist Confessions of Faith*, rev. and ed. by Bill Leonard (Valley Forge, PA: Judson, 2011).

9. Lumpkin, *Baptist Confessions of Faith*, 18–22.

10. Lumpkin, *Baptist Confessions of Faith*, 19.

11. Lumpkin, *Baptist Confessions of Faith*, 20.

12. Lumpkin, *Baptist Confessions of Faith*, 21.

13. Lumpkin, *Baptist Confessions of Faith*, 21.

defending the Swiss Brethren against the teachings of the "Spiritualist Anabaptists" in southern Germany.[14] These articles were akin to a confession of faith and ultimately achieved a role of authority among the Brethren.[15]

The fifth article, "Pastors [*Hirten*] in the Church,"[16] echoes biblical instructions in 1 Timothy 3 about selecting church leaders (*episkopoi*, "bishops" or "overseers"): "The pastor in the church of God shall, as Paul has prescribed, be one who out-and-out has a good report of those who are outside the faith."[17] The reference to Paul and the clear allusion to 1 Timothy 3:1–7 makes it clear that these early Anabaptists were equating the role of bishop or overseer with "pastor." Additionally, the article speaks to disciplining wayward "pastors" and draws on 1 Timothy 5:19–20, instructions offered about dealing with "elders" (*presbyteroi*) who sin: "But if a pastor should do something requiring discipline, he shall not be dealt with except [on the testimony of] two or three witnesses. And when they sin they shall be disciplined before all in order that the others may fear."[18] In this earliest confession, Anabaptist leaders equate the title "pastor" with "bishop" and "elder" and privilege it when addressing the role of church leaders or describing their responsibility.

The Schleitheim Confession also describes the role and responsibility of pastors in the parish: "His office shall be to read, to admonish and teach, to warn, to discipline, to ban in the church, to lead out in prayer for the advancement of all the brethren and sisters, to lift up the bread when it is to be broken, and in all things to see to the care of the body of Christ, in order that it may be built up and developed, and the mouth of the slanderer be stopped."[19] Already in 1527, pastors occupied an office of some sort within the Anabaptist congregations. These early fellowships were gathering for Bible study and prayer, and they depended on their pastors to provide leadership. They were practicing church discipline (the ban), and they authorized pastors to play a leading role in that process. The celebration of the Lord's Supper was in the hands of the pastor, as was the pastoral care of the body of Christ. Should a pastor be banished or martyred, the confession admonishes the congregation

---

14. Anabaptist Michael Sattler, a young leader of the conference, had a large influence in composing the articles. John C. Wenger and C. Arnold Snyder, "Schleitheim Confession," *Global Anabaptist Mennonite Encylopedia Online*, updated January 15, 2017, https://gameo.org/index.php?title=Schleitheim_Confession.

15. Lumpkin, *Baptist Confessions of Faith*, 22.

16. John H. Yoder translates this as "Shepherds in the Church." *The Schleitheim Confession* (Scottdale, PA: Herald Press, 1977).

17. Lumpkin, *Baptist Confessions of Faith*, 27–28.

18. Lumpkin, *Baptist Confessions of Faith*, 28.

19. Lumpkin, *Baptist Confessions of Faith*, 27–28.

to ordain another immediately, "so that God's little flock and people may not be destroyed."[20]

Another confession of 1527—Discipline of the Church, How a Christian Ought to Live, likely penned by Hans Schlaffer—focuses on the practicalities of discipleship in the Christian community.[21] The fifth article addresses the work of the ministry: "The elders [*Vorsteher*] and preachers," it states, "chosen from the brotherhood shall with zeal look after the needs of the poor, and with zeal in the Lord according to the command of the Lord extend what is needed for the sake of and instead of the brotherhood (Gal. 2; 2 Cor. 8, 9; Rom. 15; Acts 6)."[22] Note the different terminology ("elders" and "preachers") and the absence of any shepherd-flock imagery in this document.[23]

In 1580, Hans de Ries and Lubbert Gerrits drew up the Waterland Confession, a more detailed and complete statement of faith. John Smyth, the leader of the English Separatist congregation that eventually formed the first General Baptist Church in England, requested its republication, and a reprint appeared in 1610.[24] Articles 25–30 address issues of the church's ministry. Article 25 says Christ "has ordained an evangelical ministry." Those who serve in this ministry are responsible for teaching the divine Word, offering the holy sacraments, caring for the poor, exercising fraternal admonition, and administering the ban on the impenitent. This confession refers to congregational leaders as the "evangelical ministry," "ministers," "teachers," and "the teaching office." The words "bishop" and "elder" occur in the confession, but in context they seem to refer to people other than the ordained minister.[25] Neither the title "pastor" nor any specific shepherd imagery occurs in this document as a way of describing or defining the role of congregational leadership.

The Dordrecht Confession (1632) became the most influential of all Mennonite confessions.[26] Article 9 is devoted to "The Election, and Offices of Teachers, Deacons, and Deaconesses in the Church."[27] No specific title for min-

---

20. Lumpkin, *Baptist Confessions of Faith*, 28.

21. Lumpkin, *Baptist Confessions of Faith*, 31–36.

22. Lumpkin, *Baptist Confessions of Faith*, 34.

23. The Hutterite communities in Moravia were thriving collective farms. Lumpkin notes that "at the head of each *bruderhof* was a bishop or shepherd, elected for life, who kept in touch with business managers and ministers and, along with the elders, maintained oversight over the communities. Some ministers were appointed as apostles and sent out to preach and baptize." *Baptist Confessions of Faith*, 38.

24. Lumpkin, *Baptist Confessions of Faith*, 42–61. The language of the Waterland Confession is echoed in the short confession of 1610 issued by Thomas Helwys's party.

25. See the reference to bishops in article 26 and the reference to elders in article 28.

26. Lumpkin, *Baptist Confessions of Faith*, 61.

27. For the entire text of the Dordrecht Confession, see Lumpkin, *Baptist Confessions of Faith*, 61–74.

isters appears. The confession gives a comprehensive list of apostles, prophets, evangelists, pastors, and teachers, alluding to Ephesians 4:11. The document refers to Jesus as "the Great Shepherd" and the church as "his flock." These church leaders govern the church, feeding, watching over, and protecting the flock. The function of church leadership portrayed in this confession is essentially pastoral, imitating Jesus, the Great Shepherd.

Early English Baptists Confess Their Faith

Early English Separatist-Baptists drew up a confession in 1596 titled A True Confession. The seven Particular Baptist Churches of London used this as a model when they composed their first confession in 1644.[28] This confession describes the office of the ministry in article 19 as "Ministrie of Pastors, Teachers, Elders, Deacons, Helpers to the instruction, government, and service of his Church."

John Smyth's Short Confession of Faith in XX Articles of 1609 asserts in article 16, "That the ministers of the church are, not only bishops ('Episcopos'), to whom power is given of dispensing both the word and the sacraments, but also deacons, men and widows, who attend to the infirm of the poor and sick brethren."[29] An English confession (A Declaration of Faith of English People) issued in Amsterdam in 1611 employs the title "elder" to describe the office responsible to "feed the flock concerning their soules" (article 20).[30]

In 1644, Particular (Calvinist) Baptists in London composed the London Confession to distinguish themselves from both the General Baptists and the Anabaptists.[31] Lumpkin asserts that "perhaps no Confession of Faith has had so formative an influence on Baptist life as this one."[32] Article 36 affirms that "every Church has power given them to choose to themselves meet persons into the office of Pastors, Teachers, Elders, Deacons, being qualified according to the Word, as those which Christ has appointed in his Testament for the feeding, governing, serving, and building up of his Church, and that none other have power to impose them, either these or any other." In later editions of this confession, "Pastors" and "Teachers" are omitted. Even with the eventual omission of "Pastors," the language of article 37 calls on them

---

28. Lumpkin, *Baptist Confessions of Faith*, 75–91.

29. Lumpkin, *Baptist Confessions of Faith*, 95.

30. Lumpkin, *Baptist Confessions of Faith*, 112.

31. Particular Baptists represented a more Calvinistic theology, affirming that Christ died only for the elect (limited atonement). General Baptists, on the other hand, confessed that Christ died for all people.

32. Lumpkin, *Baptist Confessions of Faith*, 140.

to "carefully feed the flock of Christ committed to them," alluding to Acts 20:28 and 1 Peter 5:1–3.

In the Second London Confession (1677), the Particular Baptists revised their description of the church's ministry.[33] Chapter 26, paragraph 8, says that the church officers are "Bishops or Elders and Deacons." Bishops and elders are mentioned synonymously again in paragraph 9. The language then shifts. Paragraph 10 speaks of "the work of Pastors," and paragraph 11 equates bishops and pastors. Although these three titles are used interchangeably, Particular Baptists began to prioritize the title "elder."

The Standard Confession (1660) served as an essential confession among General Baptists (non-Calvinists).[34] Article 25 of this document equates "Elders" and "Pastors," "which God hath appointed to oversee, and feed his Church." As in the key biblical passages (Acts 20:28; 1 Pet. 5:1–3), this confession equates the terms "pastor," "elder," and "overseer." Following the Second London Confession of the Particular Baptists, the General Baptists produced a more comprehensive document in 1878 known as The Orthodox Creed.[35] Article 31 affirms that the officers in the church of Christ are "Bishops, or Messengers; and Elders, or Pastors; and Deacons, or Overseers of the poor," distinguishing the role of bishop and elder/pastor.[36]

American Baptists Confess Their Faith

The New Hampshire Confession (1833) became a touchstone for Baptists in America. Its language continues to appear in confessional statements well into the twenty-first century. The Baptist Convention of New Hampshire said of the "Gospel Church" that "its only proper officers are Bishops or Pastors, and Deacons, whose qualifications, claims, and duties are defined in the Epistles to Timothy and Titus."[37] The Articles of Faith of the National Baptist Convention follows this same language regarding congregational leadership. The language is similar in the Baptist Faith and Message (1925, 1963, 2000), a confession based on the New Hampshire Confession (1833) and used by many Southern Baptist Convention churches.

Regarding church officers, Southern Baptists have omitted the title "bishop," stating simply, "Its Scriptural officers are pastors and deacons" (article 6). Southern Baptists also added to the Baptist Faith and Message (2000) a qualify-

---

33. Lumpkin, *Baptist Confessions of Faith*, 216–97.
34. Lumpkin, *Baptist Confessions of Faith*, 202–15.
35. Lumpkin, *Baptist Confessions of Faith*, 298–348.
36. Lumpkin, *Baptist Confessions of Faith*, 328.
37. Lumpkin, *Baptist Confessions of Faith*, 382.

ing statement about the role of pastor: "While both men and women are gifted for service in the church, the office of pastor is limited to men as qualified by Scripture" (article 6). The term "elder" dropped out of use among Baptists in America beginning with the New Hampshire Confession but has found its way back in the late twentieth century with a revival of Reformed theology and the emergence of an elder-based polity.[38]

Baptists around the World Confess Their Faith

Swedish Baptists offered The Confession of Faith of the Swedish Baptist (1861), setting forth the church's offices as "shepherds or overseers, and deacons."[39] In 1879 and 1924, French Baptists published Confession of Faith and Ecclesiastical Principles of the Evangelical Association of French-Speaking Baptist Churches. The section "Ecclesiastical Principles" addresses the titles used for their clergy: "The Scriptures establish no distinction in rank or authority between bishops (overseers), as pastors or elders. The pastors or elders are particularly charged to watch over the teaching and spiritual health of the church."[40] The Baptist Union of Victoria, Australia, simply referred to their clergy as "ministers" in their 1888 confession.[41] Russian evangelicals, closely associated with the Baptist movement, composed a brief confession of faith in the early twentieth century, Religious Doctrine of the Evangelical Christians. This document was ratified in 1966 by the All Union Conference of Evangelical Christian-Baptists in Moscow.[42] Russian evangelicals affirmed that presbyters, "called in other parts of Holy Scripture—pastors, bishops," comprised the church's leadership.[43] A 1944 Confession of Faith enunciated

38. The role of elders in church governance has revived among Southern Baptists in America since the 1980s. Mark Dever suggests that the resurgence may have come in part from influence outside the denomination, such as the teachings and practices of John MacArthur, and in part from pastoral frustration with the cumbersome congregational polity of twentieth-century committee- and council-governed congregations; see Mark Dever, "Baptist Polity and Elders," *Journal for Baptist Theology and Ministry* 3, no. 1 (2005): 5–37; see also Benjamin L. Merkle, "The Scriptural Basis for Elders," in *Baptist Foundations: Church Government for an Anti-Institutional Age*, ed. Mark Dever and Jonathan Leeman (Nashville: B&H Academic, 2015), 243–52; Merkle, "The Biblical Role of Elders," in *Baptist Foundations: Church Government for an Anti-Institutional Age*, ed. Mark Dever and Jonathan Leeman (Nashville: B&H Academic, 2015), 271–90. This same period has seen a renewal of Calvinist theology among Southern Baptists; see Keith Hinson, "Calvinism Resurging among SBC's Young Elites," *Christianity Today* 41, no. 11 (October 6, 1997): 86–87.
    39. Lumpkin, *Baptist Confessions of Faith*, 426.
    40. Lumpkin, *Baptist Confessions of Faith*, 432.
    41. Lumpkin, *Baptist Confessions of Faith*, 436–37.
    42. Lumpkin, *Baptist Confessions of Faith*, 422–35.
    43. Lumpkin, *Baptist Confessions of Faith*, 445.

by the Alliance of Evangelical Free-church Congregations in Germany simply used a modified list of church offices taken from Ephesians 4:11: evangelists, pastors, teachers, preachers, elders, and deacons.[44]

Among Baptists in Asia, the Hong Kong Baptist Seminary, founded in 1950, affirmed in its Statement of Baptist Beliefs that "the church officers—pastors and deacons—have special responsibilities that are derived from the consent of the church, but they do not have a unique priestly status."[45] In South America, the Evangelical Baptist Convention of Peru has employed an unofficial statement of faith including the affirmation "the New Testament teaches that each church has two leadership positions: pastor and deacons."[46]

In Eastern Europe, the Baptist Union of Romania issued their Confession of Faith in 1951, which contains a lengthy statement concerning church leadership. In it they affirm, "We do not recognize hierarchical rankings. Those who are entrusted with certain duties are servants of the church and not masters to give orders."[47] The section on church leadership is titled "About the Servants of the Church." They confess that two orders of ministry existed in the New Testament to lead the spiritual and material affairs of the churches: elders (presbyters, pastors, bishops) and deacons.[48] The Romanian confession explicitly equates the titles bishop, elder (presbyter), and pastor: "All these words describe the same ministry: oversight, shepherding and spiritual leadership of the church."[49]

Around the world and through time, Baptists have designated their leaders with the biblical terms "bishop (overseer)," "elder," and "pastor."[50] Without exception, the title "priest" does not appear in these confessions but occurs only regarding the priesthood shared by all believers in Christ. Does it make a difference that Baptists have chosen primarily to recognize their congregational ministers as "pastors"? What is the theological significance of this title vis-à-vis "elder," "overseer," "priest," or even "minister"? How does our theology, in this instance, affect the practice of ministry among Baptist clergy? Those remain questions for theological reflection.

44. Lumpkin, *Baptist Confessions of Faith*, 422.
45. Lumpkin, *Baptist Confessions of Faith*, 479.
46. "El Nuevo Testamento enseña que cada iglesia tiene dos oficios—el del pastor y el de los diáconos." Lumpkin, *Baptist Confessions of Faith*, 531.
47. Lumpkin, *Baptist Confessions of Faith*, 488.
48. Lumpkin, *Baptist Confessions of Faith*, 488–89.
49. Lumpkin, *Baptist Confessions of Faith*, 489.
50. Not all Baptist confessions of faith designate titles for church leaders. For example, the statements of faith of the Nigerian Baptist Convention, the Baptist Union of South Africa, the Arab Baptist Theological Seminary in Lebanon, the Japan Baptist Union, the Malaysia Baptist Theological Seminary, the Mexican Baptist Convention, and the American Baptist Churches all omit this topic. See Lumpkin, *Baptist Confessions of Faith*, 454–532.

Theological Reflection

Cultural Models of Ministry

Baptists reflect theologically in the context of a culture that exercises a significant gravitational pull on our thinking. We breathe the air and drink the water of our culture, and its ideas shape us. Christian ministers, not to mention *Baptist* ministers, are stereotyped figures in our literature, films, television dramas and sitcoms, and jokes. Only 37 percent of Americans rate the honesty and ethical standards of clergy as "very high" in Gallup's most recent poll.[51] We place just ahead of journalists, bankers, real estate agents, and lawyers. We, whom the community once considered integral to its life, have become increasingly marginalized and impotent. In response, pastors may begin to think about the work we do in a way that conforms to a cultural understanding or that seeks its value in things the world about us counts as essential.[52] Such is the path to pastors functioning like CEOs rather than servants, becoming media gurus rather than students of Scripture, and delivering self-help TED Talks rather than preaching "the whole purpose of God" (Acts 20:27). Theological reflection on our Scriptures and our heritage are antidotes to such deadly cultural images. From a *Baptist* perspective, our call is a summons from God and the church to enter a set of relationships and to engage a set of tasks. Our gifts and training accompany us. We define and clarify our call not by turning to our culture's values but by relying on Christ, the Chief Shepherd, and studying the Christian Scriptures.

Pastoral Roles and Responsibilities

The most prominent biblical terms for congregational leaders are "elder" and "overseer" (or "bishop"). These terms speak primarily to the roles and responsibilities of the pastoral leader. Elders are responsible "to rule" (*proistēmi*)—that is, to lead or direct the affairs of the congregation (1 Tim. 5:17). Additionally, some elders are responsible for preaching and teaching. "Overseer" or "bishop" also implies roles and responsibilities. The overseer is responsible for "taking care of" (*epimeleomai*) the church (1 Tim. 3:5)

51. Megan Brenan, "Nurses Again Outpace Other Professions for Honesty, Ethics," Gallup, December 20, 2018, https://news.gallup.com/poll/245597/nurses-again-outpace-professions -honesty-ethics.aspx.

52. William H. Willimon identifies a series of images the secular and religious cultures offer pastors in the twenty-first century, including media mogul, political negotiator, therapist, manager, resident activist, preacher, and servant. He says, "Uncritical borrowing from the culture's images of leadership can be the death of specifically *Christian* leaders." *Pastor: The Theology and Practice of Ordained Ministry*, rev. ed. (Nashville: Abingdon, 2016), 55–74.

and teaching (1 Tim. 3:2). The church redefines these responsibilities as it appropriately adapts its form to the cultural context in which it serves. Being responsible for budgets, websites, or a plan to move worship online during a worldwide pandemic may be expressions of those biblical responsibilities. Neither of these titles, however, speaks powerfully to the relational aspect of pastoral ministry.

Pastoral Relationships

The title "pastor" is rooted in a relationship. One cannot be a shepherd without a flock. To be a pastor, a shepherd, is to relate in a particular way to the church. The True Shepherd of Ezekiel 34 and John 10 enriches that powerful metaphor of congregational ministry. The pastor is no hireling but one who loves and cares for the sheep. The shepherd's affection for the flock extends even to a willingness to sacrifice on their behalf. Love, care, sacrifice, and protection are not mere administrative responsibilities. Pastors accept these duties in the context of the Christian community (*koinōnia*), responding to the powerful pull of Christlike compassion for God's flock. As Peter says, we tend the flock of God "not under compulsion but willingly, as God would have [us] do it—not for sordid gain but eagerly" (1 Pet. 5:2). Love for Jesus Christ motivates pastoral care for the flock he loves (John 21:15–17). Paradigms of pastoral ministry focusing merely on roles and responsibilities and not on relationships may produce technically competent managers or communicators, perhaps, but not pastors.

Pastoral Domains

The term "pastor" has an advantage over other potential titles because it comprehends both the relational and the role/responsibility aspects of the work. I have often visited with children in Sunday school or Vacation Bible School classes at the request of their teacher to talk about what pastors do. I approach that assignment no differently than I do with seminary students in the classroom. I start by explaining that the biblical word for pastor also means "shepherd." I tell the children that even the English word "pastor" once meant "shepherd." I ask them, "If the pastor is a shepherd, then who are the sheep?" They catch on rather quickly. I read from Psalm 23, John 21:15–21, and 1 Peter 5:1–3. Then I ask, "What is it that shepherds do for the sheep?" Even the suburban kids have enough exposure to the metaphor to respond with some prodding: they feed the sheep, they take care of the sheep, and they lead the sheep. We just play with the analogy from that point on.

These three shepherd tasks are the domains of pastoral ministry: proclamation (including teaching and discipleship), leadership and administration, and pastoral care. A Venn diagram of three overlapping circles representing the domains helps me understand that my ministry to the congregation shows up in these three highly relational areas. I am seldom doing only one of them. Preaching becomes an expression of both care and leadership. Genuine pastoral care prepares people to hear my sermons and to cooperate in matters of church leadership. Whether I am preaching a sermon, visiting a hospital room, or sitting in a committee meeting, I am the pastor of the people I am serving. My call is to love them and live with them. "Elder" and "overseer" do not take me to that place of understanding this relational dimension of the call to ministry. "Pastor," however, does that without shirking responsibility for the work of leadership and oversight.

CONCLUSIONS

That morning on the golf course with Mike, I began to think about myself a bit differently. I "owned" my pastoral identity in a way I had not done before. Such ownership of the role does not take who one is and falsely confuse that with what one does. Being a pastor is more integral to life than that. If I were, like Mike, an engineer, I could punch a clock on Friday and walk away from work until Monday. Being a pastor, however, is not like that. The role makes demands on the pastor's character, the pastor's relationship with Christ that empowers the work, and the pastor's affection for the congregation, which precludes clocking out at five on Friday. One may rest from the tasks but not from the relationships. We are pastors all the time.

Pastoral identity develops as we respond to a summons from God and an invitation from God's people. Ordination serves as a public way of answering that dual calling, saying yes to both. Ordination changes nothing in the pastor. One receives no infusion of power or authority. However, when the weight of the ordaining hands disappears, one rises to enter a realm of service uniquely binding the shepherd to the flock of God. One becomes a pastor.

FOR FURTHER REFLECTION

1. Which biblical passages determine your understanding of what it means to be a pastor? Which biblical images or metaphors most shape your

thinking? What do these biblical materials contribute to your concept of pastoral ministry?

2. If you wrote a confession of faith about the church, what would you have to say about its leaders—who they are, their responsibilities, and how the church chooses them?

3. This chapter argues that the title "pastor" better represents both the role/responsibility issues and the relational issues that accompany church leadership. Do you agree? Do you see any advantages to the use of other titles? Any disadvantages to the title "pastor"?

4. Pastoral identity, understanding oneself as a pastor, is described in this chapter as being something one does not conveniently lay aside. Is that different from being overly identified with the work one does? How?

2

The Call to Ministry

More Than a Job

Every Godsent Christian minister is as much called to preach the gospel as was that apostle who spake of "the Lord, even Jesus, who appeared unto me in the way."

—Charles Haddon Spurgeon, *The Sword and the Trowel*

I, Paul, have been called and sent by Jesus, the Messiah, according to God's plan.

—Paul (1 Cor. 1:1 Message)

The concept of a "called ministry" has etched itself deeply into Baptist life and practices.[1] Contemporary men and women professing a call to ministry ("this") connects in Baptist thought directly to the calls received by ancient prophets and apostles ("that") narrated in Scripture. Although no single biblical text speaks about being called into ministry, God consistently issues a summons to men and women in the biblical story who become divine

1. The term "called ministry" refers to the Baptist understanding that those whom it recognizes as its pastors have satisfactorily demonstrated a sense of responding to a call from God and that they manifest the character and gifts required to serve in that role.

instruments—teaching, leading, and encouraging God's people. Anthony Thiselton says of Paul's call, "Paul sees his apostleship not as an instrument of power but as a call to become a transparent agency through whom the crucified and raised Christ becomes portrayed through lifestyle, thought, and utterance."[2] These biblical call experiences unite the church of the apostles with the church throughout history.[3]

Biblical Foundations

Not every story of a call tells of a call to ministry. However, these narratives still fit the paradigm of call and obedience. For example, Abram's call is an invitation from Yahweh to leave his former life in Haran and become a holy vagabond, following God's leadership to a land of promise (Gen. 12:1–9). The definitive aspect of a call experience is the presence of a Caller, who is God. This reality affirms that the journey from Haran to Canaan was a venture initiated not by Abram but by the God who called him. The choices of the one receiving the call are clear: one may obey or disobey the call.[4] Paul testifies to King Agrippa, "I was not disobedient to the heavenly vision" (Acts 26:19). Paul did not decide on his own to preach Christ to the gentiles. Christ called him to that mission.

The call stories told by or about Israel's prophets follow this pattern: God calls, and the prophet chooses obedience or disobedience. At times, the called prophets may protest their lack of qualifications, as in the cases of Moses (Exod. 3:1–4:17), Isaiah (Isa. 6:1–13), and Jeremiah (Jer. 1:4–10). Moses issues a series of excuses as to why he should not be the one to confront Pharaoh and liberate Israel: "Who am I?" "Who are You?" "They won't believe me." "I'm not a good communicator" (see Exod. 3:11, 13; 4:1, 10). Isaiah asserts his sinfulness as a disqualifier (Isa. 6:5). Jeremiah claims he is too young and inexperienced to serve as Yahweh's spokesman to Judah's kings and people (Jer. 1:6).

2. Anthony C. Thiselton, *The First Epistle to the Corinthians* (Grand Rapids: Eerdmans, 2000), 45.

3. L. R. Scarborough writes, "I think no doctrine is more thoroughly taught in God's Word than the doctrine of the divine call to service of his ministers. It was true of the prophets. It was true of the priests of the old dispensation, especially if we consider the continuous call in the offspring of Aaron to the priesthood. It was tremendously emphasized in the apostolic group. Christ called each of them and gave them a holy, inner, spiritual ordination to their divinely outlined task." *My Conception of the Gospel Ministry* (Nashville: Sunday School Board of the Southern Baptist Convention, 1935), 16.

4. Other "calls" that are not issued to prophets include the call of various judges (Judg. 3:9), such as the call to Gideon to lead God's people against the Midianites (Judg. 6:11–40) and the call of David to be king (1 Sam. 16:1–13).

In each instance, God remedies the prophet's perceived deficiency and authorizes him to speak. God promises to be with Moses in response to Moses's claim to be a persona non grata in Egypt ("Who am I?"). God reveals the name "Yahweh" in response to Moses's appeal that he does not know God's name and will be unable to tell the people of Israel who sent him. God provides a series of convincing signs for Moses to perform so that Israel will believe his message. And God reminds Moses that his brother Aaron, who is eloquent, can be the spokesman to Israel and Pharaoh. As each excuse melts away, Moses chooses to obey the call of God.

In Isaiah's vision, God responds to his guilt and shame ("I am a man of unclean lips") by sending one of his heavenly servants, a seraph, to take a coal from the temple's altar and touch his lips, purifying them. After that, Isaiah is eager to serve ("Here am I; send me!"). God parries Jeremiah's protest of youthful inexperience with the same promise given to Moses centuries before: "I will be with you." Jeremiah then yields to God in a commitment that would consume more than forty years of his life. That call would be the one thing that bound him to the mast of obedience when he faced rejection and persecution from his people. He often wanted to resign the prophetic role but found that to be impossible:

> If I say, "I will not mention him,
>   or speak any more in his name,"
> then within me there is something like a burning fire
>   shut up in my bones;
> I am weary with holding it in,
>   and I cannot. (Jer. 20:9)

God calls Jonah to go to Nineveh, but the prophet rebels and heads for Tarshish instead (Jon. 1:1–3). Only after experiencing the consequences of his willful disobedience does he hear the call again and respond with grudging obedience (Jon. 1:4–3:3). Amos, a farmer turned prophet in the eighth century BC, receives a call while herding sheep and growing fruit (Amos 7:12–14). Hosea, a contemporary of Amos, apparently discerned a call out of the pain of marital unfaithfulness (Hosea 1:2–8; 3:1–5). His own experience became a way for him to understand God's love for Israel despite their turning to other gods. Ezekiel's call in the seventh century BC occurs in a pastoral setting. He is a priest living among the exiles along the river Chebar. Through a series of surrealistic visions, God summons him to serve as a spokesman to Judah's kings, religious leaders, and citizens (Ezek. 1:1–3:11).

For the Old Testament prophets, God's call was the authorizing power of their ministry and message. They were "sent ones." They did not choose their ministry; Yahweh chose them for it. They did not speak their own words, but "the word of the LORD" came to them. They did not tell of their own visions but of what God had revealed to them. False prophets, says Jeremiah, are those who minister without a call, without divine authority. They speak their own mind, not the word of Yahweh (Jer. 23:16). They have not stood in the heavenly council and heard God declare a vision (Jer. 23:18). The Lord says of them:

> I did not send the prophets,
>   yet they ran;
> I did not speak to them,
>   yet they prophesied.
> But if they had stood in my council,
>   then they would have proclaimed my words to my people,
> and they would have turned them from their evil way,
>   and from the evil of their doings. (Jer. 23:21–22)

These false prophets lacked authority because they lacked a call.

New Testament call narratives, often modeled on those in the Old Testament, have served the same paradigmatic function for Baptists, providing models for understanding a call to ministry. Jesus himself received a call at his baptism (Matt. 3:13–17; Mark 1:9–11; Luke 3:21–22), which was then tested by the evil one in the wilderness (Matt. 4:1–11; Mark 1:12–13; Luke 4:1–13). Jesus began his ministry by extending a call to discipleship to Peter and Andrew (Mark 1:16–17), James and John (Mark 1:18–19), Philip (John 1:43), and Matthew/Levi (Mark 2:13–17). Like the call of God in the Old Testament, Jesus's call was an imperative: "Come, follow me." It could only be obeyed or disobeyed. One either followed him or not.[5] Some of those he called chose to disobey rather than to follow (Luke 9:57–62).

---

5. In the words of Dietrich Bonhoeffer,

When Jesus demanded voluntary poverty of the rich young man, the young man knew that his only choices were obedience or disobedience. When Levi was called from tax collecting and Peter from his nets, there was no doubt that Jesus was serious about those calls. They were supposed to leave everything and follow him. When Peter was called to step out onto the stormy sea, he had to get up and risk taking the step. Only one thing was demanded in each of these cases. That was their entrusting themselves to the word of Jesus Christ, believing it to be a stronger foundation than all the securities of the world. . . . Jesus' call broke through all of this and mandated obedience. It was God's own word. Simple obedience was required. (*Discipleship*, vol. 4 of *Dietrich Bonhoeffer Works*, ed. Geffrey B. Kelly et al. [Minneapolis: Fortress, 2003], 77)

From among the multitudes who followed him and listened to his teaching, Jesus prayerfully selected twelve to be with him and to join him in proclaiming the kingdom of God, replete with signs of healing and exorcism (Mark 3:13–19; Luke 6:12–16). Even among those twelve, one ultimately chose to disobey the call (Mark 3:19; John 6:66–71).

A call to serve God continued to play a significant role in the earliest Christian community. After prayerful discernment and casting lots, the Jerusalem congregation called Matthias to fill the vacancy left by Judas's death (Acts 1:15–26). God's call came through the wisdom of the community again as the Hellenistic Jewish Christians selected seven to serve the widows among them (Acts 6:1–7). Once more, in Antioch, the worshiping, praying, fasting church leaders heard the call of God that fell on Saul and Barnabas and obediently laid hands on them, setting them apart for a ministry to the gentiles (Acts 13:1–3). Baptist practices of calling, licensing, and ordaining men and women for ministry echo the congregation's role in expressing God's call to individuals.

Paul's call narrative is the most familiar one in the New Testament. Luke found the event so central to the early church's story that he included it three times in the book of Acts, offered once in the narrator's voice (Acts 9:1–19) and twice in Paul's testimony (Acts 22:6–16; 26:12–18). Although some continue to refer to Saul's experience as a "conversion," scholars have increasingly recognized that the event represents his "call." He does not convert to a new religion in that moment but responds to a heavenly invitation. Paul himself clearly understood it that way.[6] The risen Christ met him on the road to Damascus and called him to be his servant, his apostle to the nations. Paul regarded himself as a "called apostle" (*klētos apostolos*) (Rom. 1:1; 1 Cor. 1:1). Like the calls of Old Testament prophets, this calling authorized Paul's ministry and message, and he frequently appealed to that experience. As with Jeremiah, the call kept him obedient despite setbacks and persecution. As with Isaiah, the call purified this sinner by grace so that God could send him. The most direct, first-person perspective on Paul's call experience appears in his Letter to the Galatians. In Galatians 1:11–2:10, he narrates the experience that formed his life, beginning with the subjective encounter on the Damascus Road, where God "reveal[ed] his Son" to Paul and called him to "proclaim him among the Gentiles" (1:15–17); then he moves on to the confirmation of his call that he received from the Jerusalem apostles (1:18–2:10). Paul prioritized his subjective experience on the Damascus Road over approval

---

6. For an exhaustive study of Paul's reflection on his Damascus Road call throughout his letters, see Seyoon Kim, *The Origin of Paul's Gospel*, Wissenschaftliche Untersuchungen zum Neuen Testament 2/4 (Tübingen: Mohr Siebeck, 1981).

by Jerusalem's leaders (2:6). If they had refused to confirm his ministry, one suspects he would have proceeded without their blessing.

In Paul's letters to his churches, he frequently uses the term "called" to refer not only to himself but also to all believers. If he is a "called apostle" (*klētos apostolos*) (Rom. 1:1; 1 Cor. 1:1), his recipients in Corinth are "called saints" (*klētois hagiois*) (1 Cor. 1:2). He refers to their "calling" as an act of God's grace rather than something they earned or deserved (1 Cor. 1:26–31). For Paul, to become a believer is to respond obediently to a call from God (Rom. 8:30; 1 Cor. 7:17–24). This call places ethical demands on the lives of the saints. Paul urges them to live in a manner worthy of those called to follow Jesus Christ (Eph. 4:1). In these instances, Paul is referring not to a "call to ministry" but to every believer's call to follow Christ. He does not speak of calling in his instructions to church leaders found in the Pastoral Epistles. On the contrary, he speaks of one "aspiring" (*oregō*) to the office of bishop or overseer, not being "called" to it (1 Tim. 3:1).

Baptists have turned to these stories of God's people in both the Old and New Testaments to interpret the experience of those who profess a call from God to proclaim the good news of God's kingdom and serve God's people in roles of leadership. The ancient stories make sense of contemporary ones. In the accounts of called prophets and apostles, we have also found an affirmation that the call of God comes in a variety of ways: subjectively in worship or prayer, spectacularly through burning bushes and visions, silently in caves or among almond groves or fig trees. The summons may come as the voice of the community of faith or through the cry of the oppressed. The call is a prerequisite to serving as a pastor to God's people and has never been optional among Baptists.

Historical Bypaths

Baptists have universally insisted on the significance of a "called ministry."[7] According to John Broadus,

> The preacher should be a person with a call from God. Ministers are a class of professionals, but they should never be persons with just a "profession." They

7. Pamela R. Durso, *This Is What a Preacher Looks Like: Sermons by Baptist Women*, Baptist Women in Ministry (Macon, GA: Smyth & Helwys, 2010), 520; Herschel H. Hobbs, "The Pastor's Calling," in *Baker's Dictionary of Practical Theology*, ed. Ralph G. Turnbull (Grand Rapids: Baker, 1967); Claude L. Howe, "The Call, Placement, and Tenure of Ministers," *Baptist History and Heritage* 15, no. 1 (January 1980): 3–13; J. B Tidwell, *Concerning Preachers: What All Preachers Should Know* (New York: Fleming H. Revell, 1937), 23.

are people with a divine calling. Paul declared that he was "called as an apostle, set apart for the gospel of God" (Rom. 1:1). Spurgeon asserted, "I am as much called to preach as Paul was." And so it has been with every true preacher. The impulse to preach comes from God. Moreover, this call is intensely personal. It comes to people of all ages and classes in a variety of ways. . . . Regardless of how the call comes, it must be present.[8]

This insistence has marked the Baptist movement from its beginning.[9]

Baptists use the term "calling" equivocally, however, expressing a variety of experiences. Every believer is "called" by Jesus Christ to follow in faithful discipleship.[10] A believer may be "called" by God to the gospel ministry, whether to serve a local church or to serve in a cross-cultural "missionary" role.[11] Additionally, a local church may "call" (not "hire") someone to serve as its pastor.[12] All three of these calls are relevant to a Baptist understanding of a called ministry. In what follows, therefore, we must first clarify the various ways we use the term to understand how Baptists view a call to Christian ministry.

Because calling is an experiential notion, it is best illustrated narratively from the stories of men and women who have experienced God's call to serve. Once we are clear about the meaning of the term, we will attend to stories of the call experiences of four Baptist pastors: Menno Simons, an early Anabaptist leader; Frances Townsley, one of the first women ordained as a Baptist pastor in the United States; George W. Truett, a North Carolinian who came to Texas and whose leadership among Baptists extended to the Baptist World Alliance; and Dr. Martin Luther King Jr., the iconic civil rights leader and co-pastor alongside his father at the Ebenezer Baptist Church in Atlanta.[13]

Who Are "the Called"?

To be a believer in Jesus Christ is to be among those called by God (1 Cor. 1:2, 26–31; 7:17–24; Rom. 8:30). Baptists have always recognized this universal

8. John A. Broadus, *On the Preparation and Delivery of Sermons*, 4th ed. (San Francisco: Harper & Row, 1979), 13–14.

9. John J. Kiwiet, "Call to the Ministry among the Anabaptists," *Southwestern Journal of Theology* 11, no. 2 (1969): 29–42.

10. Howe, "Call, Placement, and Tenure," 4–5.

11. Some would restrict the call to ministry to those called to preach and to foreign missionary service. T. A. Patterson wrote in the *Baptist Standard* of October 4, 1961, "Those who insist that there is no difference simply reveal one thing—they have never been called to preach." Quoted in Howe, "Call, Placement, and Tenure," 5.

12. L. R. Scarborough wrote in 1935, "Pastorates are not jobs to be sought, and preachers are not 'hands' to be hired." *My Conception of the Gospel Ministry*, 48.

13. For other Baptist call stories, see Maurice Martin, "Cross-Cultural Perspectives on the Call to Ministry," *Vision* 12, no. 2 (2011): 70–78.

call to discipleship and to service. For every believer, baptism is their moment of ordination to ministry, in a sense.[14] To follow Christ is to minister in his name, serve others, bear witness to his love, and tell his story.

Nevertheless, Baptists have also believed that God calls some from among the church to a distinctive role. On October 7, 1892, B. H. Carroll preached to Texas Baptist pastors at their annual convention, "The divine Lord of the harvest sends forth his laborers into the harvest. He separates them from the masses of Christian people. He kindles on the altar of their hearts an unquenchable desire to preach his gospel. He counts it as rendered to himself the treatment they receive. An audience given to them is given to him. Their message scorned is his message scorned. Therefore every minister should magnify his office."[15] But how have Baptist believers understood this call and the manner in which it comes?[16]

Although we have not closely attended to how God extends this call to ministry, Baptist experience indicates that various agencies and influences may contribute to a personal sense that God has called one to ministry.[17] In the experience of a divine call, the individual's inner life with God often intertwines with the shared life within Christian community. Menno Simons recognized that the call might come to the person from God or through the church.[18] For example, John Mason Peck was part of the New Durham church in New York in 1811. Even before receiving baptism, he says, nearly every male member of the church spoke to him in private about considering whether God was calling him to the ministry, asking something like, "Don't you think you ought to preach the gospel?" The pastor of the church pressed the matter as well. Peck continued to struggle with a call for several months following his

14. Bent Hylleberg, "Baptism as Commitment to Ministry and Mission: A Consideration of the Rites for Baptism and Ordination in the Nordic Baptist Churches," in *Rites of Ordination and Commitment in the Churches of the Nordic Countries: Theology and Terminology* (Copenhagen: Museum Tusculanum, 2006), 355–76.

15. J. B. Cranfill, *Sermons and Life Sketch of B. H. Carroll, D.D.* (Philadelphia: American Baptist Publication Society, 1893), 108.

16. Baptists frequently refer to a call to ministry as being "called to preach." Understanding the call as simply a call to preach can prove frustrating, since pastoral ministry requires so much more than a Sunday sermon or a teaching ministry. Calvin Miller satirizes the professionalization of ministry that separates the pastor from such duties as pastoral care in favor of merely occupying a teaching role. See *O Shepherd, Where Art Thou?* (Nashville: B&H, 2006).

17. James Winston Crawley, "Call to Foreign Mission Service," in *Encyclopedia of Southern Baptists* (Nashville: Broadman, 1958).

18. "According to the Scriptures the mission and vocation of Christian preachers takes place in two ways. Some are called by God alone without any human agent as was the case with the prophets and apostles. Others are called by means of the pious as may be seen from Acts 1:23–26." Menno Simons, *The Complete Writings of Menno Simons, c. 1496–1561* (Scottdale, PA: Herald Press, 1986), 159.

baptism, so the pastor encouraged him to make his feelings known to the congregation. The church urged him to "improve his gifts" and invited him to preach the next afternoon. In three months, the church extended the limits of Peck's ministry to neighboring churches and finally to "wherever Divine Providence might open the door."[19]

For some, the call might be almost entirely an internal experience until announced to the church. Paul Beasley-Murray identifies several components of a call to ministry.[20] He begins with the observation that the individual must sense the call. No single pattern, either in Scripture or in Christian experience, is to be imposed on this experience, however. It may or may not have some dramatic component, like Isaiah in the temple (Isa. 6) or Saul on the Damascus Road (Acts 9). Such a call can come quietly—for example, young Jeremiah's response to God (Jer. 1) or the simple response of the fishermen to Jesus's invitation "Follow me" (Mark 1:17). What authentic call experiences hold in common, however, is an "inward sense of constraint (1 Cor. 9:16) and a real desire to serve the Lord in such a way (1 Tim. 3:1)."[21] J. B. Tidwell describes this as both a sense of duty and a deep desire to preach.[22]

The congregation has a role to play at this point. The church can observe whether the requisite gifts, abilities, and character accompany the professed desire to preach. The candidate submits their subjective sense of calling to the church for confirmation. Claude Howe observes, "In the Baptist heritage, an individual who professed a call to the gospel ministry might be granted the privilege by the church to 'exercise his gifts' before the church or in surrounding areas. The privilege might be extended or restricted in various ways. In this manner the church could assess the validity of the call and the qualifications of the individual in relation to it. On the other hand, a church might take the initiative and encourage a capable member in this direction."[23]

Tidwell also sees a significant role for the church in the process of discerning a call. He does, however, allow for the individual's conscience in the matter to prevail. He writes, "Certainly one's own church should publicly endorse the conviction of the one entering the ministry. The young man may not see his defects as others do. The church should make known any adverse judgment

19. John Mason Peck, *Forty Years of Pioneer Life: Memoir of John Mason Peck, D.D.* (Philadelphia: American Baptist Publication Society, 1864), http://hdl.handle.net/2027/nyp .33433082250386.

20. Paul Beasley-Murray, "The Ministry of All and the Leadership of Some: A Baptist Perspective," in *Anyone for Ordination? A Contribution to the Debate on Ordination*, ed. Paul Beasley-Murray (Tunbridge Wells, UK: MARC, 1993), 157–74.

21. Beasley-Murray, "Ministry of All," 168–69.

22. Tidwell, *Concerning Preachers*, 24–25.

23. Howe, "Call, Placement, and Tenure," 6.

it has. This should be done in great kindness, but done nevertheless. If the church doubts his call, the candidate should re-examine his heart experience with reference to it. If, after such re-examination, he still believes he ought to preach, he may go on, since he alone can decide the will of God for him."[24] Tidwell's conclusion accords with the Baptist principle referred to as "the soul competency of the believer."[25]

If the church affirms the sense of call, then the candidate's training, ordination, and call to serve in a specific congregation can follow.[26] Brian Brewer writes, "Echoing Luther's sentiments, John Colwell argues that the call to Christian ministry is 'inherently ecclesial; Jesus does not by-pass his Church; he mediates his call through his Church.' Thus is a person's call to vocational ministry tested and confirmed. The church acts on behalf of Christ to declare and confirm this calling."[27]

Baptists also refer to this final step of serving in a particular congregation as a "call." Churches "call" a pastor.[28] Among the charges opponents leveled against early English Baptists was that their ministers, being independent of apostolic succession, lacked authorization for their work. These criticisms may have led those who drafted the London Confession to take up the call to ministry in article 36: "Every church has power given them from Christ for their better well-being, to choose to themselves meet persons into the office of

---

24. Tidwell, *Concerning Preachers*, 25.

25. Edgar Young Mullins is one of the most articulate theological proponents of this Baptist distinctive. He writes, "If there is any one thing which stands out above all others in crystal clearness in the New Testament it is Christ's doctrine of the soul's capacity, right, and privilege to approach God directly and transact with him in religion." *The Axioms of Religion: A New Interpretation of the Baptist Faith* (Philadelphia: Griffithe & Rowland, 1908), 63.

26. Beasley-Murray, "Ministry of All," 170.

27. Brian C. Brewer, "A Baptist View of Ordained Ministry: A Function or a Way of Being? Part 2," *Baptist Quarterly* 43, no. 4 (October 1, 2009): 224.

28. Increasingly, Baptists along with other denominations employ more secularized language in this regard. They "hire" pastors rather than "call" them. They pay pastors a "salary" rather than "support" them. The theological and practical implications of this change in language could be more far-reaching than churches suspect. Those who are hired are easily fired. This language appears not just in ordinary conversations with church members but in publications as well. See, for example, the titles of the following articles: Rob Boston, "Exceptional Power: Supreme Court Says 'Ministerial Exception' Trumps Civil Rights Laws When Religious Organizations Hire Clergy," *Church & State* 65, no. 3 (March 2012): 52–54; John William Kennedy, "Booming Churches, Barred Pastors: How Visa Policies Make It Hard to Hire Ministers," *Christianity Today* 57, no. 6 (July 2013): 13–14; Michael G. Smith, "Let Your Minister's Wife Be the Minister's Wife: We Hire the Pastor, but Not His Wife," *Christianity Today* 27, no. 15 (October 1983): 92–93. The originally covenantal relationship between pastors and congregations has become contractual; see Joe E. Trull and R. Robert Creech, *Ethics for Christian Ministry: Moral Formation for Twenty-First-Century Leaders* (Grand Rapids: Baker Academic, 2017), 57.

Pastors, Teachers, Elders, Deacons, being qualified according to the Word, as those which Christ has appointed in his Testament, for the feeding, governing, serving, and building up of his church, and that none other have power to impose them, either these or any other."[29] Christ's authority expressed through the church authorizes those the church calls to be its leaders. The call to serve a particular congregation is a significant dimension of the Baptist insistence on a "called ministry."

As we will see when we take up the question of ordination in chapter 3, Baptists in North America have more recently extended the understanding of calling and ordination to other ministerial roles besides that of preacher or pastor.[30] It has long been the practice of Southern Baptist churches to speak of one's being "called to foreign missions." In fact, they have required evidence of such a call before commissioning missionaries to serve.[31] Additionally, Baptist theological seminaries often expect those who apply for theological training to enunciate a sense of calling to ministry, whether they plan to pursue pastoral ministry or some other form of service.[32] Should they later seek ordination, the ordination council or ordaining congregation will ask them to recount their testimony of calling as well.[33]

Baptist Call Narratives

James McClendon argues that biography can serve as a source for theological reflection. He writes, "If by attending to those lives, we find ways of reforming our own theologies, making them more true, more faithful to our ancient vision, more adequate to the age now being born, then we will be justified in that arduous inquiry. *Biography at its best will be theology.*" Those who live as part of a "convictional community" (such as Baptists) may, by the lives they lead, exemplify the convictions that the community professes. "Such lives," McClendon says, "by their very attractiveness or beauty, may serve as data for a Christian thinker, enabling her more truly to reflect upon the tension between what is and what ought to be believed and lived by all. To engage in such reflection, however, is the proper task of Christian theology."[34] The call

---

29. Ian Birch, "'An Intolerable Usurpation': Theology and Practice of Ministry among Early Particular Baptists," *Baptistic Theologies* 8, no. 2 (2016): 49.

30. Wilburn T. Stancil, "Divergent Views and Practices of Ordination among Southern Baptists Since 1945," *Baptist History and Heritage* 23, no. 3 (July 1988): 42–43.

31. Crawley, "Call to Foreign Mission Service."

32. Stancil, "Divergent Views," 44.

33. Beasley-Murray, "Ministry of All," 168.

34. James McClendon, *Biography as Theology: How Life Stories Can Remake Today's Theology* (Eugene, OR: Wipf & Stock, 2002), 22.

narratives that follow serve as data for us as we consider Baptist convictions about the nature of a called ministry.[35]

The Call of Menno Simons (1496–1561)

Menno Simons was an early Anabaptist leader in Holland. His call reflects the combination of an inner subjective experience and an interaction with the community of faith. Menno had been preaching and teaching in his church for a time. Then, in 1537, several people whose personal piety he respected asked him to assume a leadership role in the congregation. Menno objected at first but saw the need. He wrote,

> Finally, after much prayer before the Lord and his Church I gave these conditions: That they and I would pray fervently for some time. Then, if it should be pleasing to his holy will that I could or should serve to his praise, he would give me such a heart and mind to declare with Paul, "Woe is me, if I preach not the Gospel." And if not, that God might provide the means so that nothing would come of it, for Christ says, "If two of you agree on earth about anything they ask, it shall be done for them by my father in heaven. For where two or three are gathered in my name, there am I in the midst of them" (Matt. 18:19–20).
>
> See, dear reader, in this way I was called to this service, . . . unworthily by a people who were prepared to accept Christ and his Word, lead a penitent life in the fear of God, serve their neighbors in love, bearing the cross. . . . So it was that I, a miserably great sinner, was enlightened of the Lord; converted to a new mind; fled from Babel; entered into Jerusalem; and finally, though unworthily, came into this high and holy service.
>
> When the persons mentioned persisted in their entreaty and my own conscience made me somewhat uneasy, although weak, for I saw the great hunger and need as noted above, I surrendered myself to his grace. I began to teach and to baptize in keeping with his holy Word, to work in the Lord's field with my limited talent, to build up his holy city and temple, and to mortar back into place the stones which had fallen away, et cetera.[36]

In Menno's case, the church initiated the call but he confirmed it subjectively. Part of Menno's clarity in the discernment process grew out of his awareness of the congregation's need. He saw "the great hunger" they had for God and their need for a shepherd.

35. For additional stories of Baptist pastors' call experiences, see Winthrop Still Hudson, "The Pastoral Ministry: Call and Ordination," *Foundations* 5, no. 3 (July 1962): 238–49.

36. Menno Simons, *"Confession of My Enlightenment, Conversion, and Calling": The New Birth and Who They Are Who Have the Promise*, Mennonite Sources and Documents 5 (Lancaster, PA: Lancaster Mennonite Historical Society, 1996), 19–20.

The Call of Frances E. Townsley (1849–1909)

Frances E. Townsley was one of the first women ordained as a Baptist pastor in America. Like Menno Simons, her call to ministry reflects an interplay between her own subjective experience with God and the wisdom of some within her Christian community. As Townsley tells the story, her friend Nell, an Episcopalian, told Frances of a revelation she had experienced. "Dear," she said, "I am convinced that you are to preach the everlasting Gospel of our precious Lord!"[37]

Townsley wrote, "If a flash of light from the opening heavens had burst upon me the effect would have been little more vivid or impressive. I walked home to think, to wonder, to pray and to 'be silent unto my God.'" For several days, she went about "in a strange dazed wonder" as to how God was to use her life. She did not trust Nell's vision and began to think through every possible obstacle to its fulfillment. "But," she says, "a great cry after God rose in my heart, and at last I prayed, 'Take away the horror, the doubts, the heart-ache, and let me see Thee. Thou art better than work—than visions, THOU, O CHRIST, ART ALL I WANT.'"[38]

After an itinerant ministry of preaching and evangelism, Townsley began serving as pastor of the Baptist Church at Fairfield, Nebraska, in 1885. After three months, it came time to celebrate communion. Baptist custom required her to ask for an ordained minister to come and conduct the service. Her church and other Baptist bodies in the region urged her to seek ordination. She warned them that doing so would "cause a commotion" but eventually acceded.

Representatives from fourteen Baptist churches formed a council, and she sat for three hours of examination. Their inquiry focused on three matters: her Christian experience, her call to ministry, and her views of Bible doctrine. The council voted to ordain her despite her gender. A determining factor in their decision, they reported, was the clarity of her sense of calling. In a summary statement, the council's clerk wrote,

> The council was not unmindful that this would be regarded as a new departure by many other denominations as well as members of our own. The council had been called by a unanimous vote of the church. Then came before it this cultured, Christian lady with an experience that made all feel that she had seen Jesus. *Then came her call to the ministry, which was so clearly defined and beautifully and simply explained, as to make every minister present feel that*

37. Frances E. Townsley, *A Pilgrim Maid: The Self-Told Story of Frances E. Townsley* (Butler, IN: Higley, 1908), 135.

38. Townsley, *Pilgrim Maid*, 136.

she, too, had been led over his own pathway. Her views of Bible doctrine were so clearly defined, and orthodox, exhibited such an amount of careful reading and study, as would have done honor to any graduate of our theological schools. Here is evidently one called of God to the public ministry of the Word and has demonstrated the fact by years of successful ministerial work. The vote to ordain was unanimous.[39]

Townsley's story underscores the importance that Baptists place on a confirmed call to ministry. Her call account led Baptist leaders to recommend a woman's ordination as a pastor and preacher of the gospel, although their preconceptions disinclined them to do so. Part of the "this is that" Baptist vision was the conviction that obedience, regardless of the cost, is the proper response to a call from God. Men and women in the biblical story had faithfully demonstrated such sacrificial obedience. Evidently, to those Baptist pastors present for the ordination council, Frances's testimony of a call to ministry resonated with their own. Although it meant going against a traditional Baptist reading of Scripture and previous practices, they recommended her ordination to serve as pastor for the Fairfield congregation.[40] Their response echoed, in a way, that of Simon Peter when he explained to the Jerusalem leaders why he had baptized gentiles in Caesarea: "If then God gave them the same gift that he gave us when we believed in the Lord Jesus Christ, who was I that I could hinder God?" (Acts 11:17). That argument proved persuasive to both the Jerusalem leaders and the Nebraska presbyters (Acts 11:18).

The Call of George W. Truett (1867–1944)

George W. Truett was spiritually formed and educated in the Blue Ridge Mountains of southwestern North Carolina, where he served as a schoolteacher and a faithful church member. He moved to Texas with his brother in 1889 and settled in Whitewright, a small town in Grayson County sixty

---

39. Townsley, *Pilgrim Maid*, 278–79 (emphasis mine).

40. In her autobiography, Townsley cites unfavorably an article from a leading Eastern Baptist paper reporting her ordination:

"The council is understood to give for their reason for their action, that they were convinced that Miss Townsley had a deep conviction of having been called of God to preaching the gospel." Well did this editorial add, "This is a feeble justification." Certainly! I fully agree with the writer that "a conviction though genuine maybe a mistaken one." But not a report sent out by that council ever hinted at such a "reason." An ordination council is called partly to decide whether the conviction of the candidate is a "genuine" or "a mistaken" one. They referred to my conviction, but stated as a reason for voting to ordain, *their own united, unanimous conviction.* (*Pilgrim Maid*, 279)

miles north of Dallas, about twenty miles from the Texas-Oklahoma state line. He joined the local Baptist church and served faithfully as a layperson.

Truett began studies at Grayson Junior College to prepare for a legal career. He taught a Sunday-school class at the church and soon became the Sunday-school superintendent. The pastor often called on George to preach in his absence. Truett's sermons created a stir among the members, who began talking to him about becoming a pastor. Truett assured them that God had called him to be a lawyer. As Keith Durso describes it, "Eventually, his fellow church members took matters into their own hands."[41]

The church held its monthly business meeting on a Saturday evening in 1890. Truett was surprised to find the sanctuary filled since business meetings usually did not attract a crowd. After the meeting, the pastor preached and then a deacon stood and spoke, making a motion to the body that they "call a presbytery to ordain Brother George W. Truett to the full work of the gospel ministry."[42] Someone seconded the motion, but before the church could vote, Truett rose to speak. "You have me appalled," he said. "You simply have me appalled!" He asked them to wait six months, but they said they would not wait six hours. The church voted unanimously to ordain Truett. Years later he wrote, "There I was, against the whole church, against a church profoundly moved. There was not a dry eye in the house—one of the supremely solemn hours in a church's life. I was thrown into the stream and just had to swim."[43] Truett was examined and ordained the next day.

Truett's story is not unique. Churches have often had a strong hand in calling out the called from among them, as the testimonies of both Menno Simons and Frances Townsley bear witness.

The Call of Martin Luther King Jr. (1929–1968)

Martin Luther King Jr. preached a trial sermon at Ebenezer Baptist Church in the fall of 1947. He was ordained in February 1948 and entered Crozier Theological Seminary that fall. His call to ministry had not been a spectacular Damascus Road event but one of prayer, reflection, and discernment. In 1959, Joan Thatcher, the publicity officer of the American Baptist Convention, wrote to King and asked for a description of his call experience. She was concerned about younger people struggling with the concept of being called. She wrote to King, "Apparently many of our young people still feel that

41. Keith E. Durso, *Thy Will Be Done: A Biography of George W. Truett* (Macon, GA: Mercer University Press, 2009), 30.
42. Durso, *They Will Be Done*, 31.
43. Durso, *They Will Be Done*, 31.

unless they see a burning bush or a blinding light on the road to Damascus, they haven't been called."[44]

King replied on August 9, 1959, describing his realization of God's call.[45] King explains that his "call and pilgrimage to the ministry" was undramatic and unspectacular. He denies any miraculous vision or Damascus Road experience. Rather, the call emerged over time as a kind of "inner urge" that gradually become clear to him. He felt a deep desire to serve God and humanity and a sense that his gifts and commitment could best be employed in the ministry. Although he considered a career in medicine or law, it was the ministry that appealed to his heart. During his senior year in college, he acknowledged that calling. He soon preached his sermon and, a few months later, entered theological seminary.

King does not mention any outside influences on his thinking at this time. Although both his father and his two grandfathers were ministers, he describes no role that his family might have played in his decision. Neither does King describe any influence by his church or personal mentors. Perhaps these men and women did not directly appeal to King about considering a call to preach, but they had undoubtedly shaped him in such a way that when he began to look for a way to serve, the ministry made his list. McClendon argues that King's life cannot be fully understood apart from his religious upbringing, "the religion he had drunk in almost with his mother's milk."[46]

King describes his call as an inward and personal working out of God's will for his life. Part of the circumstances that shaped his experience was his awareness of human hurts and hopes that surrounded him and his growing compassion within his soul for those people. He wanted to serve God and humanity, but neither law nor medicine satisfied that desire. The process of prayerful discernment led King to a commitment to ministry instead. God was calling him to preach.

Theological Reflection

Sources of a Call to Ministry

Both the biblical materials we surveyed and the historical bypaths we followed indicate that for Baptists the call to ministry ultimately comes from

44. Joan Thatcher to Martin Luther King Jr., July 30, 1959, "My Call to the Ministry," The Martin Luther King Jr. Research and Education Institute, February 16, 2015, https://kinginstitute .stanford.edu/king-papers/documents/my-call-ministry.
45. King's response to Thatcher is available at https://kinginstitute.stanford.edu/king-papers /documents/my-call-ministry.
46. McClendon, Biography as Theology, 48.

God. Still, one may encounter it in a variety of ways. The diversity of sources represented in the biblical stories—burning bushes, profound silence, temple worship, ecstatic visions, and blinding lights—echo in the accounts from our heritage. Some hear the call coming from the lips of a fellow Christian. Others receive it from the entire congregation, which recognizes it even before the recipient, as in the testimonies of Menno Simons, Frances Townsley, or George Truett. Yet others may discern a call while prayerfully considering the needs of the church or the world, as did Menno Simons and Martin Luther King Jr. The call may come secretly in a silent place like Elijah's cave at Mount Horeb or as publicly as George Truett's church business meeting. In teaching about God's call, the church must keep this diversity of sources in mind. Perhaps the further one is from God's purposes, the louder the call might need to be for one to hear it. The more one is humbly open to finding that purpose, perhaps, the easier it is for God to speak in a whisper instead of a shout. Saul of Tarsus (Acts 9:1–19) and young Samuel of Shiloh (1 Sam. 3:1–21) have quite different call experiences. To give the impression that every call to ministry is as dramatic as that of Saul of Tarsus may keep many from hearing and responding to the voice of God when it is manifest by other means.

Testifying to a Call

The practice of recounting one's call goes back as far as Abraham. The call narratives of Abraham, Moses, Samuel, Isaiah, Jeremiah, Ezekiel, Amos, Hosea, Peter, Andrew, James, John, Matthew, and Paul make it clear that these are important stories for the community to hear and to remember. A call implies a Caller.

For Jeremiah to claim, "The LORD called me to proclaim his word to Judah," (11:6) is to say that God is interested and actively involved in the lives of his people, even (or especially) in their sin and rebellion. Testimony to the call of God is not simply about God's activity in the life of an individual. Such stories affirm God's involvement in the life of the whole people of God—indeed, the life of the world.

These calls to ministry take place *within* a community of faith, and they are *for* that community of faith. The call is always to serve the broader community in some way. Reggie McNeal affirms,

> The call is a mystery. It begins and ends with God, but it loops through a very human individual. It is personal, but bigger than the person. The call comes out of who we are as well as shaping who we are. It has both being and doing components. The call involves relationship at its core, not just function or task,

though it clearly carries task components. . . . Those who describe themselves as called mean that they have made a commitment of life into God's service, to be at his disposal, to be in his employ for the efforts of accomplishing his agenda.[47]

So, telling the story of one's call is not to boast, "God has called *me*," but to affirm, "God is active among *us*."

In addition to call narratives affirming God's active engagement with us all, the stories serve to validate the message of those whom God calls. A call does not make one infallible, but it gives one boldness to speak and to lead that might otherwise be absent. The story of one's call should contribute to humility, not pride, and to a servant's posture, not an authoritarian stance. The community of faith receives that story, not by mindless subjection to the will of the one professing a call, but with respect for the obedience and commitment offered in response to the call (1 Thess. 5:12–13; Heb. 13:17). The call stories, ancient and contemporary, need to be told. "This is that."

Calling Out the Called

The church has a role in helping its members discern a call to ministry. The church took the initiative to select Matthias to join the apostles' company (Acts 1:12–26). The congregation sought out seven men they trusted to serve the Hellenistic Jewish Christian widows in Jerusalem (Acts 6:1–7). Church leaders in Antioch, in obedience to the Holy Spirit's leadership, chose Paul and Barnabas to initiate a mission to the gentiles (Acts 13:1–3). The responsibility of the church in calling out the called resounds through Baptist experience as well. The stories of Menno Simons, Frances Townsley, and George Truett are a few of many such testimonies. The local church provides an environment where men and women come to faith in Christ and mature spiritually. Young believers should not need to wait until they are involved in a parachurch organization in college before considering a call to ministry. Neither should we expect youth ministers alone to raise the issue with the adolescents they serve. Churches should challenge older adults who are approaching retirement into what Mary Catherine Bateson calls "Adulthood II" to listen for the call as they think about another fifteen or twenty years of active life with time, resources, energy, and experience at their disposal.[48] This is the responsibility of the entire church.

---

47. Reggie McNeal, *A Work of Heart: Understanding How God Shapes Spiritual Leaders* (San Francisco: Jossey-Bass, 2011), 95.

48. Mary Catherine Bateson, *Composing a Further Life: The Age of Active Wisdom* (New York: Vintage, 2011), 14.

Pastors and mature believers in the congregation need to remain sensitive to those among them who display evidence of gifts and character that might signal God's call on their lives. Sermons and lessons dealing with the call ought to become ordinary parts of the congregation's diet. Pastors should occasionally refer to their own story of calling as a way of both publicly reaffirming their commitment to it and inviting others to consider God's call in their lives. If a called ministry is as vital a conviction for Baptists as it appears, then creating an environment in which people learn to listen for and obey God's call would be a reasonable extension of our theology into our practice.

Sustaining a "Long Obedience"

A call from God received in his youth sustained Jeremiah over forty years of frustrating rejection of his message (Jer. 1:4–21). When he wanted to give up, to abandon the ministry, his call held him fast (Jer. 20:9). Jeremiah was not the only one who pressed on under difficulty because of a call from God. Paul rehearses the suffering he endured as a result of his obedience to a call (2 Cor. 11:21–33). That call, however, kept him faithful to the task (Phil. 3:12–14). These called servants lived what Eugene Peterson termed "a long obedience in the same direction," borrowing language from Friedrich Nietzsche.[49] They persevered. Their conviction that God had called them supported them during persecution, rejection, and apparent failure in both cases.

In 2013 and 2014, Dr. Angela Reed and I used a grant from Baylor University's Oral History Department to interview ten Texas Baptist congregational ministers. Each of them had been in vocational ministry for more than twenty years. We were interested in what had sustained them over two decades when others were no longer serving in churches for one reason or another. Reed later wrote,

> One of the most consistent findings was a certain clarity about their invitation from God to faith in Christ and their calling to ministry. . . . None of the ministers have truly doubted the notion that God has called them to congregational ministry. A few describe a temptation to quit or pursue another path at some point, but none question that God initiated a personal calling to ministry and invited their response. This invitation and response has become an important aspect of their relationship with God, a sense that God has created them for a purpose and will sustain them along the way. . . . Holding on to the calling

49. Eugene H. Peterson, *A Long Obedience in the Same Direction: Discipleship in an Instant Society* (Downers Grove, IL: InterVarsity, 2000), 13; Friedrich Nietzsche, *Beyond Good and Evil* (London: SDE Classics, 2019), 81–82.

from God and returning to it as a "benchmark," in the words of [one of the pastors], seems to be a key to longevity for these ministers.[50]

The same sense of a calling has kept God's servants at their task for thousands of years. Obedience to the call has allowed men and women to endure through conflicts, rejection, doubts, and persecution. The contemporary call that sustains is the ancient call that kept prophets and apostles through the most challenging circumstances.

CONCLUSIONS

The notion of a called ministry is at the heart of Baptist pastoral theology. Professing a call from God is not optional for those who would serve our congregations as pastors. We insist that calling and character matter more than anything else. Although Baptists have a history of establishing institutions of higher education to train those called to ministry, a theological degree cannot take the place of a call. The "this" of a Baptist pastor's testimony to a call from God is an echo of the "that" of the biblical call stories.

FOR FURTHER REFLECTION

1. Ask your pastor to recount the story of his or her call to ministry. Ask questions. What would you say were the primary factors in that call? People? The church? The needs of the church or the world? Personal discernment? An ecstatic experience of some sort?
2. Are you called to ministry? Write out your call story. Include all the factors that prepared you to hear that call—your family, your community of faith, circumstances in your life or the world, the needs around you.
3. Who in your circle of Christian friends may be showing evidence of a call to ministry? What is that evidence? Gifts? Character? How would you speak with your friend about that?
4. Describe a time when your sense of calling sustained you through a period of temptation, burnout, or difficulty.

50. Angela Reed, "Rooted in Relationship: Longevity in Congregational Ministry," *Review & Expositor* 113, no. 3 (August 2016): 310.

3

Ordination

Set Apart to Serve

At least one statement may be made about the Baptist view of ordination without any possibility of successful contradiction: Baptists anywhere in the world have never totally agreed on the question of ordination.

—Robert Baker, "Ordination: The Baptist Heritage"

Do not lay hands upon anyone too hastily and thereby share responsibility for the sins of others.

—Paul (1 Tim. 5:22 NASB)

For most Baptist pastors, the path that commenced with a call to ministry and continued with their congregation's affirmation culminated in ordination. Hershel H. Hobbs defines ordination as "the ceremony whereby those who have a vocation and have given some evidence of ability for the ministerial office are set apart for the work of their calling."[1] Given the ubiquity of that ceremony among Baptists, we might expect to find a unified

---

1. Hershel H. Hobbs, "Ordination," in *Encyclopedia of Southern Baptists* (Nashville: Broadman, 1958), 2:1056.

understanding of the necessity, significance, and practice of ordination. We would be disappointed.[2]

During the past four centuries, Baptists have not fully agreed about whether ordination is biblical and, if not, whether we should practice it at all. We have disagreed about who is to be ordained, who is to ordain, and who is to participate in the laying on of hands. We have not seen eye to eye about the significance of ordination—whether it is merely functional, setting one apart to a particular place of service, or whether it bestows a standing on an ordinand that remains for life. Some have come to understand ordination more sacramentally. Others have seen it as mere practicality so that pastors approved by one congregation can freely move to other fellowships of like faith and order.

Additionally, Baptists have struggled to make sense of the practice and meaning of ordination alongside other theological affirmations such as the priesthood of all believers, the local church's autonomy, and the separation of church and state. This chapter explores the biblical basis of ordination and some of the historical and theological tensions surrounding Baptists' practice.

Biblical Foundations

The first place for Baptists to turn in our effort to justify a practice in our communities is Scripture. We look for a "that" to undergird the "this" of what we do or how we do it. In the case of ordination, we have found that principle has required stretching our interpretive efforts. Founding the "ceremony" (to use Hobbs's term) of ordination on biblical examples or teachings cannot be done confidently.

The Old Testament offers some precedent for religious ceremonies associated with selecting and setting aside religious leaders among God's people.[3] The practice of laying on of hands appears early in the Old Testament as

2. William H. Brackney understates the case: "Across the Baptist family there is a wide variety of opinions and practices." "Ordination in the Larger Baptist Tradition," in *Baptists and Ordination: Studies Conducted by Baylor University and the Baptist General Convention of Texas*, ed. William H. Brackney, NABPR Special Studies Series 13 (Macon, GA: National Association of Baptist Professors of Religion, 2003), 61. Brackney's edited volume is a valuable compendium of articles related to Baptist ordination practices, history, and theology, and I rely heavily on it in this chapter.

3. For a review of the Old Testament passages and practices relating to ordination, see Thomas V. Brisco, "Old Testament Antecedents to Ordination," in Brackney, *Baptists and Ordination*, 1–17; Susan M. Pigott, "A Response to 'The Old Testament Antecedents to Ordination' by Thomas Brisco," in Brackney, *Baptists and Ordination*, 18–23; and R. Alan Culpepper, "The Biblical Basis for Ordination," *Review & Expositor* 78, no. 4 (December 1, 1981): 471–74.

Jacob blesses Joseph's sons, Manasseh and Ephraim (Gen. 48:1–22). The law codes in Exodus, Leviticus, and Numbers instruct the priest to lay hands on Israel's sacrifices and offerings (as in Exod. 29:10, 15, 19; Lev. 1:4; 3:2, 8, 13; 4:4, 15, 24, 29, 33; 8:18; Num. 8:12). Two incidents involving the laying on of hands have exercised considerable influence on the thinking and practice of both Jewish and Christian traditions of ordination: the account of Moses passing on the leadership role to Joshua (Num. 27:15–23; Deut. 31:7–8, 14–15, 23; 34:9) and the cleansing and dedication of the Levites for sacred service (Num. 8:5–26).[4] Other texts anticipating the church's practice of ordination, especially the laying on of hands, include the reference to Israel's universal priesthood (Exod. 19:5–6), the sprinkling of the blood of the covenant (Exod. 24:1–18), and the consecration of Aaron and his sons (Lev. 8; Exod. 29).[5] These examples from the Old Testament connect with the Baptist practice of ordination only tangentially. True, they are ceremonies in which the laying on of hands occurs. In some instances, these passages involve setting apart religious leadership. What is not clear is whether the early church relied on these passages when commissioning people to leadership roles, since New Testament writers do not cite them to that end.

Hobbs, nevertheless, says that ordination is "based upon" scriptural practice and calls on several New Testament passages to bear the weight of the Baptist practice.[6] Even that claim stretches the texts he cites, which would apply to a ceremony of ordination only indirectly at best. Hobbs mentions four passages (John 15:16; Acts 14:23; 1 Tim. 2:7; Titus 1:5), each containing the word "ordain" in the King James Version.[7] However, "ordain" is not found in any modern English translations of these passages, and its use in the King James Version does not reflect the contemporary practice of ordination to ministry.[8] The references to "appointing" elders simply refer to their

---

4. Briscoe, "Old Testament Antecedents to Ordination," 1–2.

5. Pigott, "Response," 18–23.

6. Hobbs, "Ordination," 2:1056. For a review of all biblical texts bearing on the practice of ordination in both the Old and New Testaments, see Culpepper, "Biblical Basis for Ordination," 471–72. See also David E. Garland, "The Absence of an Ordained Ministry in the Churches of Paul," in Brackney, *Baptists and Ordination*, 25–37; Todd D. Still, "Historical Anachronism and Ministerial Ordination: A Response to David E. Garland," in Brackney, *Baptists and Ordination*, 38–44; Sharyn Dowd, "'Ordination' in Acts and the Pastoral Epistles," in Brackney, *Baptists and Ordination*, 45–56; R. Robert Creech, "A Response to '"Ordination" in Acts and the Pastoral Epistles' by Sharyn Dowd," in Brackney, *Baptists and Ordination*, 57–59; Heber F. Peacock, "Ordination in the New Testament," *Review & Expositor* 55, no. 3 (July 1958): 262–74.

7. Hobbs, "Ordination," 2:1056.

8. Loren L. Johns, "Ordination in the King James Version of the Bible," in *The Heart of the Matter: Pastoral Ministry in Anabaptist Perspective*, ed. Erick Sawatzky (Telford, PA: Cascadia, 2004), 105–17.

selection from among the congregation on the basis of their ability, character, and gifts. As in the passages that follow, Acts 14:23 and Titus 1:5 envision the community praying for these people as they take on a new role among them. They do not become "ordained" people at this point, at least not on the basis of anything in the biblical texts.

The inclusion of 1 Timothy 2:7 in Hobb's list above does not reflect a full Pauline context.[9] To read this as a reference to Paul's "ordination" is to misread it seriously. Paul is adamant that his appointment as a herald and an apostle had nothing to do with any human agency (Gal. 1–2). His authority came uniquely from the risen Christ on the Damascus Road.

Nevertheless, the earliest church's practices have provided a basis for some to claim a scriptural basis for ordination. However, using these accounts as anything other than suggestive of ordination in the ecclesiastical sense is problematic. Yet Baptists have often claimed them as the "that" to which the "this" of ministerial ordination corresponds.

In Acts 6, for example, the Hellenistic Jewish Christians in Jerusalem chose seven men of good character and spiritual maturity from their community to care for the widows who felt slighted in the food distribution.[10] Their administration of this matter would free the apostles to focus on their calling to prayer and teaching (6:4). After selecting them, the church "had these men stand before the apostles, who prayed and laid their hands on them" (6:6). The practice of laying on of hands does not indicate a formal setting apart of these seven for a lifetime of congregational ministry. Instead, the laying on of hands is better understood as a simple practice of prayerfully setting these men to a task for which they have been chosen and affirming the community's support of them.

9. The critical issues of authorship of the Pastoral Epistles (1 Timothy, 2 Timothy, and Titus) are well known and much discussed. My assumption is that these epistles at least represent the Pauline stream of Christian thought and process in the early church. I cannot rule out Pauline authorship. George W. Knight surveys the data and the arguments and writes, "Our conclusion is that the [Pastoral Epistles] were indeed written by the apostle Paul to his colleagues. This conclusion is based not only on the clear self-testimony of the letters to Paul as their author, their frequent personal references to Paul, their basic Pauline teaching, and their basic Pauline vocabulary and style, but also on the satisfactory resolution of the perceived or real differences, which in the end point toward rather than away from that authorship." *The Pastoral Epistles: A Commentary on the Greek Text*, New International Greek Testament Commentary (Grand Rapids: Eerdmans, 1992), 51–52.

10. Baptist interpreters have often associated the office of deacon in the church with these seven, although Luke does not use that title anywhere in Acts. The verbal form of *diakonos* is used to describe their activity (to wait on tables) (Acts 6:2). But this word is also used in the New Testament to describe the work of Jesus (Mark 10:45), Paul (Rom. 15:25), Onesimus (Philem. 13), and others. That does not make them deacons.

Acts 13 presents a similar case. The prophets and teachers in Antioch had been worshiping and fasting. They received a Spirit-inspired prophetic utterance: "Set apart for me Barnabas and Saul for the work to which I have called them" (13:2). In obedience, the church leaders responded: "Then after fasting and praying they laid their hands on them and sent them off" (13:3). This event could hardly be considered Paul and Barnabas's "ordination." By this time they had been doing church planting, evangelism, and pastoral ministry for years. They received prayer and the laying on of hands to bless this new calling to take the gospel to the gentiles. Never does Paul imply that this prayer meeting had anything to do with his calling, authority, or ministry. Once more, the laying on of hands implies no further authorization than the call they had received from God. It demonstrates prayerful support, recognition of their dependence on God, and the community's support of the mission.

We occupy shaky ground when we turn to a narrative work like Acts to settle normative church practices. The book of Acts does not claim to be setting forth a description of *how* we do church. Instead, Luke tells the story to demonstrate *who* the church is. He reveals how our witness in the world functions as a ministry of Jesus Christ through the Holy Spirit working in the church.[11] If the New Testament Gospels are "narrative Christology," we could describe Acts as "narrative ecclesiology."[12] The book of Acts simply does not address such issues as forms of worship, structure, authority, interdependence among congregations, or many other modern ecclesiastical questions. Asking Acts to answer such questions is anachronistic and is hermeneutically unjustified.

11. Kimlyn Bender makes a sharp distinction between the church as the body of Christ graciously *assumed* by Jesus through the Holy Spirit and the body Christ *assumed* in the incarnation. Yet it remains appropriate to think of the church's ministry as a continuation of Christ's ministry. Bender says, "The language of a free assumption of this body is thus not unfitting if properly qualified. Christ assumes the corporate life of the church through the Spirit insofar as he takes up its members' service and even suffering to be indirectly his own. . . . But the identities, agencies and activities of Christ and of the church cannot be collapsed or directly identified." Bender further explains this relationship: "Nevertheless, the language of assumption, in its disciplined and carefully designed sense, is not strictly inappropriate, for the formal relation of Christ to his church, one marked by intimacy, differentiation, and irreversibility, reflects the logic of the incarnation itself, and one that might be set forth in Chalcedonian terms. Everything hinges, however, in recognizing that the assumption of the flesh, and the assumption of the church and its service and suffering, are qualitatively and categorically different in nature and effect." "Christ's Body and the Body of Christ: Reflections on Identity, Difference, and Ordered Relations" (paper for the Evangelical Theology Society Annual Meeting, 2020), 11, 12.

12. Jason Ripley, "'Those Things That Jesus Had Begun to Do and Teach': Narrative Christology and Incarnational Ecclesiology in Acts," *Biblical Theology Bulletin* 44, no. 2 (May 2014): 87–99. Ripley argues that Luke presents a continuity between the ministry of Jesus and the life of the church.

Two passages mention the laying on of hands in Timothy's life (1 Tim. 4:14; 2 Tim. 1:6). These refer to church leaders prayerfully setting him to the work he would share with Paul and Barnabas. Perhaps this experience occurred when Timothy joined the missionary team on Paul's second journey (Acts 16:3). Luke tells nothing of such a ceremony, but 1 and 2 Timothy allude to it. Church leaders (elders) and Paul laid hands on Timothy and prayed for him as he embarked on this new direction in his life. To claim that he was thus "ordained" to the gospel ministry requires reading the church's much later practices back into the earliest church's experience.

Even if we accept the references in 1 Timothy 4:14; 5:22; and 2 Timothy 1:6 as references to the "ordination" of leaders, some official setting aside of an unspecified category of leaders through prophetic utterance and the laying on of hands, we have no hermeneutical justification for thinking that such was the practice in all the churches.[13] We certainly have nothing in the New Testament on ordination equivalent to Jesus's mandate for baptism (Matt. 28:18–20). We have only an account of a single location (Ephesus) and only evidence from some Pauline congregations. Did the Johannine Christians in Ephesus set apart their leaders in such a way? We have no way of knowing.

The quest to justify contemporary Baptist practices scripturally, following "the New Testament church," contains some problematic assumptions. We must assume that, although twenty centuries separate us, we can accurately identify some entity as the New Testament church (as opposed to New Testament churches). We would need to assume that all the Pauline churches organized and practiced their faith in the same way so that any reference in any epistle would be universally true.

Even less likely is the assumption that the Pauline churches organized themselves and practiced their faith in the same way as did, say, the Johannine communities. This uniformity is not a fact that we can know, however. We are more likely projecting an idealized time in the past when the divisions of theology and practice we face now did not plague the church.[14] We have naively assumed that the earliest church experienced a homogeneity that probably did not form until the New Testament documents circulated widely, encouraging a cross-pollination of terminology, theology, and tradition. Such assumptions,

---

13. David Garland surveys the Pauline Epistles and concludes, "There is a lack of any evidence of an ordained ministry in Paul's churches." "Absence of an Ordained Ministry," 36.

14. James D. G. Dunn, *Unity and Diversity in the New Testament: An Inquiry into the Character of Earliest Christianity*, 3rd ed. (London: SCM, 2006); Frank J. Matera, *New Testament Theology: Exploring Diversity and Unity* (Louisville: Westminster John Knox, 2007). Both Dunn and Matera underscore the diversity present in the earliest days of Christianity. Dunn finds the unity in the New Testament to be centered on Jesus Christ, and Matera finds unity based on the master story of salvation.

however, have not deterred Baptists from identifying our practices with those of "the New Testament church."

The references in the Pastoral Epistles also raise problematic issues of consistency in our Baptist theology. We have wanted to claim 1 Timothy 4:14 to support the practice of ordination but have not found equally appealing the implication that the ritual action bestows spiritual gifts of ministry. This notion smacks too much of sacramentalism for most Baptists' theological palates.[15]

In our Baptist zeal to be responsive and obedient to Scripture's teachings, we have often overinterpreted these texts and offered exaggerated claims. Given James McClendon's principle of a "this is that" reading of Scripture at the core of the Baptist vision, ordination as a ceremony setting apart those who profess a call to ministry and who have demonstrated abilities has little correspondence to biblical practices. On the contrary, careful exegesis raises the substantive issue of how Baptists justify our contemporary ordination practices scripturally. A more honest hermeneutic might lead us to claim less biblical support for how and why we ordain persons to vocational ministry. Instead, we turn to historians rather than biblical scholars to understand the pragmatic needs that have shaped our practices.[16]

Historical Bypaths

The bibliography on the history of ordination among Baptists is rich and thick, and a section of a single chapter cannot do justice to the fullness of the arguments and examples.[17] Instead, I shall briefly describe its history and summarize the main points of contention among Baptists. Readers may further pursue those matters that attract their interest.

The Origin of Ordination among Baptists

Ordination among the Early Anabaptists

Early on, a pattern appears among the Anabaptists closely resembling that followed by Baptists until now. The local church elected or called its

---

15. Sharyn Dowd writes, "Again, Baptists always want to deny that the gift is given because of the ritual and stress that the ritual is the community's recognition of gifts already given by God. This position can be supported by the texts in Acts but requires a good bit of hedging on the plain sense of the Greek in the Pastorals." "'Ordination' in Acts and the Pastoral Epistles," 55n49.

16. For a summary of the postapostolic development of ordination and the post-Reformation Baptist adaptation, see Clyde Penrose St. Amant, "Sources of Baptist Views on Ordination," *Baptist History and Heritage* 23, no. 3 (July 1988): 6–8.

17. See Chung-Yan Joyce Chan, "Ordination in the Baptist Experience: A Selected Bibliography," in Brackney, *Baptists and Ordination*, 205–15.

own ministers. According to the Waterland Confession (1580), the ministers of the church and the members together, depending on the leadership of the Holy Spirit, "call" or "elect" new ministers to their office (article 27).[18] The church set apart or ordained those they called to that work by the "laying on of hands by the elders of the people in the presence of the congregation" (article 28). The ordained were charged with teaching, preaching, and the administration of baptism and the Lord's Supper (articles 30–34). The church reserved these specific functions for those they had ordained to the ministry. Mennonites today continue to debate whether they ordain ministers to an office or a function.[19]

Ordination among Early English Baptists

Early English Baptists practiced a form of ordination that gradually changed over time. By the early eighteenth century, they had settled into a standard process involving prayer, fasting, and the laying on of hands.[20] Congregations typically fasted for a day before selecting a pastor, involving all the members in choosing and setting aside their leaders. Brackney cites the 1662 case of Thomas Ewins: "After severall dayes for Consideration, and Election of Persons fitt for each place, ye Church Mett by appointment upon ye 24th day of ye 4th month, or June, Anno 1662, for setting aparte ye persons chosen, by fasting and Prayer."[21] Although the practice was well founded and continued into the 1700s, it died out by the end of the century.

The earliest full description of an English Baptist ordination service appears in Thomas Crosby's *History of the English Baptists (1738–41)*.[22] A congregation had selected Joseph Burroughs as pastor following the death of the former minister, Richard Allen. Crosby attended the service. According to his account, the ceremony began with the reading of 1 Timothy 3–4. They prayed for the church, for those called to serve it as its officers, and

---

18. William L. Lumpkin, *Baptist Confessions of Faith*, 2nd rev. ed. (Valley Forge, PA: Judson, 2011), 56.

19. Ross T. Bender, "That Some Would Be Pastors," in Sawatzky, *Heart of the Matter*, 15–23.

20. As early as the Short Confession (1610) of Thomas Helwys's party, English Separatists affirmed that the offices of teacher, elder, or deacon were limited to "those who are ordained thereto and not to every particular common person" (article 24). The calling or election of these officers is "performed by the church, with fasting, and prayer to God" (article 25). Article 26 declares that "although the election and vocation to the said offices is performed by the aforesaid means, yet, nevertheless, the investing into the said service is accomplished by the elders of the church through the laying on of hands." Lumpkin, *Baptist Confessions of Faith*, 101–2. This language closely follows that of the Waterland Confession, articles 24–28.

21. Brackney, "Ordination in the Larger Baptist Tradition," 64–65.

22. Brackney, "Ordination in the Larger Baptist Tradition," 66.

for that day's proceedings. Benjamin Stinton preached from Philippians 1:1 a sermon aimed at explaining the duties of both elders and deacons (the church also ordained two deacons later that day). Then Nathaniel Hodges preached from Titus 1:5, explaining and defending the form of ordination. After the sermon, the ministers serving as messengers invited members of the ordaining church to gather with them where the communion table usually stood. Spectators remained in the gallery. One of the messengers presented a report recommending Joseph Burroughs as their elder or overseer in the Lord. The congregation affirmed the report by raised hands. The moderator then turned to Burroughs to ask his response. Burroughs offered a humble acceptance speech. The pastor's acceptance of the call was followed by prayer for him and the laying on of hands. As the ministers placed their right hands on Burroughs's head, Stinton, who had delivered the ordination sermon, made this pronouncement of ordination: "Brother Joseph Burroughs, we do in the name of the Lord Jesus Christ and with the consent of this church, ordain thee, to be an elder, bishop, or overseer of this church of Jesus Christ." Then Stinton prayed for both Burroughs and the church.[23]

Up to the nineteenth century, British Baptists agreed on a few aspects of ordination. They saw the office of ministry as essential to the church's life. They understood presiding at the Lord's Table as a role generally reserved for pastors. They concurred that having other ministers present at ordination services served to protect the larger Christian fellowship and that these ministers should lay hands on the ordinand. They also agreed that ordained Baptist ministers served primarily in congregational contexts but concurred that they might work in other settings.[24]

Ordination among Baptists in America

Across the Atlantic, meanwhile, the customs of English Baptists influenced practices in the colonies. Isaac Backus was called to be the pastor of a Separatist church in 1747. Other Separatist pastors, along with a large crowd, gathered for his ordination. The service included Backus's testimony of conversion, two sermons, a formal vote by the church to receive him as their

23. Thomas Crosby, *History of English Baptists from the Reformation to the Beginning of the Reign of King George I* (London: Robinson, 1740), 4:183–89. For a description of standard contemporary ordination services among Baptists in America, see Bill J. Leonard, "The Ordination Service in Baptist Churches," *Review & Expositor* 78, no. 4 (December 1981): 549–61; and William L. Hendricks, "Ordination: A Composite View and Practical Suggestions," *Southwestern Journal of Theology* 11, no. 2 (1969): 87–96.

24. J. Ithel Jones, "British Baptist Views of Ordination," *Southwestern Journal of Theology* 11, no. 2 (1969): 46–47.

pastor, and the laying on of hands by the other Separatist pastors. In 1756, Backus reorganized the congregation as a Baptist church and sought a second ordination. The church invited Baptist elders from around New England to the solemn gathering.[25]

Brackney notes the degree of formality about ordination that developed among New England Baptists. He cites Elias Smith, a Baptist pastor, who comments with some disdain, "They proceeded according to the order of the Baptist denomination. There was nothing said about the order of the New Testament; it is not likely that any one in the council thought of that, and I am certain it never entered my mind; because it was a fixed point with me that the Baptists order was in all things according to the scriptures of truth."[26] Among the matters that disturbed Smith were the pomp, the in-folio wigs, the sounding boards, and the ritual—all items that Thomas Baldwin assured him were "to make our denomination respectable."[27]

In the Middle Colonies, churches based their practices on the Philadelphia Confession of Faith (1742), which was rooted in the Second London Confession (1677). Ordination was a lengthy and careful process that moved from a "call" to a "pastoral settlement."[28] The congregation "called" a pastor, who commenced a trial period of service. Eventually, the church convened a presbytery of local Baptist pastors to examine and recommend the candidate (or not) to the congregation. The congregation then voted to affirm the pastor and organized a service of ordination. The laying on of hands was optional. According to Brackney, "The essence of ordination, then, in the Philadelphia Association, involved a call, a vote, and a designation to the work."[29]

In the North during the nineteenth century, the Baptist association played a prominent role in the ordination process. Hezekiah Harvey affirmed, "In the ordination of a minister there is evident propriety in inviting the cooperation of other churches; for it is desirable that he should be recognized as a minister and should perform ministerial functions outside his own church."[30] When a candidate required ordination, churches called a council of pastors from

25. William G. McLoughlin, *Isaac Backus and the American Pietistic Tradition* (Boston: Little, Brown, 1967), 77–81, 93–94.

26. Brackney, "Ordination in the Larger Baptist Tradition," 69.

27. Brackney, "Ordination in the Larger Baptist Tradition," 69.

28. Francis W. Sacks, *The Philadelphia Baptist Tradition of Church and Church Authority, 1707–1814: An Ecumenical Analysis and Theological Interpretation*, Studies in American Religion 48 (Lewiston, NY: Mellen, 1989), 340–59.

29. Brackney, "Ordination in the Larger Baptist Tradition," 70.

30. H. Harvey, *The Church: Its Polity and Ordinances* (Philadelphia: American Baptist Publication Society, 1879), 85.

all neighboring churches, not just Baptists. Ordination consisted simply of prayer, fasting, and laying on of hands.[31]

Baptists on the frontier operated with less formality. Licensed preachers often served several churches. However, when one of these preachers accepted a permanent call to serve a single congregation, the church ordained their pastor. The dearth of preachers among the settlers on the frontier often meant that ordination was a no-frills matter. Local churches ordained pastors without the benefit of a presbytery of other local ministers. For similar reasons, such an expeditious approach to ordination also arose in Baptist missionary work.[32]

Black churches in America also contributed to the evolving ordination practices among Baptists. In the early days of the colonies, Black Baptist pastors received their recognition, or ordination, from White ministers who were members of the Baptist associations. George Liele was the first Black Baptist ordained in America (1775), founding churches in Georgia before leaving for Jamaica as a missionary. Joseph Willis (1762–1854), a freeman from South Carolina, immigrated to Mississippi in 1798 and served as a missionary to the Opelousa Indians in Louisiana Territory. He was finally ordained in 1812, when he founded the first Baptist church in Louisiana at Bayou Creek.[33] Eventually, "Negro" associations were organized, and ordination became a more common practice, separate from White churches.

As in the churches on the frontier and mission fields, the demand for ordained Black pastors often outstripped the supply, and so expediency ruled. Associations quickly ordained those professing a call to the ministry so that they might serve a church or start one. Brackney outlines a more careful process that Black Baptist churches often follow now.

> A senior pastor sponsors a candidate who has been licensed to preach and a council is called. The candidate is catechized rather than preparing an "ordination paper" and the examination follows upon the catechetical material. Usually pastors of the local Black Baptist associations participate (sometimes there are both open and closed examinations) and, in a worship service the laying on of hands is conducted, with the issuance of a certificate in the name of the association to follow. Ordination is a recognition of gifts (especially preaching) and may still precede education by a long period.[34]

These practices, of course, will vary somewhat among Black Baptists across the country and even from association to association and church to church.

31. Brackney, "Ordination in the Larger Baptist Tradition," 70.
32. Brackney, "Ordination in the Larger Baptist Tradition," 71.
33. Brackney, "Ordination in the Larger Baptist Tradition," 72.
34. Brackney, "Ordination in the Larger Baptist Tradition," 73.

Ordination Issues for Baptists

Should We Ordain at All?

One of the issues Baptists face is the tenuous connection between the biblical witness and ordination. Not only does Scripture provide no clear evidence of ordination, but Baptist theological principles also appear to stand in tension with the practice. A few Baptists have raised their voices in protest. Some have claimed that since ordination has no clear biblical basis, we should not be doing it. Some have rejected the practice as a relic of Anglicanism or Catholicism. Others argued that, although it may be helpful for various practical reasons, it is an unnecessary practice. One may be a pastor with or without ordination. Brian Brewer describes certain differences of opinion and practice:

> The nineteenth century, ironically, also saw the diminution of the rite of ordination among many Baptist churches in Britain and the United States. In part because of the influence of Spurgeon and others, Baptist churches began to practice ordination less regularly. A pervasive anti-Catholic sentiment directed Baptists to oppose any rite which might smack of ritualism. Baptists began to interpret the word "ordain" as "appoint" and argued that a ceremony after a pastor's selection by a congregation was unnecessary. Thus, while some nineteenth-century theologians and church officials welcomed ordination as demarcating the pastor as authoritative, in other Baptist circles the practice was on the wane and seen as inessential and even "Catholic."[35]

Considering the issues raised by these voices of protest may shape our theological reflection on the practice.

As early as the seventeenth century, some Baptist voices were challenging the practice and necessity of ordination. Edmund Chillenden, a member of the Parliamentary Army under Oliver Cromwell, argued for the legitimacy of preaching without ordination. He wrote a tract titled *Preaching without Ordination, or, a Treatise Proving the Lawfulnesse of All Persons . . . to Preach and Set Forth the Gospel* in 1647, insisting that the sole requisites of a gospel minister were a calling and an opportunity.[36] He asserted, "There is not one Parish of tenn that hath one of your men that is able to preach Christ." He went on to say the "ordained" ministers of the established church were "Drunkards, uncleane persons, dumb Idoles, or at best cruell Malignants."[37]

---

35. Brian C. Brewer, "A Baptist View of Ordained Ministry: A Function or a Way of Being? Part 1," *Baptist Quarterly* 43, no. 3 (July 2009): 165–66.

36. Edmund Chillenden, *Preaching without Ordination, or, a Treatise Proving the Lawfulnesse of All Persons . . . to Preach and Set Forth the Gospel* (London: George Whittington, 1647).

37. Chillenden, *Preaching without Ordination*, 2–3.

In 1738, after describing an ordination service in London, Thomas Crosby declared,

> I must observe here, that there are some among the Baptists, who object against this form of ordination, tho' it is thus usually performed in their churches, believing it favours too much of mens assuming great power to themselves, in the setting others apart to the ministry; and also believing, that the apostles themselves in ordination, used not this form, *We ordain thee*. And therefore decline pronouncing any words of ordination, and only pray to God for a blessing on the pastor elect, laying their hands upon his head, which they hold is ordination sufficient, and all that they know with certainty respecting the practice of the Apostles, who laid their hands on persons whom they set apart, and prayed to God on their behalf.[38]

Crosby is not clear whether he is himself one of those Baptists who find ordination unbiblical.

Andrew Fuller (1754–1815), a Particular Baptist theologian who helped form the Baptist Missionary Society, viewed ordination merely as a "brotherly concurrence." Brewer says that Fuller "rejected the notion that through ordination a minister was given the authority to preach the Word or administer the ordinances."[39] Although Fuller encouraged congregations to permit outside preachers to participate in the ordination of its minister, he refused the notion that such ordination might imply "my having to impart to another minister some power or authority."[40] Fuller saw ordination as a prudent but not an essential practice.

One of the most strenuous voices raised in the nineteenth century against the practice was that of Charles H. Spurgeon, the renowned pastor of London's Metropolitan Tabernacle. In an article titled "Fragments of Popery among Nonconformists," first published in *The Sword and the Trowel* in June 1874, Spurgeon laid out his objections to the ceremony. He also objected to using the word "reverend" to designate or address an ordained pastor, resisting the sacerdotal view of ministry implied by such titles.[41] He saw it all as "priest writ large."

38. Crosby, *History of English Baptists*, 187–88.
39. Brewer, "Baptist View of Ordained Ministry: Part 1," 163.
40. John H. Y. Briggs, *The English Baptists of the Nineteenth Century*, History of the English Baptists 3 (London: Baptist Historical Society, 1994), 37.
41. Charles H. Spurgeon also objected to assigning certain practices to "the ordained" alone, such as pronouncing the benediction at the end of the service, administering baptism, presiding at the Lord's Table, officiating at marriages and burials, and visiting the sick and dying. "Fragments of Popery among Nonconformists," *The Friend* 14, no. 165 (August 1, 1874): 195.

Spurgeon critiqued the various elements of an ordination service, such as the ordination prayer, usual questions, address to the church, and address to the pastor. These elements of ceremony smacked too much of ritualism and legalism. The laying on of hands seemed to him an echo of Catholicism's apostolic succession. "Whence comes the whole paraphernalia of ordination as observed among some Dissenters?" he asked. "Since there is no special gift to bestow, why in any case the laying on of empty hands? Since we cannot pretend to that mystic succession so much vaunted by Ritualists, why are men styled 'regularly ordained ministers'?"[42]

Spurgeon believed that a call from God and a call from a church composed sufficient "ordination" to ministry. He wrote,

> Is not the Divine call the real ordination to preach, and the call of the church the only ordination to the pastorate? The church is competent, under the guidance of the Holy Spirit, to do her own work, and if she calls in her sister churches, let her tell them what she has done, in such terms that they will never infer that they are called upon to complete the work. The ordination prayers should be prayed in the church meeting, and there and then the work should be done; for other churches to recognize the act is well and fitting, but not if it be viewed as needful to the completion of the act itself.[43]

Spurgeon does admit some practical value to ordination. "We do not object," he says, "to a recognition of the choice of the church by its neighbours and their ministers; on the contrary, we believe it to be a fraternal act, sanctioned by the very spirit of Christianity; but where it is supposed to be essential, is regarded as a ceremony, and is thought to be *the* crowning feature of the settlement, we demur."[44]

What Does Ordination Mean?

The question of the meaning of ordination for Baptists also occupies a tension between two poles. On the one hand, some Baptists have regarded ordination and the pastor's role as a *functional* matter, setting apart one member of Christ's body to perform a particular set of tasks or serve in a specific place. At the far end of this spectrum, some argue that ordination applies to one congregation. Were one to take on the pastoral role in another church, ordination to that position would be appropriate. On the other hand, other Baptists have considered ordination as being set apart to occupy an office for life, unless revoked. The extreme

42. Spurgeon, "Fragments of Popery among Nonconformists," 195.
43. Spurgeon, "Fragments of Popery among Nonconformists," 195.
44. Spurgeon, "Fragments of Popery among Nonconformists," 195.

version of this position understands ordination sacramentally as if the laying on of hands conveys a specific power or authority or an ontological change occurs.

The functional view of ordained ministry has dominated Baptist thinking and practice. This perspective has helped Baptists negotiate the apparent contradiction of professing the priesthood of all believers and yet ordaining some to an office that sets them apart from the rest of the body. G. Thomas Halbrooks surveyed the beliefs and practices of Southern Baptist Convention churches over the first hundred years of their history and concluded, "The diversity Baptists expressed in their views on qualifications was also in evidence on the issue of what ordination conferred. But Baptists were almost unanimous in their opinions of what it did not confer. They repeatedly asserted that it did not confer any grace, spiritual gifts, abilities, power, priestly authority, special rights or privileges, mysterious virtues, or magic 'fluid.' Nor did it place the minister in any line of succession. For Baptists, ordination was by no means a sacerdotal action."[45] A functional view still obtains among most Baptists.

Leon McBeth summarizes a radically functional perspective offered by T. W. Dean, who served as a professor at both Southwestern Baptist Theological Seminary in Fort Worth, Texas, and Hardin-Simmons University in Abilene, Texas. Dean called for structuring Baptist ordination practices in light of three central Baptist values—biblical teachings, the priesthood of all believers, and the local church's autonomy. He argued that the Bible does not provide enough evidence for us to base our practices on Scripture. The only biblically based argument for ordination resided within the concept of the autonomy of the local church. The church holds the authority to choose, set apart, or ordain any of its members for a particular task or ministry by prayer and the laying on of hands. He contended that one's ordination did not extend beyond the local church that had called the person to the task. Further, he maintained, if an ordained pastor moved to serve another congregation, that congregation should ordain them as they assume the new position. Dean denounced what he called "an enlarged clerical cult" and called on Baptist pastors to become laymen again for the sake of the gospel.[46]

A more sacerdotal view of ordained ministry has increased among Baptists in the late twentieth and early twenty-first centuries.[47] The tendency toward

45. G. Thomas Halbrooks, "The Meaning and Significance of Ordination among Southern Baptists, 1845–1945," *Baptist History and Heritage* 23, no. 3 (July 1988): 28.

46. H. Leon McBeth, "Texas Baptists and Ordination," in Brackney, *Baptists and Ordination*, 91–92.

47. Brian C. Brewer, "A Baptist View of Ordained Ministry: A Function or a Way of Being? Part 2," *Baptist Quarterly* 43, no. 4 (October 1, 2009): 224. See 228n67 for a bibliography of Baptists advocating a more sacramental view of ordination.

a sacramental interpretation of ordination is almost inherent to the act. To set someone apart in such a ceremony and affirm that such ordination authorizes the individual to administer baptism and the Lord's Supper, for example, clearly tips the scales in the direction of assuming that ordination conveys some sort of spiritual or religious authority. Baptists felt this tension early on when it was the more common understanding that the ordinances were to be administered only by the ordained.[48] J. R. Graves and the Landmark Baptists especially emphasized that position. Over time, and partly in reaction to the Landmark movement, some Baptists raised their voice to oppose such a requirement.[49] More recently, others have offered a theological basis for a Baptist sacramental understanding of both the church's ordinances and the church itself.[50]

The change in legal status also energized a more sacramental understanding of ordination accorded ordained ministers in America. The law exempts them from the military draft and offers certain tax advantages, such as ministerial housing allowance and optional participation in Social Security. Further, the state delegates authority to ordained ministers to officiate at weddings and to sign marriage licenses. This special status granted by the state contributes to the clergy-laity distinction that was already a part of those denominations that took a more sacramental view. Baptists were easily influenced in that direction since our clergy claimed the same benefits and acted as agents of the same state.

Brewer argues that Baptists must learn to live with a both-and understanding of ordination. The tension is not resolved merely in terms of one end of the spectrum or the other. He writes,

> From this review of historical evidence and theological reflections it appears that ordination, out of necessity, carries qualities both functional and ontological. Baptists ordain their ministers to the "Gospel ministry," typically understood as the function of proclaiming the gospel of Christ. Additionally, Baptists join most other Protestants in seeing the pastor as the normative representative, on behalf of the congregation, to administer the ordinances or sacraments, and as one particularly gifted and qualified for pastoral care and leading the congregation in theological reflection. This understanding is pragmatic; it serves an ecclesial purpose.[51]

48. Halbrooks, "Meaning and Significance," 28.
49. Halbrooks, "Meaning and Significance," 28.
50. See, for example, the two volumes edited by Anthony R. Cross and Philip E. Thompson, *Baptist Sacramentalism*, Studies in Baptist History and Thought 5 (Carlisle, UK: Paternoster, 2003); and *Baptist Sacramentalism 2*, Studies in Baptist History and Thought 25 (Milton Keynes, UK: Paternoster, 2008); as well as the work of Curtis W. Freeman, *Contesting Catholicity: A Theology for Other Baptists* (Waco: Baylor University Press, 2014).
51. Brewer, "Baptist View of Ordained Ministry: Part 2," 225.

Ordination sets the pastor apart for a particular service to the church (functional). Still, it recognizes specific gifts and asks for certain qualifications, both in calling and in character (ontological). The tension between the two remains.

Who Ordains Baptist Pastors?

Baptists have also experienced tension in our practice of ordination around the source of authority to ordain someone to ministry. In light of their notion of the local church's autonomy, some have argued that only the local congregation may ordain. When a church convenes a presbytery from the association, that group merely bears witness to the event. The notion of local church autonomy also raises the question of who appropriately lays hands on the candidate: only other ordained ministers or the congregational members? Others have argued that assembling a presbytery offers a practical advantage of assuring the doctrinal integrity of the pastoral role and connecting the candidate with those who can serve as mentors and support in the work. But for some, to have the presbytery lay hands (Spurgeon called them "empty hands" since they convey no power or authority) on the candidate too closely resembles apostolic succession.

Because Baptists usually consider ordination to extend for the minister's entire life, others besides the ordaining congregation have a stake in who is ordained. The ordination certificate becomes a kind of union card affirming that a church of like faith and order has observed the candidate's character and gifts and has examined them as to their profession of faith, their experience of a divine call, and their doctrinal integrity. As they move from place to place in service, that ordination accompanies them. Also, a Baptist pastor represents Christ, the congregation, other Baptists, and even other Christians when interacting with the community in which they serve. That outside world assumes this perspective, whether one desires it to do so or not (1 Tim. 3:7). The fact that the broader Baptist family is a stakeholder in those whom their churches ordain is an argument for the involvement of other pastors and churches in the process.

At the same time, the autonomy of the local church is a core value for Baptists. Jesus Christ alone is the head of the church. No district superintendent, area presbytery, association, bishop, or denominational official exercises authority in the least decision of the smallest Baptist congregation. This autonomy extends to whom the church calls as its pastor and whom the church ordains. This point of Baptist faith prompted Spurgeon to write,

> I detest the dogma of apostolic succession, and dislike the revival of the doctrine by delegating power from minister to minister. I believe in the glorious principle

of Independency. Every church has a right to choose its own minister; and if so, certainly it needs no assistance from others in appointing him to the office. You, yourselves, have chosen me; and what matters if the whole world dislikes the choice? They cannot invalidate it: nor can they give it more force. It seems to me, that other ministers have no more to do with me as your minister, than the crown of France has to do with the crown of Britain.[52]

These two realities, interdependency and autonomy, keep another area of tension alive in Baptist faith and practice.

The most common practice among mainstream Baptists, outside the Southern Baptist family, is to use associational resources alongside those of the local church. The congregations of the American Baptist Churches USA rely on denominational ordination and follow a rigorous process. Black churches tend to rely on a local presbytery in the process.[53]

Churches of the Southern Baptist Convention have most often considered ordination a local church matter. For example, Texas Baptists, in accordance with their emphasis on the autonomy of Baptist churches, have traditionally viewed ordination as strictly an issue for the local church. In practice, however, these churches often cooperate voluntarily, frequently inviting pastors in the local association to participate in ordination councils. Although Baptist denominations that rely on denominational ordination may establish criteria for ordination, such as formal theological training, the emphasis on local church autonomy rules out any commonly held standards for ordination. Each church determines a candidate's qualification for the work.[54] This stress on local church autonomy has proved challenging to local associations and denominations with regard to women's ordination, as we shall see in chapter 4.

Theological Reflection

The Priesthood of All Believers

Baptists have retained a ceremony by which they set apart those who have a vocation and evidence of ability to serve in the ministerial office. We have not always been clear about how such practice aligns with our principle of the priesthood of all believers. Other Protestants have wrestled with this tension

---

52. C. H. Spurgeon, *The Autobiography of Charles H. Spurgeon*, vol. 1, *1834–1854* (Chicago: Fleming H. Revell, 1898), 357.

53. Brackney, "Ordination in the Larger Baptist Tradition," 75.

54. William M. Pinson Jr., "A Response to 'Ordination in the Larger Baptist Tradition' by William H. Brackney," in Brackney, *Baptists and Ordination*, 77–78.

as well.[55] We have maintained a clergy-laity distinction whose consistency with our doctrine is difficult to explain without sounding like double-talk. All believers are priests and have full and equal access to God through Jesus Christ, our High Priest. All believers are ministers, authorized by their baptism to serve Christ in the church and the world. But we lay hands on some, call them pastors, expect more of them morally, and accord them privilege, respect, and sometimes an authority that other believers do not receive. How do we account for this?

Baptists have not fully resolved the tug-of-war between the authority bestowed on pastors by ordination and the concept of the priesthood of all believers. Lisa Matthews argues that the two "irritate each other in a fruitless tension."[56] Those who follow Spurgeon in rejection of ordination pull away from the pole of pastoral authority toward the believer-priests.[57]

Baptists have attempted to resolve these two contending notions in one of three ways. First, the tension disappears if one rejects the importance of the priesthood of all believers, as did the Southern Baptist 1988 resolution on the subject.[58] Second, the problem also goes away if one eliminates ordination,

55. Brewer, "Baptist View of Ordained Ministry: Part 1," 164.
56. Lisa Grabarek Matthews, "Professional Ministry: Ordination, the Baptist Tradition," *Foundations* 20, no. 3 (July 1977): 215.
57. Brewer, "Baptist View of Ordained Ministry: Part 1," 164.
58. On June 1, 1988, in San Antonio, Texas, messengers to the Annual Meeting of the Southern Baptist Convention approved the following resolution:

> WHEREAS, None of the five major writing systematic theologians in Southern Baptist history have given more than passing reference to the doctrine of the priesthood of the believer in their systematic theologies; and
>
> WHEREAS, The Baptist Faith and Message preamble refers to the priesthood of the believer, but provides no definition or content to the term; and
>
> WHEREAS, The high profile emphasis on the doctrine of the priesthood of the believer in Southern Baptist life is a recent historical development; and
>
> WHEREAS, The priesthood of the believer is a term which is subject to both misunderstanding and abuse; and
>
> WHEREAS, The doctrine of the priesthood of the believer has been used to justify wrongly the attitude that a Christian may believe whatever he so chooses and still be considered a loyal Southern Baptist; and
>
> WHEREAS, The doctrine of the priesthood of the believer can be used to justify the undermining of pastoral authority in the local church.
>
> Be it therefore RESOLVED, That the Southern Baptist Convention, meeting in San Antonio, Texas, June 14–16, 1988, affirm its belief in the biblical doctrine of the priesthood of the believer (1 Peter 2:9 and Revelation 1:6); and
>
> Be it further RESOLVED, That we affirm that this doctrine in no way gives license to misinterpret, explain away, demythologize, or extrapolate out elements of the supernatural from the Bible; and
>
> Be it further RESOLVED, That the doctrine of the priesthood of the believer in no way contradicts the biblical understanding of the role, responsibility, and authority of the

declining to accord any special status to ministers. The third option attempts to reconcile the two, which is the challenge. Reconciliation requires recognizing the necessity of a set-apart ministry to the church and on behalf of the church. Yet it also requires the church to affirm that they have set the pastor apart to serve Christ and the congregation and to lead and equip God's people to bear witness in the world. The pastor's role does not put them above the other church members but instead places them as servants to Christ among the believers. The laying on of hands conveys no special grace but denotes a responsibility to the flock affirmed by the church and accepted by the pastor.

Ordination does, however, affect one's life. For example, a couple must learn what it means to live as married persons once they exchange vows and establish a new relationship. The newly formed marriage reshapes how they live their lives. The wedding ring, although having no sacramental significance, identifies one as married. Similarly, when one emerges from the waters of baptism, a disciple of Jesus must learn what it means to live as a baptized person (Rom. 6:1–4). Passing from death to life requires a new way of living. Baptism, without any necessary sacramental power, identifies one as a follower of Jesus. Even so, answering the call of God to ministry, responding to the invitation of a congregation to serve as their pastor, and receiving the laying on of hands—all of this ushers one into a set of relationships with God and God's people that necessitates living as an ordained person. Without the need to affirm sacramental significance to the moment, ordination nevertheless identifies one as a pastor.

Ordination does not impart grace through the touch of the presbytery or the congregation. Neither does it provide authority passed on by succession.[59] Instead, ordination forms a covenant between the pastor (the shepherd), the church (the flock), and Christ (the Chief Shepherd). In the call to ministry, God makes a motion in calling a person to ministry. In ordination, the congregation seconds the motion. They, too, see the calling evident in the gifts and character of a brother or sister. And the candidate willingly and obediently steps into the role of shepherd to Christ's flock. As a believer-priest among

      pastor which is seen in the command to the local church in Hebrews 13:17, "Obey your leaders, and submit to them; for they keep watch over your souls, as those who will give an account"; and

      Be finally RESOLVED, That we affirm the truth that elders, or pastors, are called of God to lead the local church (Acts 20:28). (H. Leon McBeth, *A Sourcebook for Baptist Heritage* [Nashville: Broadman, 1990], 521–22)

59. J. L. Dagg, nineteenth-century Baptist theologian and former president of Mercer University, argued a position that approached apostolic succession regarding authorization to perform the rite of baptism. See *Manual of Theology* (Charleston, SC: Southern Baptist Publication Society, 1859), 357.

others, as a minister of Christ among others, the pastor promises to lead out in care, in the ministry of the Word and worship, and in equipping others to discover their calling and ministry in the body of Christ.[60] This role is not sacerdotal but a service that requires recognition, cooperation, and support from the congregation for a pastor to carry it out effectively.

The Separation of Church and State

The separation of church and state was an issue of contention between the earliest Anabaptists and their culture. To be baptized as an infant made one both a citizen of one's country and a member of one's church, whether Catholic or evangelical. The Anabaptist insistence on believer's baptism opened a chasm between the two. Because in the American colonial period, and even in the early years of the republic, church and state remained connected, Baptists sometimes experienced persecution or incarceration for their faith. Baptist pastors Isaac Backus and John Leland consequently played a leading role in advocating with James Madison and Thomas Jefferson to obtain religious liberty guarantees in the First Amendment to the US Constitution.[61] But long before the Bill of Rights or Thomas Jefferson's exchange with the Danbury Baptist Association explicating the establishment clause, Baptists had advocated for what Jefferson called "a wall of separation" between the church and the state.[62]

In 1925 the Southern Baptist Convention adopted its first official confession of faith, The Baptist Faith and Message, basing it on the New Hampshire Confession (1833). The new confession introduced ten additional articles not addressed by the earlier document, including a statement on religious liberty.[63]

---

60. Lisa Matthews contends that this covenantal promise is the distinctive aspect that makes some church ministries "ordainable" and others not. She says, "The three suggested arguments fail in their task to distinguish the two ministries [ordainable and not ordainable] because they fail to approach ordination as a commitment, as a promise. Thus, they fail to focus on the distinguishing content of that promise. The proper question to pose is: What do the ordained promise to do that the nonordained do not necessarily promise to do? Only in this way is it possible to establish a Baptist interpretation of ordination which is in harmony with the biblical precedent for ordination and the principle of the priesthood of all believers" ("Professional Ministry," 218). Matthews argues that the thing the ordained promise to do is to earn their living from the work of ministry, to work faithfully as "professional" ministers. This, she says, is the only way to resolve the tension between ordination and the priesthood of all believers.

61. Joe L. Coker, "Isaac Backus and John Leland: Baptist Contributions to Religious Liberty in the Founding Era," in *Faith and the Founders of the American Republic*, ed. Mark David Hall and Daniel L. Driesbach (New York: Oxford University Press, 2014), 305–37.

62. Daniel Dreisbach, *Thomas Jefferson and the Wall of Separation between Church and State*, Critical America (New York: New York University Press, 2002).

63. Baptist Faith and Message (1925), article 18, reads,
   God alone is Lord of the conscience, and he has left it free from the doctrines and commandments of men which are contrary to his Word or not contained in it. Church and

"Church and state should be separate," it said. The church should not resort to the state to accomplish its work. The government should not favor one ecclesial group over another. A free church in a free state is the ideal situation.

As if the issues surrounding the practice of ordination were not complicated enough among Baptists, in the United States the government gets involved.[64] Ordination exempts pastors from military service and training. Ordained ministers receive tax benefits derived by exempting housing allowance from their taxable income. This exemption itself represents a significant advantage to many pastors. Additionally, since interest paid on a home mortgage is also deductible, the ordained may "double-dip" if they itemize their deductions. Ordained ministers may choose to opt out of paying Social Security Tax at the time of their ordination if they affirm that they conscientiously object to receiving government insurance for work done as a minister of the gospel, which becomes a permanent decision on the part of the minister. Finally, the state grants authority to ordained ministers to solemnize a marriage and sign a marriage license.[65] All of these matters introduce the temptation to pursue ordination for reasons never contemplated by our Baptist ancestors.

Consider the issue of weddings. The state has authorized ministers to act as its agents in officiating at weddings and signing marriage licenses for many years, primarily as a convenience to the state. Many faithful followers of Jesus have requested their pastors to conduct their wedding ceremonies. They desired to enter the covenant of marriage in the presence of both their

---

state should be separate. The state owes to the church protection and full freedom in the pursuit of its spiritual ends. In providing for such freedom no ecclesiastical group or denomination should be favored by the state more than others. Civil government being ordained of God, it is the duty of Christians to render loyal obedience thereto in all things not contrary to the revealed will of God. The church should not resort to the civil power to carry on its work. The gospel of Christ contemplates spiritual means alone for the pursuit of its ends. The state has no right to impose penalties for religious opinions of any kind. The state has no right to impose taxes for the support of any form of religion. A free church in a free state is the Christian ideal, and this implies the right of free and unhindered access to God on the part of all men, and the right to form and propagate opinions in the sphere of religion without interference by the civil power.

This statement was included in both the 1963 and the 2000 revisions of the confession.

64. For a discussion of some of the legal implications of ordination for Baptist ministers, see Porter Routh, "Ordination: Contemporary Problems," *Southwestern Journal of Theology* 11, no. 2 (1969): 71–85.

65. Marriages are a matter of state rather than federal law, and each state is free to handle the process differently ("Marriage Laws," Legal Information Institute, https://www.law.cornell.edu/wex/table_marriage). In some states the application of the laws are quite lax and the credentials of the officiants are not on file or audited. Consequently, people may utilize online ordination sites to obtain "credentials" to solemnize marriages and sign the license. Such is the state of affairs when the church becomes the agent of the state. What for many is a sacred matter (ordination) becomes available for a fee.

physical and spiritual families. However, many others have sought out "a preacher" to marry them, with no intent to live together and serve Christ in the church. This cultural reality has often put pastors and churches in an ethical bind. Were a pastor or church to define themselves more clearly, they might find themselves out of the wedding business. Baptists might be more consistent in our affirmation of the separation of church and state if we allowed government officials to solemnize marriages and only officiated over a Christian celebration of it in the context of a church and when the couple intends to form a Christ-centered home.[66]

If ordained Baptist pastors are to continue to accept the state's benefits (let him who is without sin cast the first stone), we might need to rethink our full position on church-state separation. To allow ordination to do anything other than set us apart for service to Christ's church may be to denigrate its significance. To permit the state to define us in a way that separates clergy and laity impinges on our view of the priesthood of all believers and our advocacy for a free church.

CONCLUSIONS

Although Baptists claim to root "faith and practice" in biblical teachings, an honest self-appraisal raises questions about the degree to which we look to Scripture to dictate the practice of ordination versus the degree to which we have assumed a practice and then sought biblical justification for it. Scholars are nearly unanimous in concluding that the New Testament offers no precedent for such a practice. Historically, Baptists have not always agreed on the propriety, much less the necessity, of the ordination of pastors. This

---

66. The curmudgeonly Baptist pastor Will D. Campbell relates his own awakening to the way that weddings turn pastors into agents of the state. In a conversation with his brother Joe, about Joe's divorce, he realized that a marriage license was merely a contract with the state and that he was signing it on the state's behalf. He writes,

I was never again to say, "By the authority vested in me by the State of Tennessee." If my authority as priest comes from the State, then I have no authority at all. From that time on I began all my weddings by saying, "Render unto Caesar the things that are Caesar's's. If you have a license, we will sign it at this time." And then saying to the couple, "Now what we have just done is to endow you with a legal contract. It has nothing to do with Christian marriage. It is nothing more than a contract between you and this state which gives you the right to sue one another if you should ever desire to do so." And the document is tossed casually and sometimes contemptuously aside. "Now the passage which begins 'Render unto Caesar the things that are Caesar's' continues. And render unto God the things that are God's." And the *wedding* begins at this point. (*Brother to a Dragonfly* [New York: Continuum, 2007], 213)

near-universal Baptist practice is especially difficult to justify on the basis of McClendon's "baptist vision": "this is that."

Nevertheless, most of us have practiced setting apart our ministers, replete with ceremony and certificates. Our practices regularly bump up against our professed principles. We advocate for the priesthood of all believers, yet we set some apart in a nearly sacerdotal role. We argue for the autonomy of the local church but turn to others to ordain our pastors. We reject apostolic succession but often have only those who are ordained lay hands on the candidate. We confess a conviction regarding the separation of church and state, yet our ordained ministers find themselves intrinsically caught up in the state's affairs as recipients of its benefits. The practical and spiritual advantages of ordination for our churches and our pastors have kept the custom in place. Yet we seem to need to justify the practice theologically or biblically. For four hundred years we maintained the tradition, but we have always felt the tensions that it produces to some degree. Ordination remains a topic for Baptist practical and systematic theologians to incorporate into our vision for being the church at the beginning and the end of the age.

FOR FURTHER REFLECTION •

1. How would you define or describe ordination to a secular friend who asked you what it means?

2. Do you believe that ordination is necessary for a person to serve as a Baptist pastor? What are the reasons for your position? Does ordination convey any authority that the nonordained do not possess?

3. How do you connect the practice of ordination with such Baptist convictions as (1) the priesthood of all believers and (2) the separation of church and state?

4. Who do you believe has the authority to ordain someone? The local church? The local association? The denomination? Who should lay hands on the candidate? Anyone in the church? Ordained persons only? Who should examine the candidate?

5. Do you believe a Baptist pastor should access the state's various benefits, such as exemption from military service, tax benefits, or authority to officiate at weddings? What are your reasons for your convictions?

4

Women in Ministry

Your Daughters Shall Prophesy

The council of fourteen Baptist churches, came, gave me a close examination of three hours, retired, prayed, talked, assured one another that they were in for honor, logic, and straightforward action, the only real issue being, *"In his gifts and callings, is the Holy Ghost limited by the fact of sex?"*

—Frances E. Townsley, *A Pilgrim Maid*

But this is that which was spoken by the prophet Joel; And it shall come to pass in the last days, saith God, I will pour out of my Spirit upon all flesh: and your sons and your daughters shall prophesy, and your young men shall see visions, and your old men shall dream dreams: And on my servants and on my handmaidens I will pour out in those days of my Spirit; and they shall prophesy.

—Simon Peter (Acts 2:16–18 KJV)

Women's roles in Baptist ministry relate directly to the questions of pastoral identity, call to ministry, and ordination raised in the first three chapters. Whom does God call to this task of shepherding the people of God? Who is to be set apart for that work by prayer and the laying on of hands? Men only? Or women as well? In parts of Baptist life, this has not been an issue. For some Baptist groups, both men and women exercise pastoral ministry with little controversy. In other expressions of the Baptist vision, only men have served in that role, without discussion. And in certain realms of Baptist life these days, the question is still being debated.[1] Baptists want to answer that question biblically: What does Scripture say? We also want to know what the practice among us has been over the past four centuries. And we want to pray and reflect on the full implications of our theology as we discern our own beliefs and practices in the matter. Baptists on both ends of the spectrum of conviction on this matter appeal to Scripture, Baptist tradition, and reasoned theology. Regardless of where a congregation or individual emerges on this question, substantive biblical, historical, and theological reflection still provides the guardrails that can keep us from running into either ancient or contemporary cultural ditches.[2]

Biblical Foundations

A thorough exegesis of all the relevant biblical texts on this subject is impossible in this limited space. Nor is that necessary, since books and articles abound. I do want to illustrate, however, that Baptists at both poles of opinion have sought to form their convictions out of the Baptist vision described earlier, which is the effort to shape the church's faith and practice in response to the biblical witness: "this is that." People at one pole may unhelpfully accuse those at the other of various motives for their convictions on this issue (for example, legalism, liberalism, conforming to contemporary cultural values, mindlessly sanctifying the customs of an ancient culture, misogyny, patriarchy). I cannot judge the motives behind the convictions of either, but I wish

1. Eileen R. Campbell-Reed, "Changing Hands: The Practice of Ordaining Baptist Women," *Baptist History and Heritage* 51, no. 1 (2016): 18–26; Richard Groves, "Southern Baptist Women in Ministry," *Christian Century* 101, no. 6 (February 22, 1984): 202–3.

2. Ann Miller outlines the questions that govern the controversy among Baptists in Texas: "Can a biblically sound, Christ-honoring church ordain women, although Jesus was male, and some people teach that God is male? Although Adam was created before Eve? Even though Eve was the first to sin in the Garden? Although Jesus chose twelve men for his closest followers? Although some teach that the Epistles restrict pastoral leadership to men? And remain faithful to Baptist practice? Even though Baptists have not yet reached consensus on this issue? What might Baptists risk in ordaining qualified women? What do Baptists gain in ordaining qualified women as well as men?" "The Ordination of Women among Texas Baptists," in *Baptists and Ordination: Studies Conducted by Baylor University and the Baptist General Convention of Texas*, ed. William H. Brackney, NABPR Special Studies Series 13 (Macon, GA: National Association of Baptist Professors of Religion, 2003), 132–33.

to point to the sense of commitment to understand and obey the Scripture that both profess to bring to the process.

Two passages in the New Testament appear to restrict women's roles in church leadership, and they are the ones most frequently cited in debates on the topic: 1 Timothy 2:8–15 and 1 Corinthians 14:33–36. On the surface, they are clear-cut statements forbidding women from speaking in church or teaching men. However, these words are heavily entangled with cultural elements that interpreters need to unravel. One passage addresses the church's strained situation in Corinth, and the other attends to problems arising in the church at Ephesus. Despite the differences between an ancient cultural context and ours, those who argue for a restricted role for women in the church often rely on these texts to provide biblical authority for their position.[3]

Taken at face value, which Baptists have often done, these passages preclude women from teaching men, having authority over men, or even speaking aloud in the congregation. Paul roots this instruction in the creation and fall (1 Tim. 2:13–14; cf. Gen. 2:7, 22; 3:1–7): the reason women are not to exercise authority over men or teach men is that "the man was first in creation and the woman was first in the Edenic fall (1 Tim. 2:13ff.)."[4] The list of qualifications for the office of overseer in 1 Timothy 3:1–7 likewise describes the candidate as being "husband of only one wife" (literally, "a one-woman man").[5] That would,

3. The rationale of most who restrict the role of women in the church goes beyond a handful of biblical texts, expressing a theological perspective about the inherent relationship between men and women intended by God in creation. Evangelicals refer to this position as "complementarianism," which defines men and women as "equal" but with different, "complementary" roles in family, church, and society. Additionally, some have bolstered their argument about limiting women in church leadership with the observation that Jesus chose twelve men to be the apostles, but no women. Some Baptists teach that God is a gender-specific being, "eternal, all-powerful, all-knowing, holy and male" (Miller, "Ordination of Women among Texas Baptists," 133). Consequently, they contend, a male pastor can represent God in a way that a female could not.

4. This is the language used in the 1984 Southern Baptist Convention resolution on "Ordination and the Role of Women in Ministry." H. Leon McBeth, *A Sourcebook for Baptist Heritage* (Nashville: Broadman, 1990), 520–21.

5. The "literal" meaning of this phrase is unclear. Does it address the gender of the bishop, or the bishop's morals? According to Daniel C. Arichea and Howard Hatton,

This looks as if it does not need further explanation, but the statement is more complicated than it seems. Does it mean, for example, that *bishops* should be married, and that unmarried men are disqualified? Or is this a statement against polygamy, so that a man with more than one wife cannot become a bishop? Or again, does this prohibit second marriages, so that a man who desires to be a bishop should not get married again, even though he is divorced or even if his first wife dies? . . . Or, finally, does this put stress on faithfulness to one's wife? (See, for example, NEB: "faithful to his one wife.") This last interpretation assumes that the person is married, but it does not rule out polygamy, divorce, and remarriage, and does not necessarily prohibit a widower from marrying again. All four options are possible, although the last option may have some advantages,

some contend, eliminate women from consideration for the office. Baptists who would argue that the church ought to be free to ordain women and call them to serve as pastors must address these texts without dismissing them.[6]

The cultural context of each of these passages complicates our reading of them. Women are forbidden to speak in the church in 1 Corinthians 14:33–36, but in 1 Corinthians 11:5 they are permitted to pray and proclaim God's word as long as their heads are covered. How can both these actions be allowed? Women are not to teach or have authority over a man (1 Tim. 2:11), and neither are they to wear their hair in braids nor adorn themselves with gold or pearls (1 Tim. 2:9). How do we sort out which of the statements in a single passage are universal instructions to the church and which are cultural matters irrelevant to our practices? Such issues suggest that something is going on in these texts rooted in ancient Greek, Roman, or Jewish culture and that moving directly from those instructions to the church through the ages may be problematic.

Despite claims to the contrary, the biblical evidence does not quickly and simply lead to a clear conclusion. If it did, Baptists would not have such varieties of practice over the years and such differences of opinion. Todd Still writes, "It should be noted that our questions and concerns regarding women in ministry are not explicitly or systematically addressed in Scripture. Therefore, when people maintain that the Bible is crystal clear on this matter or that clearer texts are to interpret unclear texts on this issue, you have every good reason to take such assertions with a grain of salt. Sound bites and shibboleths serve us poorly, especially on this subject."[7]

What other biblical evidence must Baptists deal with on this issue? Advocates for an unrestricted role for women in Baptist churches have argued that listening to all of Scripture requires attending to the clear examples of God's work in the past. What *has* God done, and how *has* God used women to lead Israel and the church to accomplish divine redemptive purposes?

---

since unfaithfulness in the marriage relationship was a common occurrence in the world of the New Testament. (*A Handbook on Paul's Letters to Timothy and to Titus*, UBS Handbook Series [New York: United Bible Societies, 1995], 66)

6. Scot McKnight writes in *The Blue Parakeet* about how we best read and apply Scripture to our lives, setting out a set of principles that lead to valid interpretation. In part 5 he uses the topic of women and ministry in the church as a test case, tracing his own change of mind on the subject from the more literal end of the spectrum to a position that is open to women serving in the church in the same roles as men. McKnight offers a reading of these more restrictive passages in 1 Timothy and 1 Corinthians. Whether one accepts his interpretation or not, McKnight's work represents a clear and concise reading of these controversial texts. See *The Blue Parakeet: Rethinking How You Read the Bible*, 2nd ed. (Grand Rapids: Zondervan, 2018), 194–261.

7. Todd D. Still, "Women in Ministry: Biblical, Theological, and Practical Reflections," George W. Truett Theological Seminary, Baylor University, https://www.baylor.edu/content/services/document.php/144245.pdf.

The biblical story testifies that women have led people into God's presence in worship. One of the earliest corporate worship experiences described in detail followed the exodus, that significant experience in which God redeemed Israel and set them apart. God brought the people safely through the Red Sea. Miriam, Moses's sister, stood and led a group of women in singing praises to God, and it seemed to please the Lord (Exod. 15:20). Other women regularly ministered outside the tent of meeting, helping to facilitate God's people in worship (Exod. 38:8; 1 Sam. 2:22).

Through the ages, in both the Old and the New Testaments, women delivered divine messages to God's people. In both Testaments, prophets speak for God. They are preachers declaring the divine will and mind to God's people. Miriam was a prophetess (Exod. 15:20), which indicates that God gives the gift of prophecy to both men and women. In Micah 6:4, God rebukes the people of Israel for their failure to respond over the centuries. One of the accusations God leveled against them was this: "I sent Moses to lead you, also Aaron and Miriam" (NIV). Deborah was a prophetess and a judge and ruler over Israel as well (Judg. 4). The armies of Israel went to her for their instruction. Barak, the leader of Israel's army, was preparing for battle against Sisera and said he would not go to war unless Deborah also agreed to go, since she represented God among them.

The king of Israel sent priests to Huldah the prophetess to hear God's word and understand God's purposes (2 Kings 22:14). Isaiah refers to his wife as "the prophetess" (Isa. 8:3). The prophet Joel foresaw a time when the Messiah would come and God would pour out the Holy Spirit, a prophecy fulfilled on Pentecost (Acts 2:1–21). Joel says,

> Then afterward
>   I will pour out my spirit on all flesh;
> your sons and your daughters shall prophesy,
>   your old men shall dream dreams,
>   and your young men shall see visions.
> Even on the male and female slaves,
>   in those days, I will pour out my spirit. (Joel 2:28–29)

In the last days, both men and women will be spokespersons for God among the people of God and to the world. They will be prophets and prophetesses.

Luke's infancy narratives introduce an older woman named Anna, who ministered in the temple of God in Jerusalem and who awaited the Messiah's birth. Luke describes her as a prophetess, a spokesperson of God to Israel (Luke 2:36–38). Peter stood on the day of Pentecost and said, "This is what was spoken through the prophet Joel" (Acts 2:16–18), as both men and women bore witness to God's mighty acts (Acts 1:14; 2:4, 11). Philip was an evangelist in the early church and one of the seven selected to serve the Hellenistic Jewish believers in Jerusalem (Acts 6:1–6). He had four daughters who never married, and all were prophetesses (Acts 21:9). Paul encouraged women who prophesy in the church to conform to the cultural practice of covering their heads when they spoke (1 Cor. 11:5).[8] God has used women to address both Israel and the church, declaring the divine will.

Women serve as role models for discipleship and piety in the Gospel stories, especially in Luke's Gospel.[9] In the Gospel of John, the first person to whom Jesus appears after his resurrection is one of his devoted female followers, Mary Magdalene, while the men were cowering in fear and guilt back in their dens (John 20:11–18).[10] She was the first one commissioned to go and announce the resurrection. All four Gospels offer some variation of this event, but in every story the women are the first to proclaim the Easter message: "Christ is risen!" It was not women who betrayed Jesus or denied him. The women in the New Testament appear as followers and devotees of Jesus, whose stories function as paradigms of discipleship. A poor widow places her gift in the temple treasury, and Jesus commends her above all others, holding her up as an example (Mark 12:41–44). Martha serves Jesus, and Mary sits at his feet, learning from him (Luke 10:38–42). During the last week of Jesus's life, Mary anoints him proleptically for burial (John 12:1–8). Even Jesus's parables are replete with stories of both men and women who symbolize God's kingdom.

God used women in the early church as leaders and servants in various ways. When Paul discusses spiritual gifts, he never makes giftedness a gender issue.[11] He identifies no male gifts and female gifts so that men, for example, receive gifts such as apostle, prophet, teacher, and pastor, while women are assigned gifts such as helping or mercy. Paul simply describes the Spirit's gifts

8. For a reading of 1 Cor. 11:2–16 as restricting women's roles in the church, see Thomas R. Schreiner, "Head Coverings," in *Recovering Biblical Manhood and Womanhood: A Response to Evangelical Feminism*, ed. John Piper and Wayne Grudem (Wheaton: Crossway, 1991), 124–39. For a reading arguing for an egalitarian position in the church, see the works by Lucy Peppiatt and Scot McKnight, *Unveiling Paul's Women* (Eugene, OR: Wipf & Stock, 2018) and *Rediscovering Scripture's Vision for Women: Fresh Perspectives on Disputed Texts* (Downers Grove, IL: IVP Academic, 2019).

9. See Greg W. Forbes, *Raised from Obscurity: A Narratival and Theological Study of the Characterization of Women in Luke-Acts* (Eugene, OR: Pickwick, 2015).

10. Karen Heidebrecht Thiessen, "Jesus and Women in the Gospel of John," *Direction* 19, no. 2 (1990): 52–64.

11. Boubakar Sanou, "Spiritual Gifts, Pastoring, and Gender: An Ongoing Dialogue," *Journal of Applied Christian Leadership* 11, no. 2 (2017): 84–91.

that God sovereignly bestows on men and women who make up the body of Christ. In the New Testament, men and women alike specifically receive the gift of prophecy.

Paul sometimes closes his letters by acknowledging his friends or sending greetings from those who are with him. Bible readers often pay no more attention to those closing passages than they do to biblical genealogies. We simply overlook them. But these passages have a story to tell about life in the early church. In Romans 16:1–2, for example, Paul writes, "I commend to you our sister Phoebe, a deacon of the church at Cenchreae, so that you may welcome her in the Lord as is fitting for the saints, and help her in whatever she may require from you, for she has been a benefactor of many and of myself as well." Most modern interpreters understand that Phoebe was a deaconess at the church in Cenchreae.[12] She is the person to whom Paul entrusts the Letter to the Romans—the scroll he has written—to deliver it from Corinth to Rome. The most important document written in Christian history, perhaps, is placed in Phoebe's hands, a deaconess from the church of Cenchreae.

Paul mentions Prisca and Aquila in Romans 16:3 and 2 Timothy 4:19.[13] This couple first appears in the New Testament in Acts 18:1–3, when Paul joined them in their tent-making trade. After some time in ministry together in Corinth, they accompanied Paul to Ephesus, where he left them to lay groundwork for the church, promising to return (Acts 18:18–21). During Paul's absence, a man named Apollos arrived in Ephesus. He was a brilliant scholar and orator familiar with the Old Testament and with the preaching of John the Baptist (Acts 18:24–25). However, he had not yet heard the gospel of Jesus Christ. When he taught in the synagogue, Aquila and Priscilla heard him.

After the synagogue service was over, they invited him to their home, where "they took him aside and explained the Way of God to him more accurately" (Acts 18:26). *They* instructed him. *Priscilla*, along with Aquila, taught Apollos. Paul writes later to Timothy, who was working in Ephesus, "I permit no woman to teach or to have authority over a man; she is to keep silent" (1 Tim. 2:12). Given the story of Priscilla's work in Ephesus, we must assume some kind

12. The Greek text describes Phoebe as a *diakonon*, a masculine noun that elsewhere in the New Testament describes the office of deacon (Phil. 1:1; 1 Tim. 3:8, 11). Some versions translate the word in Rom. 16:1 as "servant," usually with a footnote indicating the word can also be transliterated as "deacon" (KJV, ESV, NASB). Other English versions transliterate it as they do in Phil. 1:1 and 1 Tim. 3:8, 11, rendering it as "deacon" or "deaconess" and implying that it refers to the office in the early church. The NRSV includes a note with the alternative translation "minister."

13. These two are mentioned several times, always together, in Acts and Paul's Epistles (Acts 18:2, 18; 26; Rom. 16:3; 1 Cor. 16:19; 2 Tim. 4:19). In most cases, Prisca (or Priscilla) is mentioned first (Acts 18:2 and 1 Cor. 16:19 are exceptions).

of cultural context where the silence Paul enjoins is the exception rather than the rule since the practice appears to be otherwise in Paul's missionary work.

In Romans 16:6, Paul speaks of Mary, who is a hard worker in the church, and then of an intriguing couple in verse 7: "Andronicus and Junia [a man and a woman], my relatives who were in prison with me; they are prominent among the apostles, and they were in Christ before I was." Paul calls them *both* apostles.[14] Romans 16:12–15 identifies other women who played noteworthy roles in Paul's life. First Corinthians 1:11 mentions a church in Chloe's household, meaning probably a church that met at her house, where she was most likely the leader or pastor. Nympha, mentioned in Colossians 4:15, likewise leads a church meeting in her home. Euodia and Syntyche appear in Philippians as Paul's fellow workers (Phil. 4:2–3); and Lydia, the first convert in Philippi, was the person who opened her home for the church's beginnings in Europe (Acts 16:11–15).

Those Baptists who argue for women in the church to exercise a more egalitarian role frequently cite Paul's words in Galatians 3:28: "There is no longer Jew or Greek, there is no longer slave or free, there is no longer male and female; for all of you are one in Christ Jesus."[15] In this text, Paul is making a clear countercultural claim about religion, race, class, and gender. He spent most of his ministry arguing that the Jew-Greek dichotomy did not obtain in Christ's body, and his argument eventually won the day in the church. Paul's teaching against such caste divisions as slave or free was centuries from being widely recognized in the Western world. For a long time, some Baptists used an array of biblical texts to *affirm* the institution of slavery. Eventually the countercultural declaration of Galatians 3:28 bore fruit. Similarly, the gender division continues in many Christian contexts, with proponents citing texts to affirm it even as others once used the Bible to establish slavery. However, some Baptists contend that what Paul claimed for gentiles and slaves also applies to women in Christ: full equality in the church.[16]

14. Scot McKnight, *Junia Is Not Alone* (Englewood, CO: Patheos, 2011).

15. Paul's wording in Gal. 3:28 is instructive. He says there is "no longer Jew or [*oude*] Greek, there is no longer slave or [*oude*] free, there is no longer male and [*kai*] female." Why does he change from "or" (*oude*) in the series to "and" (*kai*)? He is reflecting the language of Gen. 1:27 in the LXX. God created human beings in the divine image *arsen kai thēly*, "male and female." This is the exact wording Paul uses in Gal. 3:28. He alludes to that time in the human story before the fall when "male and female" together reflected the divine image. Sin enters that relationship and male dominance follows (Gen. 3:16), but now in Christ the new creation prevails (Gal. 6:15). The equality and interdependence present in the original design for human relationships is restored (1 Cor. 11:11–12). All are one in Christ Jesus.

16. For a complementarian reading of Gal. 3:28, see Richard W. Hove, *Equality in Christ: Galatians 3:28 and the Gender Dispute* (Wheaton: Crossway, 1999). For an egalitarian reading of this and other key texts in Paul's writings, see Philip Barton Payne, *Man and Woman, One in Christ: An Exegetical and Theological Study of Paul's Letters* (Grand Rapids: Zondervan Academic, 2009).

Baptists who argue for an egalitarian relationship between men and women in ministry must come to terms with the passages that appear to silence women and relegate them to a submissive role in the church. These texts require accurate interpretation rather than dismissal. In the same way, Baptists who hear women professing a call from God to the role of pastor or the task of preaching and leading and yet would withhold that ministry from them, they also must deal with the texts that testify to the vital part that women played in God's redemptive plan in both the Old and New Testaments. They must also respond to the declaration of liberty and equality for those the first-century Jewish and Roman cultures devalued—gentiles, slaves, and women. When we Baptists have been at our best, we have come to terms with the broad teachings of Scripture: like the Bereans of Acts 17:11, we carefully attend to Scripture and form our beliefs and practices in response. In the matter of the role of women in ministry, when the biblical message is equivocal, we should not be surprised to find that Baptists have reached different conclusions over the centuries and that they all claim to have their convictions rooted in Scripture.

Historical Bypaths

One source of our faith and practice laid alongside Scripture, but never its equal in authority, is Baptist tradition, the Baptist voices of the past. How have our spiritual ancestors answered these questions? What have they practiced? Turning to them does not mean that we must do what they have done, but it does mean that we let them speak and we listen respectfully. The Yale University church historian Jaroslav Pelikan said in his 1983 Jefferson Lecture, "Tradition is the living faith of the dead; traditionalism is the dead faith of the living. And, I suppose I should add, it is traditionalism that gives tradition such a bad name."[17] We should not be surprised to learn that our Baptist ancestors do not speak with one voice on women and ministry.

Baptist Confessions of Faith

Baptist confessions of faith have historically said little about the role of women in the church and ministry. Some early Baptist confessions, such as A

---

17. Jaroslav Pelikan, *The Vindication of Tradition: The 1983 Jefferson Lecture in the Humanities* (New Haven: Yale University Press, 1986), 65. Pelikan later commented further on this notion in an interview with *U.S. News & World Report*: "Tradition lives in conversation with the past, while remembering where we are and when we are and that it is we who have to decide." Joseph Carey, "Christianity as an Enfolding Circle [Conversation with Jaroslav Pelikan]," *U.S. News & World Report*, June 26, 1989, 57.

Declaration of Faith of 1611 and The Baptist Confession of 1612, acknowledged women serving as deaconesses. Although among General Baptists women sometimes preached, no early sources mention their serving as pastors. In Principles and Inferences (1607), John Smyth allowed for deaconesses but expressly forbade women to preach.[18] In 1965 the American Baptist Convention adopted a resolution that affirmed women's equality and advocated women's ordination.[19] More recently, the Conference of Seventh Day Baptists included a statement in their Manual of Procedures (2004) affirming that the call of God leads both "men and women to dedicate themselves to professional ministry."[20] Southern Baptists, meanwhile, added a line to the Baptist Faith and Message in 2000 declaring it a doctrinal position that "while both men and women are gifted for service in the church, the office of pastor is limited to men as qualified by Scripture."[21] Other Baptist groups have confessed their faith not with documents but by what they practice, either by ordaining women to ministry or refusing to do so.

Baptist Practices

Unquestionably the dominant practice among Baptists over the past four hundred years has been to have only men preach and serve as pastors. This remains the reality among Baptists generally around the world. However, from the earliest days, and among many Baptist groups, the rule has had its exceptions. Pamela R. Durso identifies early seventeenth-century Baptist women who preached throughout England, such as Anne Hempstall, Mary Bilbrow, Joane Bauford, Susan May, Elizabeth Bancroft, and Arabell Thomas.[22] Durso cites a 1641 document claiming that these women took up the task of preaching because "there was a deficiency of good men, wherefore it was but fit that virtuous women should supply their places."[23] Mrs. Attaway, who preached in the 1640s, was a member of a General Baptist church in London.[24]

18. McBeth, *Sourcebook for Baptist Heritage*, 54.
19. Eileen R. Campbell-Reed and Pamela R. Durso, "The State of Women in Baptist Life—2005," Baptist Women in Ministry, June 2006, https://bwim.info/files/State%20of%20Women%20in%20Baptist%20Life%202005.pdf.
20. Pamela R. Durso, *This Is What a Preacher Looks Like: Sermons by Baptist Women*, Baptist Women in Ministry (Macon, GA: Smyth & Helwys, 2010), 523.
21. Baptist Faith and Message (2000), article 6.
22. Pamela Robinson Durso, "Baptists and the Turn toward Baptist Women in Ministry," in *Turning Points in Baptist History: A Festschrift in Honor of Harry Leon McBeth*, ed. Michael E. Williams and Walter B. Shurden (Macon, GA: Mercer University Press, 2008), 275.
23. Durso, "Baptists," 276.
24. The General Baptists were more open to women preaching than were the Particular Baptists. Even the Particular Baptists felt the tension between a biblicism that forbade women

Her activity provoked a Presbyterian pastor, Thomas Edwards, who strenuously opposed Baptists, to label her as the "mistress of all the she-preachers on Coleman Street."[25]

Early Baptists in New England also had a share of "she-preachers." James R. Lynch identifies Catherine Scott, sister of Ann Hutchinson, as one of the earliest Baptists to move to Roger Williams's settlement at Providence, Rhode Island. Lynch cites John Winthrop's *Journal*, in which Winthrop describes her as having been "infected with Anabaptistry." Winthrop also credits Scott's influence over Roger Williams for his making a public profession of believer's baptism, being baptized by Ezekiel Holiman, and then baptizing those who became part of the first Baptist church in America.[26] Scott later became a Quaker. In 1658 she went to Boston to protest two Quakers' imprisonment and was herself imprisoned and publicly whipped for her effort.[27]

Many of the Baptist women who preached in the early days of the colonies were members of Separate Baptist churches, a group of Baptists, primarily in the South, growing out of the Great Awakening. Martha Stearns Marshall, sister of Baptist evangelist Shubal Stearns, was a prominent preacher among these Baptists. Daniel Marshall, her husband, was a pastor and considered her preaching to be an appropriate demonstration of her spiritual giftedness. Robert Semple, an early nineteenth-century Baptist historian, described her as a woman "of good sense, singular piety, and surprising elocution," who on "countless occasions melted a whole congregation into tears by her prayers and exhortations."[28] Many Baptists were scandalized by her ministry, however.[29]

Durso traces the historical record of "firsts" among Baptist women in America.[30] Free Will Baptists were likely the first Baptist churches to formally

---

to speak in church and the calling and gifting of some of the women among them. See Ian Birch, "The Ministry of Women among Early Calvinistic Baptists," *Scottish Journal of Theology* 69, no. 4 (2016): 402–16.

25. Dorothy P. Ludlow, "Shaking Patriarchy's Foundations: Sectarian Women in England, 1641–1700," in *Triumph over Silence: Women in Protestant History*, ed. Richard L. Greaves, Contributions to the Study of Religion 15 (Westport, CT: Greenwood, 1985), 96.

26. James R. Lynch, "A Preliminary Check List of Baptist Women in Ministry through 1920," *American Baptist Quarterly* 13, no. 4 (December 1994): 319.

27. Lynch, "Preliminary Check List," 304.

28. Robert Semple, *History of the Rise and Progress of Baptists in Virginia* (Richmond, 1810), 374, cited by Durso, "Baptists," 277.

29. Lynch provides a table listing all the Baptist women in ministry he could document between 1638 and 1920 ("Preliminary Check List," 308–9).

30. Durso puts "first" in scare quotes to indicate, apparently, that these are approximations ("Baptists," 277). Lynch says, "I really don't think enough substantive research has been done in the field to warrant proclaiming anyone 'the first.'" "Preliminary Check List," 307.

recognize women ministers, licensing Ruby Bixby to preach in 1846.[31] The first documented ordination of a Baptist woman occurred in 1876 when the Belle Vernon Free Will Baptist Church recognized M. A. Brennan as a minister. Other women were ordained among the Free Will Baptists in the years immediately following. The first ordination of a woman among Northern Baptists (now American Baptist Churches, USA) took place in 1882, when May C. Jones was set apart for ministry by the Baptist Association of Puget Sound in Washington. Three years later, Frances E. Townsley was ordained by Northern Baptists in Nebraska. In 1885 Seventh Day Baptists ordained Experience Fitz Randolph Burdick in New York, where she served several churches.[32]

In the twentieth century, other firsts occurred. In 1922 Edith Gates was the first British Baptist woman ordained to the ministry, followed two years later by Maria Living-Taylor. Then, notes Durso, "for a period of forty years, from the early 1920s to the early 1960s, no other 'first' ordinations of Baptist women have been discovered and documented."[33] In 1962 a church associated with the National Baptist Convention, USA, ordained Arlene Churn. The first Southern Baptist woman ordained to ministry was Addie Davis, who in 1964 was set apart by the Watts Street Baptist Church in Durham, North Carolina. She could not find a place to serve in a Southern Baptist church and so became pastor of the First Baptist Church of Readsboro, Virginia, an American Baptist Convention congregation. In 1972 Druecillar Fordham, who had been ordained in an American Baptist Convention church, served as pastor of an American Baptist congregation in New York City. Her church later joined the Metro New York Baptist Association, affiliated with the Southern Baptist Convention. She then became both the first woman to serve as pastor of a Southern Baptist church and the first Black female to do so. Over the next thirty years, Baptists in Australia, the Philippines, Cuba, Brazil, and Mexico called and ordained women for the first time.[34]

Karen Bullock observes that opportunities for Baptist women worldwide shifted significantly during the last quarter of the twentieth century. "In Japan, China, Africa, and Western Europe, for example, women found greater freedom to minister. Indeed, 11 percent of the pastors in the Japanese Baptist

31. Other Free Will Baptist women had preached earlier, including Nancy Savage and Sally Parsons in the late eighteenth century. Other early nineteenth-century women who preached among Free Will Baptists include Almira Bullock, Hannah Fogg, Susan Humes, Judith Prescott, Mrs. Quimby, Betsey Stuart, Sarah Thornton, Clarissa Danforth, and Martha Spaulding, according to Lynch, "Preliminary Check List," 305.

32. Durso, "Baptists," 278–79.

33. Durso, "Baptists," 280.

34. Durso, "Baptists," 281.

Convention were women in 1995."[35] In the United States, however, the shift
was more substantial in the opposite direction. In 1984 the largest Baptist body,
the Southern Baptist Convention, adopted a resolution opposing women's
ordination.[36] In 2000 they revised the Baptist Faith and Message (their confession of faith) to exclude women from serving as pastors. Women are finding
a place in ministry among some Baptist groups in the twenty-first century,
but the numbers remain relatively small.[37]

Baptist Stories

Ruby Bixby (1818–1877)

In June 1846 the Home Mission Board of the Free Will Baptists commissioned Ruby Bixby and her husband, Rev. N. W. Bixby, to serve in Iowa, where
they finally settled a year later. Their journey to Iowa took them from Vermont
to a seminary in Whitestown, New York, and then to Wisconsin. In Wisconsin,
the Honey Creek Quarterly Meeting of the Free Will Baptists licensed Ruby to
preach. Her license was renewed when she arrived in Iowa, where she and her
husband organized a church at Lodomillo in Clayton County. The church's
records list Ruby as the minister from 1849 until her death in January 1877.
Ruby was born in January 1818 in Huntington, Vermont, to Peter and Olive
Knapp. Her obituary in the *Morning Star* on January 24, 1877, observes that
"her mother was a preacher before her." The obituary contains a summary
of her life and character:

> The love element was predominant in her nature, her daily example, and her
> ministry. She was not a subordinate, secondary helpmate, merely, but an indepen-
> dent, self-reliant preacher. Her discourses were characteristically persuasive, and
> she was more than ordinarily successful. She preached much with churches as

35. Karen Bullock, "Baptists and Women and the Turn toward Gender Inclusion," in Williams and Shurden, *Turning Points in Baptist History*, 218.
36. McBeth, *Sourcebook for Baptist Heritage*, 520–21.
37. "When the first 'State of Women in Baptist Life' report was published in 2005, 102
women were identified as pastors or co-pastors of [Baptist] churches [in the United States]. . . .
By 2015, the total number of women pastors and co-pastors had grown to 174, which is a 71%
increase over the last ten years. These increases indicate that incremental change is taking place."
Pamela R. Durso and Kevin Pratano, "State of Women in Baptist Life Update," Baptist Women
in Ministry, revised July 2016, 10, https://bwim.info/wp-content/uploads/2016/11/SWBL-2015
-revised-7-11-16.pdf. According to Eileen Campbell-Reed, none of the forty-seven thousand
Southern Baptist Convention churches have a female pastor ("The State of Clergywomen in the
U.S.: A Statistical Update October 2018," https://eileencampbellreed.org/state-of-clergy/). See
also Tracy L Hartman, "Already but Not Yet: The Status of Women Baptist Pastors," *Review &
Expositor* 110, no. 1 (2013): 65–76; and Eileen R. Campbell-Reed, "Baptists in Tension: The Status of Women's Leadership and Ministry, 2012," *Review & Expositor* 110, no. 1 (2013): 49–64.

a pastor, and much as an evangelist. She enjoyed many revivals, and hundreds of souls will, in the day of the Lord, rise up and call her blessed. . . . Her last illness was, humanly judging, induced by her exhaustive labors in a revival, a few miles distant which she had conducted for weeks.

Ruby Bixby was the first woman licensed as a Free Will Baptist preacher that historians can document.[38]

Addie Davis (1917–2005)

Addie Davis was the first woman ordained by a Southern Baptist Convention church. She was born in Covington, Virginia, on June 29, 1917, and was a lifelong Southern Baptist. Even as a child she sensed a call to preach, but in a context where women were not allowed to do so, she never spoke openly about that. After graduation, Davis attended Meredith College and served as a director of religious education in a Baptist church. But her calling, she believed, was to be a pastor. At that time, Southern Baptist seminaries would not train women for ministry, so Davis applied to and was accepted at both Yale Divinity School and Duke Divinity School. Before she could matriculate, family responsibilities called. Her father died, and her mother needed her to help run the family furniture business. For the next decade, until her mother's retirement, Davis worked alongside her mother. During that time, she served six months as the interim pastor at the Lone Star Baptist Church outside Covington, preaching weekly and offering pastoral care.

In 1960, at age forty-three, Davis returned to seminary for theological training when Southeastern Baptist Theological Seminary began to receive female students. She and five other women were among the first graduates of the seminary. In her last year at Southeastern, Davis attended the Watts Street Baptist Church. Eventually, she approached Warren Carr, the pastor, asking for ordination. Carr was open but insisted that Davis join the church and serve actively so that the people of Watts Street might have the opportunity to know her. He also insisted that she not be ordained until a congregation called her as pastor. The church eventually licensed her to preach in March 1963, just two months before she graduated from seminary.[39]

38. Lynch, "Preliminary Check List," 311–12.
39. The church purchased the licensing certificate from the Baptist Sunday School Board, and it read, "This is to certify that Addie Davis, who has given evidence that God has called him into THE GOSPEL MINISTRY was Licensed to preach the Gospel as he may have opportunity, and to exercise his gifts in the work of the Ministry by Watts Street Baptist Church of Durham, North Carolina, on the thirteenth day of March, 1963."

Davis's search for a pastoral position took more than a year. She was not able to find a Southern Baptist church that would consider her. Eventually, she reached out to a friend in the American Baptist Convention and made connections with the First Baptist Church in Readsboro, Vermont, who called her to serve as their pastor. Once again, Davis requested ordination from Watts Street. The church formed an ordination council and examined Davis as to her faith in Christ, her call, and her doctrine. After some dissent, the council voted unanimously to recommend ordination, with one member abstaining. Watts Street Baptist Church ordained Addie Davis on August 9, 1964. Both she and Carr received immediate backlash from Baptists who opposed the ordination of a woman. For the next forty-one years, Davis served as a Baptist pastor in Vermont, Rhode Island, and in her hometown of Covington, Virginia.[40]

Theological Reflection

I understand that many of my Baptist friends, working from the same Baptist vision as I do ("this is that"), sincerely believe that women should not preach or serve as a pastor. They are in the majority of Baptists over time. Reading Scripture, walking the historical bypaths of the Baptist story, and encountering Baptist pastors who happen to be women, however, leads me to affirm both men and women in the pastoral role. I believe that conclusion to be both scriptural and baptistic. At this point, it may be helpful to think through the way women in Baptist ministry intersect with other Baptist convictions.

The Priesthood of All Believers

The covenant with Israel at Sinai declared God's intention for them to be "a priestly kingdom" (Exod. 19:6). The Lord's promise could not merely mean that Israel would be a nation with priests among them. The other nations had priests as well. The phrase implied that the nation Israel would function as a priest, a mediator between God and people, on behalf of all other nations. Despite this special calling given to Israel, God says, "Indeed, the whole earth

40. This summary of Addie Davis's life is drawn from Pamela Robinson Durso, "Journey to Ordination: Addie Davis and Watts Street Baptist Church," *Baptist History and Heritage* 51, no. 1 (2016): 27–36. For further details on Davis's life, see Pamela R. Durso and LeAnn Gunter Johns, *The World Is Waiting for You: Celebrating the 50th Ordination Anniversary of Addie Davis* (Macon, GA: Smyth & Helwys, 2014), and Pamela R. Durso and Keith E. Durso, *Courage and Hope: The Stories of Ten Baptist Women Ministers* (Macon, GA: Mercer University Press, 2005).

is mine" (Exod. 19:5). In the New Testament, early Christians transferred the language of the universal priesthood of Israel to the church, made up of people from "every tribe and language and people and nation" of whom God makes "a kingdom and priests serving our God" (Rev. 5:9–10). The priesthood of all believers is not primarily about individuals approaching God freely without the sacerdotal mediation of an ordained priest. Instead, it is about believers being part of the body of Christ, our High Priest, and functioning in the world as mediators of God's love, mercy, compassion, forgiveness, and reconciliation. We do this within the church, serving as priests to one another. We hear one another's confessions and intercede for each other (James 5:16). We also do this for all the nations of the earth, who also belong to God. Priesthood is inherently mutual. Priesthood is intrinsically missional.

Priesthood includes all of us. From the beginning of the Baptist movement, we, along with other branches of the Reformation, have confessed this conviction. For Baptists, it became a central tenet, "the priesthood of all believers."[41] In the Old Testament, priesthood did not belong to everyone. To be a priest, one had to be Jewish, not gentile. One also had to be a free person; a slave could not be a priest. Additionally, priesthood required belonging to the tribe of Levi. And one had to be male, not female. In Galatians, Paul describes the new liberty found in Christ with a revolutionary claim. In 3:28 he declares that in Jesus Christ, those previous distinctions apply no longer. There is neither Jew nor Greek; both gentile and Jew can be priests before God, as faith in Jesus Christ permits them. God accepts both slaves and free people as priests, and both male and female. The priesthood includes *all* believers. God has made us all priests before our God and Father (1 Pet. 2:5, 9; Rev. 5:10; 20:6).

The priesthood of all believers affirms that God calls all of us to mutual ministry. Priesthood is an active role, not a passive one. Priests serve. They intercede for others. They direct people's attention to God in corporate worship. They listen to confessed sins. They announce God's grace and forgiveness. Inside the church's life, all believers are authorized and commissioned to serve as priests to one another. This mutual ministry does not belong to a few among us but belongs to all of us, whether male or female. The Holy Spirit gave women in the New Testament church the gift and role of being prophets, and as part of the body of Christ, women also received the role of priest. Nothing in the New Testament segregates that priesthood by gender. Women who have confessed faith in Jesus Christ, been baptized into

41. Walter B. Shurden, *The Doctrine of the Priesthood of Believers* (Nashville: Convention, 1987).

his body, and have received the Holy Spirit are as fully priests as any man in the church. This mutual ministry belongs to women just as it does to men.[42]

The priesthood of all believers is intrinsically a missional notion. The "kingdom of priests" that God established at Sinai and expanded to take in believers from all languages, ethnicities, and cultures has a responsibility to reach beyond ourselves. That priestly responsibility extends to all of God's world, all the nations of the earth. The "kingdom of priests" testifies to the world of God's love, Christ's sacrifice, and the Spirit's presence.[43] This task of bearing witness belongs to both our daughters and our sons, whom God calls to testify (Acts 2:17). On the day of Pentecost, both men and women proclaimed this message to the people gathered in Jerusalem (Acts 2:11). Their testimony was a priestly service not limited by gender. Both men and women are part of the body of Christ. Both have gifts for ministry. God has called both to priestly service. Both experience an ordination at baptism that sets them apart for God's purposes.

The only "ordination" found in Scripture may be the ceremony for the cleansing and dedication of the Levites (Num. 8) and the consecration of Aaron and his sons as priests (Lev. 8; cf. Exod. 29).[44] Neither kings nor prophets were publicly set apart to God like this. Similarly, the only "ordination" in the New Testament is the ordination of the priesthood, which belongs to all of God's people and transpires publicly at our baptism. Jesus Christ is the Great High Priest, under whom we are priestly people, male and female. One of the chief roles of a priest is intercessory prayer. In the New Testament, women fill that role of leadership alongside men. In Acts 1, as the early followers of Jesus—120 of them in all—gathered in an upper room and began, in obedience to Jesus, to pray for the coming of God's Spirit upon the church's life, Luke specifies that the followers of Jesus were there, as were the women who had followed him (Acts 1:14). Those women were part of the prayer meeting, asking God to fulfill the promises Jesus had spoken before his ascension.

When Herod arrested Peter and condemned him to death, his friends assembled to pray in the home of John Mark's mother (Acts 12:4–18). That

---

42. The Canadian Baptists of Atlantic Canada affirm this statement of faith regarding the priesthood of all believers: "Baptists hold that ALL believers share as equals in the church, and, in turn, have a priestly role toward each other. Every member is called to be a minister. Differences in education, wealth, gender and so on do not disqualify a person from service or from serving God through ministry to others." John McNally, "Missional Implications with Baptist Expressions of the Priesthood of All Believers," *Baptistic Theologies* 10, no. 1 (2018): 50.

43. See Susan M. Pigott, "A Response to 'The Old Testament Antecedents to Ordination' by Thomas Brisco," in Brackney, *Baptists and Ordination*, 19–20.

44. Thomas Brisco, "Old Testament Antecedents to Ordination," in Brackney, *Baptists and Ordination*, 7–11.

gathering of priestly intercessors became an instrument God used to set the apostle free and preserve his life. The priesthood of all believers indicates that God uses both men and women to intercede for divine purposes in the world. In 1 Corinthians 11:5 Paul instructs the women who pray in the church to cover their heads, but he does not tell them not to pray. Intercessory prayer is an appropriate priestly task for believer-priests.

A theology of pastoral ministry limiting the pastorate to men needs to come to terms with a more thorough articulation of the priesthood of all believers. Scripture assigns both priesthood and prophecy to men and women in the New Testament. What do pastors do that exceeds the privileges of priesthood and prophecy? What is it that male believer-priests can do as pastors that female believer-priests cannot?

The Autonomy of the Local Church

Inherent in the Baptist vision is our insistence on the autonomy of the local church. This conviction comes into play regarding ordination. If Christ, as head of the local church, has authorized the congregation to elect and ordain its leaders, what other body has any authority to challenge them? No other local church or denominational body can do so. The congregation is autonomous under the lordship of Christ. For the first time, in 1963, a Southern Baptist confession of faith explicitly declared this conviction: "This church is an autonomous body, operating through democratic processes under the Lordship of Jesus Christ."[45] For Baptists, local church autonomy was not a novel idea, however.

Baptists have extended this principle to their other organizations. Associations, for example, usually exercise their autonomy from other denominational agencies or conventions. Whether at a state or national level, Baptist conventions have no authority over either local associations or congregations. These various entities often choose to cooperate around mission and ministries but do so with a high measure of autonomy. James L. Sullivan, a Southern Baptist leader in the mid-twentieth century, referred to the arrangement as "a rope of sand."[46]

The rope holds when the cooperation is around a common mission but has often failed when doctrine is at stake. To take a recent but not isolated

45. Baptist Faith and Message (1963), article 6. Neither the Baptist Faith and Message (1925) nor the New Hampshire Confession of Faith (1833), upon which it was based, expressed this notion explicitly. The revision of the Baptist Faith and Message in 2000 retained it.

46. James L. Sullivan, *Rope of Sand with Strength of Steel: How Southern Baptists Function and Why* (Nashville: Convention, 1974).

example, First Baptist Church of Jefferson City, Tennessee, had been part of the Tennessee Baptist Convention for 140 years. In the fall of 2017, the church called Rev. Ellen Di Giosia as their pastor. Subsequently, messengers at the Tennessee Baptist Convention voted not to seat messengers from Jefferson City, effectively cutting fellowship with the church.[47]

On the one hand, First Baptist Church, as an autonomous Baptist congregation, had every right to call Di Giosia. On the other hand, the Tennessee Baptist Convention, as an independent Baptist body, had every right to decide which beliefs and behaviors it will tolerate within its fellowship. Neither is technically usurping the other's autonomy by these actions. That is not to say the state convention *ought* to have taken the step they did. They might just as easily have exercised their autonomy by allowing First Baptist to call a woman as pastor while remaining a part of their fellowship, despite most of their churches disagreeing with their sister congregation's action. This scenario has played out repeatedly among Baptists over issues of faith and practice.[48]

The decision to ordain or call a woman as pastor of a Baptist church belongs to that autonomous congregation. However, the consequences of that decision in terms of continued fellowship with other Baptist bodies will depend on the context and culture of those larger organizations. For a Baptist association to attempt to control a local congregation's decision-making process would violate this deeply held Baptist conviction. Similarly, the local church has little ground on which to stand, other than to appeal to mutual affection, if they find themselves barred from wider fellowship for their action. The autonomous association or convention retains that right as well.

The Pastoral Care of Pastors

Pastors often do a better job of maintaining their spiritual and relational health when they, too, have a pastor. In some places, the local ministerial alliance serves that purpose. A pastor may need to initiate that kind of interaction and accountability with other pastors if no established group is in place. Baptist women in the pastorate often endure the challenges of an unsupportive ministry context. When they do find their way into a pulpit, these women

47. Holly Meyer, "Congregation, Tennessee Baptist Convention Split over Church's First Female Pastor," *The Tennessean*, November 14, 2017, https://www.tennessean.com/story/news/religion/2017/11/14/tennessee-baptist-convention-church-woman-pastor-cannot-vote-annual-meeting/861855001/.

48. It is instructive to observe which issues Baptist consider serious enough to justify breaking fellowship with other Baptists and those they do not. Tolerating racist members, for example, has seldom resulted in a church being excluded from a Baptist association.

often testify that their male counterparts in the local association exclude them from needed ministerial fellowship and associational responsibilities.[49]

Men who are accustomed to church doors opening effortlessly before them because of their gender might, in Christian love and humility, ensure that those same doors open to their female colleagues as well. By listening to their sisters' stories, men might understand more fully how things do not necessarily work the same way in Baptist life for men and women. Male pastors may need to use their voice to advocate for their sisters in ministry when the system is intentionally or inadvertently shutting them out. It will undoubtedly require men to respect the calling and work of all their fellow pastors, male and female, and to demonstrate that respect with action.

Calling Out the Called

The questions of calling and ordination intertwine with the issue of women in Baptist church ministry at another practical point. Baptists who profess the importance of a called ministry must take responsibility for creating conditions in our congregations in which we call out and nurture those whom God is calling. We must ensure that women are part of that environment as well. Young girls need to see women in places of religious leadership and hear their voices from the pulpit. They will find it difficult to hear God's call to ministry when they have never seen anyone like themselves in that role. Male pastors can intentionally invite women to fill the pulpit in their absence. Churches can offer pastoral internships to female students in college or seminary who are preparing for ministry. Unfortunately, Baptist pastors or church members often discourage women who profess a call to ministry in a Baptist church from considering it. Like Eli with Samuel, pastors need to be adept at creating space where both young men and young women can hear a call from God and find that call nurtured with wise counsel and generous opportunities to exercise their gifts.

CONCLUSIONS ·

Like many other important topics, the role that women play in church life is an issue that leaves Baptists divided. For most of our history, with some clear exceptions, women's roles have been severely restricted. When twenty-

---

49. See the case study by Angela H. Reed as an illustration of this tension: "Pulpit Rotation," *Christian Century* 130, no. 12 (June 12, 2013): 32–33.

first-century Baptists debate this question, the message of Scripture, our past practices, and reflection on some of our central theological tenets will influence perspectives on the issue. Over time, Baptists are likely to see the number of women in pastoral ministry grow, but this will not take place quickly. As women respond to God's call and seek theological education, and as congregations who need pastors have viable female candidates to consider, the number of Baptist women in ministry will slowly increase. As more young women see pastors like themselves, more will be open to God's call. This cycle may eventually gain sufficient momentum that women in ministry will no longer be such a divisive issue for us. Another generation or two may pass before all of our sons *and* our daughters are permitted to prophesy.

FOR FURTHER REFLECTION

1. How did you evaluate the biblical material presented in this chapter? Are there passages not present that you would want to consider? Do you think the biblical evidence was interpreted fairly? If not, how could it have been better handled?

2. How do you integrate the biblical statements that seem to restrict women from serving as pastors with the biblical passages and examples that would support women preaching and leading God's people?

3. Before reading this chapter, how aware were you of the women in Baptist life who have served as preachers and pastors? Did you identify with any of the stories? Do you think women such as Ruth Bixby or Addie Davis were mistaken about their call from God? What evidence is there that they were or were not?

4. Do you think the Baptist conviction of the priesthood of all believers is relevant to the discussion of women in ministry? If not, why not? If so, would you make other connections beyond the ones in this chapter?

5. What are other ways churches might create environments in which women whom God is calling might be encouraged to hear and follow that call?

PART TWO

PROCLAMATION

Pastor as Prophet

5

The Preaching Ministry

Fire in My Bones

If he should give me a thousand lives, today, and ask me to choose what calling I would have them follow, I would not hesitate one moment, to choose that every one of the thousand lives should be a preacher for him.

—George W. Truett, *"Follow Thou Me"*

I can't impress this on you too strongly. God is looking over your shoulder. Christ himself is the Judge, with the final say on everyone, living and dead. He is about to break into the open with his rule, so proclaim the Message with intensity; keep on your watch. Challenge, warn, and urge your people. Don't ever quit. Just keep it simple.

—Paul (2 Tim. 4:1–2 Message)

Even though what a pastor does for twenty minutes or more in the pulpit each Sunday morning differs immensely from the ministry of ancient Hebrew prophets and first-century apostles, Baptists have connected the dots directly. The "this" of the Sunday sermon equates to the "that" of the prophets and apostles (Eph. 2:20). All are bearers of the Word of God. The gathered, worshiping congregation is doing what God's people have done all along—sitting under and submitting to the living Word of God as it is proclaimed (Neh. 8:1–8).

Biblical Foundations

The prophet's role in ancient Israel varied, from the ecstatic wandering prophets such as those to whom King Saul attached himself (1 Sam. 10:5–6; 19:18–24), to the literary masters such as Isaiah and Jeremiah. Their roles ranged from foretelling to forth telling. The Hebrew words used for the prophets reveal some of the various ministries they offered to Israel. The most frequently occurring term for prophet is *nabi'*, deriving from words meaning "proclaimer" or "called."[1] The verbal form occurs in Amos, Jeremiah, Ezekiel, Joel, and Zechariah, among the Old Testament's prophetic books, and means "to prophesy." In 2 Chronicles, the verb refers to the court prophets, both true and false, who advised the king regarding Yahweh's will (18:4–27). The same word describes the ministries of Haggai and Zechariah in Ezra 5:1. The verb distinctively refers to the temple musicians who "prophesy with lyres, harps, and cymbals" in 1 Chronicles 25:1.

The role of the *nabi'* is clarified somewhat by Exodus 4:10–17. When Moses protests his calling, excusing himself because of his lack of eloquence, the Lord assures him that his brother Aaron will assist him. Moses will hear from God and tell Aaron what to say. Aaron will speak for Moses. This relationship makes Aaron to be Moses's *nabi'*: "The LORD said to Moses, 'See, I have made you like God to Pharaoh, and your brother Aaron shall be your prophet [*nabi'*]. You shall speak all that I command you, and your brother Aaron shall tell Pharaoh to let the Israelites go out of his land'" (Exod. 7:1–2). In this sense, the prophet is God's mouthpiece. God speaks to the prophet, and the prophet speaks to the people. The typical formula found among the writing prophets is that "the word of the LORD came" to the prophet.

The Old Testament speaks of groups or schools of prophets (1 Kings 18–19; 22). Elisha led such a fellowship at Bethel, Jericho, and Gilgal (2 Kings 2–9). We can deduce that these prophets met together, shared their meals, preserved traditions, and lived modestly, although some married and had their own homes (2 Kings 4:1).[2] Women—such as Miriam (Exod. 15:21–21), Deborah (Judg. 4:4), Huldah (2 Kings 22:14–20), Noadiah (Neh. 6:10–14), and Isaiah's unnamed wife (Isa. 8:3)—prophesied as well.

---

1. Gerhard Kittel, Gerhard Friedrich, and Geoffrey William Bromiley, *Theological Dictionary of the New Testament* (Grand Rapids: Eerdmans, 1985), 954.
2. Kittel, Friedrich, and Bromiley, *Theological Dictionary of the New Testament*, 955.

Other terms appear in the Old Testament to describe this role. The phrase "man of God" (1 Sam. 2:27–36) often means the same as "prophet" and appears in the Elijah and Elisha stories in that way. Sometimes the prophet is called a "seer" (1 Sam. 9:11, 18–19; 1 Chron. 9:22), a term frequently used for Samuel.

What distinguished God's true prophets is that their vision or message was not of their own making. God inspired their vision or oracle. False prophets claimed God's authority for their words, but their message did not derive from listening to God; it was a product of their merely human imagination (Jer. 23:1–40; Ezek. 34:1–9).

This prophetic role in ancient Israel informs Baptist understanding of the task of preaching. One preaches because one is "called" to do so, like the ancient prophets. The proclamation comes from listening to God, both in prayer and in the reading of Holy Scripture. God did not call preachers to deliver their own straw-like visions but to announce the Lord's fiery word to God's people (Jer. 23:38–39).

The New Testament connection to a Baptist understanding of preaching is prominent in the ministry of the apostles. Jesus *called* these to be with him (Mark 3:13–19) and *authorized* them "to be sent out to proclaim the message, and to have authority to cast out demons" (3:14–15). The term *apostolos* in the New Testament corresponds to the Hebrew term *shaliakh* (John 13:16), referring to one legally charged to represent someone else and their cause.[3] The apostolic commission to preach the gospel recurs in the New Testament (Mark 6:6–13 // Matt. 10:5–15 // Luke 9:1–6 // 10:1–12; Matt. 28:18–20; Luke 24:44–49; Acts 1:8). These instructions of Jesus serve as directions for the contemporary preacher as well. Baptist pastors understand our authority to preach the gospel as derived from Jesus's commission to the apostles. In the pulpit, we represent him, his message, and his cause, not ourselves. Paul describes our understanding of the task: "For we do not proclaim ourselves; we proclaim Jesus Christ as Lord" (2 Cor. 4:5).

Baptist pastors do not generally claim to *be* prophets or apostles, but we see our preaching task as being like theirs, even derived from theirs. Although we may come to our message through prayer and study, we still desire to stand before God's people with a word that is more than our own, a word that has come from the God of the people to the people of God. Baptists derive this understanding of preaching from Scripture. "This" (the Sunday morning sermon) is "that" (the oracles of the prophets and the gospel of the apostles).

3. Kittel, Friedrich, and Bromiley, *Theological Dictionary of the New Testament*, 70.

The route to the Sunday sermon in a Baptist pulpit is quite different from the messages proclaimed by ancient prophets and apostles. Although Baptists are diverse enough that some indeed claim a direct, Spirit-inspired message with no preparation other than prayer, most preachers come to the pulpit by a more circuitous path. Baptists were born in an era when print technology had established itself. Consequently, we entered the world with a Bible in our hands. We identified ourselves as "people of the Book." In a Baptist context, we expect preaching to be "biblical," declaring to the congregation a message deeply rooted in what the Bible teaches. The path to the pulpit involves prayer and dependence on the Holy Spirit. But it also requires the study of a biblical text and skills in writing and rhetoric. The ancient ancestors of the contemporary preacher did not emerge from their studies with an exegetically informed message. Instead, they offered their oracles out of the immediacy of the Spirit's inspiration. Despite this difference, these figures are at the heart of a Baptist theology of pastoral preaching.

Historical Bypaths

Regardless of where they navigate the broad river of Christian doctrine, whether on the right bank, the left, or somewhere in the middle of the stream, Baptists have agreed on one thing throughout our history: the primary pastoral responsibility is preaching the Word. General and Particular, Free Will and Separatist, independent and denominational, fundamentalist, conservative, moderate, and liberal Baptists hold a common conviction about the importance of preaching. Growing up in Texas in the mid-twentieth century, we referred to our pastor as "the preacher" and the hour of worship as "the preaching service." Baptist congregations seeking a pastor are usually concerned with a candidate's ability to preach above any other asset or skill. The term "pastor search committee" has only recently replaced the more common "pulpit committee" to describe those church members entrusted with finding a new pastor for their congregation. In standard Baptist practice, the church hears a pastoral candidate "preach in view of a call" before voting on extending a call to serve as their pastor. This devotion to the centrality of preaching is evident in our practices and our language.

How have Baptists expressed our thinking about this significant aspect of our life together? Like other facets of Baptist pastoral theology, no systematic treatise on the subject has appeared, although the books explaining how to preach and collections of sermons seem endless (Eccles. 12:12).[4] A

---

4. Joel Gregory, who holds the George W. Truett Endowed Chair of Preaching and Evangelism at Baylor's George W. Truett Theological Seminary, wrote in an email to the author, "I

solid effort to derive a Baptist theology of preaching from those rich sources remains on the horizon of scholarship. A careful study of the sermons of the nineteenth-century Scottish Baptist preacher Alexander Maclaren, for example, could extract the essential theology of preaching that undergirded his work. The same possibility holds with scores of other Baptist preachers, men and women, whose sermons are accessible online or in printed volumes. A scholar could mine the myriad books that instruct preachers on their craft in the same way. This chapter will simply call attention to some of the prominent Baptist theological convictions regarding preaching that lie near the surface.

The "Call to Preach"

Baptists have consistently held to the conviction of a "called ministry." Although the call is to a role in a congregation's life encompassing all the pastoral ministry domains, Baptists have historically described it as a "call to preach."[5] Candidates for ministry were "licensed to preach." Pastors were "ordained to the gospel ministry," which was understood primarily as a ministry of preaching the gospel.

The call to pastoral ministry is a call to preach. J. B. Tidwell writes, "What is my real, outstanding task? A good minister should be able to answer: 'It is preaching.' This is the one task to which God has called me, first, last, and always. It is my business to deliver the message which God has given me."[6] This call to preach provides the Baptist link between the contemporary pastor

---

cannot think of any recent such volume by a Baptist. For the most part, Baptists have tended to write practical manuals, how-to-do-it, rather than deeper background books on the theology of preaching. . . . I cannot think of a Baptist equivalent of, for example, David Buttrick's substantial *Homiletic*" (September 30, 2020). Eric C. Rust offers one Baptist's effort to think theologically about the act of preaching: *The Word and Words: Towards a Theology of Preaching* (Macon, GA: Mercer University Press, 1982). Clyde E. Fant includes a chapter on the theology of preaching in his *Preaching for Today*, rev. ed. (San Francisco: Harper & Row, 1987). Jason C. Meyer and John Piper's work contributes to that gap in the literature but lacks the theological breadth required to address the subject fully. Meyer and Piper argue for expository preaching. The work expresses the authors' theology of preaching, appropriate to its title, *Preaching: A Biblical Theology* (Wheaton, IL: Crossway, 2013).

5. In the second half of the twentieth century, as some Baptist churches grew large enough to support multiple staff members, the concept of calling and even ordination extended beyond a call to preach to a call to ministry expressed in a variety of ways. See Pamela Robinson Durso, "This Is What a Minister Looks Like: The Expanding Baptist Definition of Minister," *Review & Expositor* 114, no. 4 (2017): 521; and Wilburn T. Stancil, "Divergent Views and Practices of Ordination among Southern Baptists Since 1945," *Baptist History and Heritage* 23, no. 3 (July 1988): 44.

6. J. B. Tidwell, *Concerning Preachers: What All Preachers Should Know* (New York: Fleming H. Revell, 1937), 181.

and the ancient prophets and apostles. According to L. R. Scarborough, "We, the ministry of this day, would, like the prophets of the other day, be the proclaimers of God's will to men. We, like the prophets, hold our first credentials from the call of God and are recognized only by presbyteries and churches on the spiritual ordination and call of God."[7] Samuel Proctor declared the same conviction, writing, "The preacher speaks for God and not as a casual observer. Preachers are agents of God's purpose, and God has not given up on the world. Preachers stand in the procession of prophets."[8] The call authorizes the preacher, and preaching fulfills the calling.

Preaching the Word

"Preaching the gospel" carries a double meaning for Baptists. On the one hand, it means to declare the essential message about what God has done in Jesus Christ. Jared Alcántara summarizes that message:

> I define the gospel as *an announcement and a call from God through Jesus Christ that welcomes us into covenant relationship.* It is an *announcement* of the good news that the triune God is reconciling the world to himself through Christ—his life, death, and resurrection—instead of counting our sins against us . . . ; and it is a *call* to individuals, systems, and the whole world to acknowledge and follow Jesus by responding to God's grace through faith . . . and by re-presenting Christlikeness through love.[9]

Gardner C. Taylor, in his majestic 1976 Lyman Beecher Lecture Series on preaching, described the essential message that the preacher proclaims:

> The preacher, then, bears tidings of another world impinging upon this sphere of flesh and blood. He comes declaring that the eternal God has chosen, and supremely in Jesus Christ, this world to be the scene of his saving work and the arena in which he wages his campaign to put down the rebellious places among us and to set the word ringing through the whole creation, "The kingdoms of this world are become the kingdoms of our Lord, and of his Christ; and he shall reign for ever and ever" (Rev. 11:15).[10]

7. L. R. Scarborough, *My Conception of the Gospel Ministry* (Nashville: Sunday School Board of the Southern Baptist Convention, 1935), 12–13.

8. Samuel D. Proctor, *Preaching about Crises in the Community* (Philadelphia: Westminster, 1988), 32.

9. Jared E. Alcántara, *The Practices of Christian Preaching: Essentials for Effective Proclamation* (Grand Rapids: Baker Academic, 2019), 15–16.

10. Gardner C. Taylor, *Lectures, Essays, and Interviews: The Words of Gardner Taylor* (Valley Forge, PA: Judson, 2001), 5:157–58.

This specific message (*kerygma*) about Jesus Christ is what God has called the preacher (*kēryx*) to proclaim (2 Tim. 1:11). The foolishness of this message about a crucified Messiah is the power of God for the salvation of the world (Rom. 1:16–17; 1 Cor. 1:17–25).

On the other hand, for Baptists, "preaching the gospel" has a related but broader meaning. The preacher's calling is to "preach the word" (2 Tim. 4:1–2 NIV). In his lectures on pastoral theology, B. H. Carroll affirmed that "the preacher's message is the Bible, nothing but the Bible, and all the Bible."[11] Jeff Ray writes in his biography of Carroll, "Because of his thoroughgoing acceptance of the whole Bible as the Word of God and his consequent reverence for it, and lifelong study of it, his sermons were literally saturated with scripture truth and loaded with scripture texts."[12] A call from God and a message rooted in Scripture function as the two foundational convictions of the Baptist preacher's authority in the pulpit.

Confidence in the Bible as God's Word is the deepest and most cherished of Baptist convictions. It lies at the heart of James McClendon's "this is that" Baptist vision. The essential question of doctrine and practice for Baptists has been "What does Scripture say?" Confessions of faith describe the Bible in terms of its God-breathed origin, its role in God's revelation to human beings, and its authority over the church's life. The New Hampshire Confession (1833) opens with the article "Of the Scriptures": "We believe the Holy Bible was written by men divinely inspired, and is a perfect treasure of heavenly instruction; that it has God for its author, salvation for its end, and truth, without any mixture of error, for its matter; that it reveals the principles by which God will judge us; and there is, and shall remain to the end of the world, the true centre of Christian union, and the supreme standard by which all human conduct, creeds, and opinions should be tried."[13] Preaching is the necessary work of reading, studying, applying, and proclaiming the truth of Scripture.

11. B. H. Carroll, "The Twentieth-Century Pastor; or, Lectures on Pastoral Theology," *Southwestern Journal of Theology* 58, no. 2 (2016): 214.

12. Jeff Ray, *B. H. Carroll* (Nashville: Sunday School Board of the Southern Baptist Convention, 1927), 75.

13. William L. Lumpkin, *Baptist Confessions of Faith*, 2nd rev. ed. (Valley Forge, PA: Judson, 2011), 378. These words were used almost verbatim in the 1925 Baptist Faith and Message. The adjective "religious" was added to modify "opinions" in the final sentence. The 1963 version added two additional matters. It describes Scripture as "the record of God's revelation of Himself to man" and affirms that "the criterion by which the Bible is to be interpreted is Jesus Christ." After more than two decades of contention about the nature of Scripture among Southern Baptists, the revision made in 2000 drops "record of" and simply affirms that the Bible "is God's revelation of Himself to man." It adds the statement "Therefore, all Scripture is totally true and trustworthy." Also, it drops the statement about Jesus Christ as the hermeneutical

Consequently, Baptists commonly speak of preaching as "biblical preaching," "expository preaching," or "exegetical preaching." Those terms describe a sermon clearly and deeply rooted in the biblical text. Baptist New Testament scholar A. T. Robertson admonished his students about the importance of such biblically grounded messages. "My beloved brethren," he once said in class, "if you never see anything else, see that there is some connection between your sermon and your text."[14] "Never get out of a text what was never in it," he warned.[15] Robertson cited John A. Broadus, his father-in-law: "If some sermons had small-pox, the text would never catch it."[16] Although other homiletical approaches, such as topical preaching or narrative preaching, make their way into Baptist pulpits, they usually show up closely connected to a biblical text.[17]

The commitment to biblically based sermons flows from these heartfelt convictions regarding Scripture as the Word of God. H. B. Charles Jr. confesses his confidence in such an approach to preaching: "My commitment to expository preaching is rooted in my firm convictions about the nature of the Bible. I believe the Bible is God-breathed Scripture (2 Tim. 3:16–17). The Bible does not merely contain the word of God; it *is* the word of God. As the Word of God, all Scripture is necessary, true, full of wisdom, without error, spiritually profitable, life-changing, clear, exclusively authoritative, and sufficient."[18] Baptists have often determined our preaching method by our theological convictions about what the act of preaching is and what it is we proclaim.

Stephen F. Olford defines preaching as "the declaration of the grace of God to human need on the authority of the Word of God with a view to claiming a verdict or converting the soul."[19] Olford's definition touches on two other aspects of Baptist preaching: addressing human need and confidence in preaching's efficacy. But here, note that the authority of preaching emerges not from the preacher's knowledge or skill but from God's Word. Olford

---

criterion for reading Scripture and adds, "All Scripture is a testimony to Christ, who is Himself the focus of divine revelation."

14. Everett Gill, *A. T. Robertson: A Biography* (New York: Macmillan, 1943), 187.

15. Gill, *A. T. Robertson*, 188.

16. Gill, *A. T. Robertson*, 180.

17. For examples of some biblically based sermons in fresh forms, see Tracy Hartman, *Letting the Other Speak: Proclaiming the Stories of Biblical Women* (Lanham, MD: Lexington Books, 2011).

18. H. B. Charles Jr., *On Pastoring: A Short Guide to Living, Leading, and Ministering as a Pastor* (Chicago: Moody, 2016), 140.

19. Paul Duaine Eppinger, "Four Great Baptist Preachers and the Theology of Preaching," *Foundations* 11, no. 2 (April 1968): 118.

continues, "Not only am I convinced that God only blesses his own Word, but the one thing the Holy Spirit owns is the Word. If I'm going to expect the Holy Spirit to implement what I have to say, it must come from what God says in his Word."[20] Confident in a call from God and the power and the efficacy of Scripture, the preacher, despite personal weakness or shortcomings, engages in what Gene Bartlett calls "the audacity of preaching."[21]

Efficacy of Preaching

Baptist pastors have preached with confidence that, having been called by God to preach and having a message from God's Word to deliver, their preaching ultimately makes a difference. God does something through the proclaimed Word that is not accounted for by the preacher's training, preparation, or skill in delivery. Preaching is efficacious.

L. R. Scarborough believed that preaching accomplishes something in the kingdom of God. He saw those effects in terms of "souls saved, character built, lives molded into Christ's holy image, lives rekindled with divine inspiration, hopes renewed, heartaches relieved, tears dried, strength of soul imparted, church revived, God glorified, and more."[22] Robert McCracken imagined preaching as a struggle in which "the preacher is wrestling with another soul." The battle, he believed, is between "the person of the preacher and the person of the man in the pew."[23] This struggle aims to present the individual with the promises and demands of the gospel and elicit a decision about the direction of the person's life. George W. Truett's confidence in the capacity of preaching to shape life's path and to form Christlike character led him to affirm that "one of God's mightiest ways is to call the people by the right kind of preaching."[24] Biblical preaching makes a difference in people's lives.

Preaching and Prayer

"The imperial two-fold task of every preacher is to '*pray* and *preach*,'" writes Scarborough in *My Conception of the Gospel Ministry*.[25] He draws on Peter and John's apostolic affirmation that they, trusting the chosen seven to care for the Hellenistic Jewish Christian widows in Jerusalem, would devote

20. Eppinger, "Four Great Baptist Preachers," 120.
21. Gene E. Bartlett, *The Audacity of Preaching*, Lyman Beecher Lectures (New York: Harper, 1962).
22. Scarborough, *My Conception of the Gospel Ministry*, 60.
23. Eppinger, "Four Great Baptist Preachers," 113.
24. George W. Truett, *Follow Thou Me* (New York: Harper, 1932), 363.
25. Scarborough, *My Conception of the Gospel Ministry*, 50.

themselves "to prayer and to serving the word" (Acts 6:4). These two activities go hand in hand in Baptist theology. Preaching is not merely about what happens for half an hour or so on Sunday morning. Before standing in the pulpit, the preacher kneels in the throne room. The preacher prepares both the sermon and the heart for the preaching event.

"It is a superlative matter for a young preacher to learn," Scarborough declares, "that there are no substitutes for prayerful intercession; not piety, not scholarship, not personal powers, not eloquent utterances, not organization; none of these is a substitute for intercession."[26] Prayer is part of the preparation process. Preachers pray through the text that they will proclaim. Preachers pray for the people who will hear. Preachers pray for passion and compassion in the moment of delivery. Preachers ask the Holy Spirit to direct their minds and hearts during the hours of preparation and to speak to the congregation as they proclaim the message. Prayer is the remedy, Truett says, for insipid, stale preaching. Prayer is where "the heart is once more set ablaze with interest and compassion for the souls of the people."[27] In his lectures to his students, C. H. Spurgeon devoted an entire chapter to the preacher's life of prayer. The pastor's responsibility week by week is not merely to prepare a message but also to prepare the messenger.

Preaching and the Human Situation

A Baptist understanding of the act of preaching operates with two indispensable foci. On the one hand, the message is Christ-centered, biblically based, and derived from time spent in the presence of God. Like the Old Testament's prophets, the preacher comes to the pulpit from time spent in the heavenly council (Jer. 23:18–19). On the other hand, the pastor preaches in a context. The congregation is on the pastor's heart while discerning and preparing the message for delivery. The people are the object of the preacher's prayer. They have needs to consider, questions to answer, struggles to face, decisions to make, ministries to perform. Gardner Taylor affirmed that "a person's preaching is infinitely sweetened as he enters, actually or vicariously, into the plight and circumstances of human hope and heartbreak."[28] The pastor's heart, the priest's intercession, and the prophet's faithfulness come together in the work of preaching.

Broadus connected the work of pastoral care and the task of pastoral preaching. Both, he affirmed, were necessary, and the two practices strength-

---

26. Scarborough, *My Conception of the Gospel Ministry*, 51.
27. Truett, *Follow Thou Me*, 235.
28. Taylor, *Lectures, Essays, and Interviews*, 193.

ened each other. The one who visits a family during a time of crisis is "the preacher, whose thorough knowledge of Scripture and elated views of life, whose able and impassioned discourses have carried conviction and commanded admiration, and melted into one the hearts of the multitude, who is accustomed to stand before them as the ambassador of God, and is associated in their minds with the authority and the sacredness of God's Word." So, Broadus declared, "When *he* comes to speak with the suffering, the sorrowing, the tempted, his visit has a meaning and power of which otherwise it must be destitute." In the same way, "when he who preaches is the sympathizing pastor, the trusted counsellor, the kindly and honored friend of young and old, of rich and poor, then 'truths divine come mended from his lips,' and the door to men's hearts, by the magical power of sympathy, will fly open at his word."[29] Preaching connects intimately with human hurts and hopes.

Carroll warned young preachers about the folly of relying on their previous sermons when opportunities to preach arose. Sermons, he believed, were not merely lectures or speeches. Preaching is an event that involves the Holy Spirit, the preacher, and the specific congregation. So he advised,

> Burn all your written sermons that you carry around in your valise. Don't you know that when you keep gnawing the same sermons they become like what a wolf leaves of a once juicy antelope—dry bones? An unchanged sermon never suits two congregations. Conditions vary. Be fresh. Be flexible. Learn proper adjustments. Study the needs of the people before you, and preach from a full heart that within that very hour has sought the Spirit's guidance as to the theme, and the Spirit's power as to the utterance.[30]

A dynamic understanding of what preaching entails underlies Carroll's counsel.

Harry Emerson Fosdick recognized that those who sat in the pews listening to his sermons were people who were up against real issues in their world and their own lives. But he realized that mere topical preaching would not address people's spiritual hunger and the issues of their lives either. "Across the years since then," he wrote, "I have seen those topical preachers petering out and leaving the ministry. If people do not come to church anxious about what happened to the Jebusites, neither do they come yearning to hear a lecturer express his personal opinion on themes which editors, columnists and radio

---

29. John Albert Broadus, *A Treatise on the Preparation and Delivery of Sermons* (New York: Armstrong & Son, 1891), 22.

30. J. B. Cranfill, *Sermons and Life Sketch of B. H. Carroll, D.D.* (Philadelphia: American Baptist Publication Society, 1893), 117.

commentators have been dealing with throughout the week. So I floundered until personal counseling gradually led me into an approach to preaching which made it an exciting adventure."[31]

Fosdick started his sermon preparation with an awareness of the human dilemma. The people he would address on Sunday faced problems in their lives every day. He said that beginning with a situation would not produce a sermon, which is more than a lecture, a discussion, or a treatise. Fosdick believed that the preacher's goal was to witness changes in the lives of those who heard the message, "not merely to discuss repentance but to persuade people to repent; not merely to debate the meaning and possibility of Christian faith, but to produce Christian faith in the lives of his listeners; not merely to talk about the available power of God to bring victory over trouble and temptation, but to send people out from their worship on Sunday with victory in their possession."[32]

Robert McCracken, who succeeded Fosdick at the Riverside Church, framed his approach to preaching as addressing the vital questions people were asking by taking them to the Word that God has spoken. He defined preaching as "an attempt to secure a person-to-person encounter whereby the preacher brings the listener to a new or deeper relationship to Jesus Christ."[33]

Black pastors have long held on to these same two foci: the powerful divine message and the reality of human need. Cleophus LaRue sees this as the distinctive hermeneutical approach among Black preachers. They have proclaimed the gospel with a clear awareness of the sociocultural context of their congregations and a profound sense that God is present in and through Scripture. "This historical, formative hermeneutic of a God who acts mightily on behalf of the marginalized and oppressed," he argues, "is the central template blacks bring to Scripture in preparation for preaching. It has been, and remains to this day, the defining, distinctive factor in African American proclamation."[34]

Taylor echoes that thought in his description of preaching. Preachers address the human dimension with the divine message. He declares,

> To seek and find God's movement in human affairs and to cry out, passionately pointing to where that stirring is discernible though scarcely ever indisputable,

---

31. Harry Emerson Fosdick, *The Living of These Days: An Autobiography* (New York: Harper, 1956), 92.

32. Fosdick, *Living of These Days*, 99.

33. Robert J. McCracken, *The Making of the Sermon* (New York: Harper & Bros., 1956), 48.

34. Cleophus James LaRue, *The Heart of Black Preaching* (Louisville: Westminster John Knox, 2000), 16.

is the preacher's task. To hear and to suffer deeply with "the still, sad music of humanity" and then to offer to it the wonderful gospel of healing and wholeness is the preacher's privilege. We are called to listen and to identify the tread of the eternal God's sovereign purpose marching in the private and public affairs of men. Hearing that approaching, fateful footfall, we are called to summon men and women, by the aid of the Holy Spirit, to "make straight in the desert a highway for our God" (Isa. 40:3), and to declare that by his will and our loyalty to that will, "Every valley shall be exalted, and every mountain and hill shall be made low: and the crooked shall be made straight, and the rough places plain: And the glory of the LORD shall be revealed, and all flesh shall see it together" (Isa. 40:4–5).[35]

The Preaching Process

The nature of preaching as addressing the human situation with a word from God carries implications for sermon preparation. The biblical text itself partakes of these two dimensions. On the one hand, it is a divine word, God-breathed, Holy Spirit–inspired. On the other hand, it is a human word with grammar, syntax, literary devices, and cultural settings. The written Word, like the eternal Word, comes to us wrapped in the swaddling clothes of human flesh.[36]

The preacher must attend to both dimensions of the text in the preparation of a sermon. Because it is a human word, we use the best study methods at our disposal to listen to its message. Because it is a divine word, we pray and depend on the Holy Spirit's leadership to understand it and to hear what this word has to say to us at this moment in our lives. Because it is a divine word, we commit ourselves ahead of time, before we even understand it, to submit to it in obedience.

All this work is the effort required to listen to the text before we proclaim it. David Wells argues that "the preacher must first be preached to, must first

---

35. Taylor, *Lectures, Essays, and Interviews*, 158.

36. My own professor of homiletics, Clyde Fant, spoke of "incarnational preaching," meaning the coming of the divine Word to us in our concrete human situation through clearly human means such as form, methodology, and delivery. He writes,

> Throughout this work I use the term *incarnational preaching*. I believe the context will suggest, if not completely define, what I do and do not mean by it. But by no means do I intend to suggest a confusion between the unique event in Christ and what happens in preaching. I do believe, however, that the incarnation is the truest theological model for the mysterious divine-human preaching event, which is neither all of the human nor all of God, but which partakes of both with precisely the same degree of mystery and humility as that reality in Jesus of Nazareth. (*Preaching for Today*, xv)

His disclaimer notwithstanding, perhaps sacramental rather than incarnational language might be more appropriate.

be addressed by the God of that truth, through the text, before attempting to preach it to others. . . . The Bible preaches to the preacher in order that the preacher might preach to others."[37] The listening process in sermon preparation includes more than the obvious need to listen to the text. Loren Johns reminds us that "when it comes to preaching well, one must listen to the biblical text, to the congregation, to scholars who have studied the text, and to the broader historical and social context in which a congregation finds itself. Even during the delivery of the sermon, the preacher must attend to the Spirit of God, listen to his or her own sermon, and watch for the communication of the congregation."[38] June Alliman Yoder observes the constant, dynamic, back-and-forth movements that take the preacher into the text, the community of scholars, the context, the congregation, and the preacher's own life as the sermon takes shape.[39]

Theological Reflection

Preaching as Sacrament

Baptists have been reluctant to use the word "sacrament" to describe the Lord's Supper and baptism, preferring the term "ordinance" instead. Despite some early exceptions and contemporary trends to the contrary, we have been quite adamant on this issue through most of our history, reacting in part to both Roman Catholic and Lutheran dogma on the topic.[40] We have not easily connected the material and the spiritual.

One act of worship that Baptists regard as near sacramental (whether we use the term or not) is the act of preaching.[41] The written Word of Christian

37. David F. Wells, "The Theology of Preaching: The Biblical Word in the Contemporary World, Part I: The Contemporary World," *Journal of the Evangelical Homiletics Society* 9, no. 1 (March 2009): 33.

38. Loren L. Johns, introduction to *The Heart of the Matter: Pastoral Ministry in Anabaptist Perspective*, ed. Erick Sawatzky (Telford, PA: Cascadia, 2004), 10–11.

39. June Alliman Yoder, "Paying Attention," in Sawatzky, *Heart of the Matter*, 179–83.

40. Early Dutch Anabaptists retained the term "sacraments" (Waterland Confession, article 25), as did John Smyth's party (*Propositions and Conclusions Concerning True Christian Religion*, paragraph 75). See Lumpkin, *Baptist Confessions of Faith*, 55, 126. See also Lloyd A. Harsch, "Were the First Baptists Sacramentalists?," *Journal for Baptist Theology & Ministry* 6, no. 1 (2009): 25–43. For evidence of a resurgence of more sacramental views of baptism and communion among Baptists, see Paul W. Goodliff, *Ministry, Sacrament, and Representation: Ministry and Ordination in Contemporary Baptist Theology, and the Rise of Sacramentalism* (Oxford: Regent's Park College, 2010).

41. Jerry M. Carter, "The Audible Sacrament: The Sacramentality of Gardner C. Taylor's Preaching," PhD diss., Drew University, 2007. Drawing from Augustine's understanding of preaching as sacramental, Carter explores Taylor's approach to preaching.

Scriptures is a material artifact—ink on paper, light reflected on the human eye's retina. The spoken Word, whether the public reading of the Bible or preaching, is a physical act. Vibrations of air travel as sound waves from the preacher's vocal cords to the eardrum of the hearer. But in these physical, material actions, Baptists believe that God speaks and accomplishes divine purposes in the church and the world. Such a notion is remarkably close to the language of sacraments.[42] In traditional Baptist church architecture, the baptistry, the pulpit, and the Lord's Supper table align. The pulpit stands in the center. This arrangement speaks to the centrality of preaching in Baptist worship, the moment when God encounters people through the Word.

No wonder then, when it comes to describing a Baptist understanding of preaching, one is tempted to reach for the language of sacraments. The eternal Word himself, Jesus Christ, through the written word of God in Scripture, speaks through the words of an all-too-human preacher to human needs in such a way that Christ himself encounters human beings and transforms them. By his Spirit he stirs forgiveness, courage, faith, clarity, character, generosity, compassion, and more in the hearers' hearts. The grace and mercy of God become realities as the congregation hears the preaching of the Word. As Paul says, "So faith comes from what is heard, and what is heard comes through the word of Christ" (Rom. 10:17), clearly referring to the preached message of Christ (10:14–15). The efficacy of preaching occurs in this mysterious interaction of the material and the spiritual. Faith forms in the physical act of hearing, the hearer trusts God, and a human life is changed.

The process of arriving at the sermon also partakes of this mysterious interaction of the human and the divine.[43] The preacher engages a physical text through physical means in the study to discern a message for God's people from God's Word. Whether one enters the pulpit with a full manuscript, a few notes, or the message committed to memory, the transformation of that study and preparation into a word from God takes place in the act of preaching.

42. Stephen Olford, in a personal interview with Paul Eppinger, said, "Preaching is absolutely central. It is above the sacraments in importance. I stand with Calvin in declaring that the preaching of the Word must come before the sacraments, for it is a sacrament itself. I believe with Dr. Farmer of Cambridge that preaching is the Word becoming flesh. There is no other ordinance or institution in which that becomes so manifest as in preaching." Eppinger, "Four Great Baptist Preachers," 118.

43. Eppinger critiques both Fosdick and McCracken for an overemphasis on the human dilemma in their theology of preaching and both Bartlett and Olford for their emphasis on the divine aspect. He offers this "inclusive theology of preaching" based on the four preachers he studied: "Preaching is the head-on constructive meeting of some problem, in which a preacher declares to persons, on the authority of the Word of God, that God has done something for man through Christ toward the goal of converting the listener." "Four Great Baptist Preachers," 125.

A sermon on paper does not become a word from God until it encounters a hearer or reader. The Holy Spirit then transforms the labor of the study into an encounter with God in the pulpit. Because such a dynamic process is involved, the sermon's preparation is marked not only by careful exegesis and diligent research but also by humble and deliberate prayer. The sermon does not become a message on its own. For that, the Spirit of God must move, leading us into truth as Jesus promised (John 16:13).

Baptists are quick to distinguish preaching and sermons from mere public speaking, whether we are comfortable with the language of sacrament or not. McCracken writes, "There is a difference between a pulpit and a platform, a sermon and a lecture, a church and an auditorium. The Christian preacher is not a lineal descendant of the Greek orator. The obligation that rests on him is not, like Socrates, to follow the argument wherever it may lead, but like Micah, to declare, 'Thus saith the LORD.' His first business is as the herald of a revelation."[44] Something else is taking place in the preaching event besides the delivering of a speech.

Preaching and the Faith Community

A theological understanding of preaching must take stock of its communal nature. No preaching occurs unless both preacher and congregation are present. Like the proverbial tree falling in the forest, a sermon preached with no hearer is no sermon. Once we accept the importance of the congregation, sermon preparation and delivery become communal events. In the study, the preacher begins to listen to and interact with those who will hear the word. How will children in the congregation hear this message? Adolescents? Newly married couples? The recently divorced? The grieving? The middle-aged engineer who has been laid off and can no longer support his family? The young mother struggling with career and family? The elderly widower who just received a cancer diagnosis? The list goes on and on. The people to whom we preach have lives and hurts and hopes. They come to sit in our pews not for entertainment but for life. We dare not waste their time with a lack of preparation or with something less than a word from God. So we invite them into the study with us, and we inquire from the biblical text on their behalf. We talk with them when the sermon is over. Preaching is inherently a communal event.

Technology has raised a challenge to the inherently communal nature of preaching. Large churches have developed multisite congregations, for ex-

---

44. McCracken, *Making of the Sermon*, 15.

ample, in which the sermon is delivered on a screen, either in a livestreaming mode or as a prerecorded video. During the COVID-19 pandemic, which is still raging as I write, most congregations, even small ones, adopted such technology when gathering would have been too dangerous. For months, congregants have been hearing the Word preached via the internet. As a congregant during these days, I have found the experience to be acceptable during such extreme circumstances but have longed to gather with God's people for the preaching event. I have spoken with dozens of pastors over the months of the pandemic and have heard the frustration of not being able to speak to human faces, to see their reactions, or to adjust to their needs in the moment of preaching. It remains to be seen how this experience will shape preaching and worship in the post-COVID-19 world.

Out-of-Control Preaching

During a period of pastoral ministry when I was facing personal difficulties, I frequently felt like I had nothing to say from the pulpit. Depressed and discouraged, I struggled each week to prepare a sermon and to preach it. If you had asked me, I would have told you that this was the driest, poorest chapter of my life. Mercifully, that time eventually passed. A few years later, I received an email from a young man I had never met. He told me that he had worshiped at our church during a one-year college internship that brought him from Mississippi to Texas. His time with us corresponded entirely with those dark days of mine. He regularly sat in the balcony, he said, but he never introduced himself and left as soon as the service ended. The man was writing to say that that year was profoundly challenging for him and that he was struggling to believe in God and stay alive. He said that every week, in the sermon, he heard just what he needed to keep going. This young man was writing to thank me. Something was taking place in the preaching of the Word of God that did not depend on me.

We do not know who sits in the pews or joins us online or in a broadcast of our services. We are not even fully aware of all that is going on in the lives of those we think we know. But God knows. God knows. That theological statement is an essential aspect of our understanding of preaching. We pray and prepare. We listen. Finally, we offer our words from the pulpit. God takes those words and does with them what each listener needs most. We have no control over that. As promised to Isaiah:

> For as the rain and the snow come down from heaven,
> and do not return there until they have watered the earth,

making it bring forth and sprout,
    giving seed to the sower and bread to the eater,
so shall my word be that goes out from my mouth;
    it shall not return to me empty,
but it shall accomplish that which I purpose,
    and succeed in the thing for which I sent it. (Isa. 55:10–11)

CONCLUSIONS ·

Preaching predominates in Baptist pastoral ministry. The declaration of the Word of the Lord to God's people is a primary task. Sunday by Sunday, as men and women take up the Bible and step into the pulpit before the worshiping congregation, contact is made between then and now—the ancient proclamation of prophets and apostles and the contemporary preaching of the gospel. The various forms of preaching may shift with changes in culture and technology, but the essence of the task will remain. Paul's rhetorical questions are still relevant: "But how are they to call on one in whom they have not believed? And how are they to believe in one of whom they have never heard? And how are they to hear without someone to proclaim him? And how are they to proclaim him unless they are sent?" (Rom. 10:14–15).

FOR FURTHER REFLECTION ·

1. How would you define preaching? How would you distinguish preaching from teaching?
2. Who is the best preacher you have ever heard? What qualities of their preaching put them in that category for you?
3. Do you think that preaching could be considered a sacramental act, the extension of God's grace through physical means? If so, how does that understanding affect your preaching? If not, what are your reasons?
4. What role do you believe prayer plays in the sermon-preparation process?
5. In what sense do you consider preaching to be a communal event? How does that affect the way you go about preparing and delivering sermons?

6

Witness to the World

Sent to Proclaim

If the command of Christ to teach all nations extends only to the apostles, then, doubtless, the promise of the divine presence in this work must be so limited; but this is worded in such a manner as expressly precludes such an idea. "Lo, I am with you always, to the end of the world."

—William Carey, *An Enquiry into the Obligations of Christians, to Use Means for the Conversion of the Heathens*

But you will receive power when the Holy Spirit has come upon you; and you will be my witnesses in Jerusalem, in all Judea and Samaria, and to the ends of the earth.

—Jesus (Acts 1:8)

In Baptist practice, pastoral ministry and authority connect directly with the ministry of Jesus and the early apostles. If Jesus is the Good Shepherd (Pastor), the Chief Shepherd, then those who care for his flock ought to model themselves after him (John 21:15–17; Acts 20:28; 1 Pet. 2:25; 5:1–4). Additionally, the apostles themselves are examples of ministry for those who serve as Baptist pastors. Just as he summoned the Twelve, Jesus has called pastors to follow him, and he has sent them to bear witness to the world about the kingdom of God.[1] At the heart of pastoral ministry is the task of witnessing to God's love for a broken world. Baptists have variously identified this task as "missions" or "evangelism."

Biblical Foundations

One of Jesus's core identities expressed in the Gospel of John is his "sentness" (5:36, 38; 6:29; 7:29; 8:42; 10:36; 11:42; 17:3, 8, 21, 23, 25; 20:21).[2] For him, God is "the one who sent me" or "him who sent me" (4:34; 5:23, 24, 30; 6:38, 39; 7:16, 28, 33; 8:26, 29; 9:4; 12:44, 45; 13:20; 15:21; 16:5) or "the Father who sent me" (5:37; 6:44; 8:16, 18; 12:49; 14:24).[3] For the Fourth Evangelist, this is at the core of the Christian message. God loved the world so much that he gave his only Son to bring eternal life to perishing people (3:16). Then he adds, "Indeed, God did not *send* the Son into the world to condemn the world, but in order that the world might be saved through him" (3:17). God sends the Son into the world as an expression of God's love for people.[4]

Jesus then sends his disciples into that same world to participate in his witness to the Father's love (John 4:38; 17:18; 20:21). Being sent into the *world*, given the world's nature as opposed to God, means that Jesus's disciples will suffer rejection and persecution even as he did (15:18–25; 16:1–4, 33). But the Paraclete, the Comforter, the Spirit of Truth whom the Father and Jesus will also send, will empower them for this task (14:26; 15:26; 16:7). At the end

1. Michael W. Stroope contends that the familiar word "mission," along with "missional" and "missionary," does not represent biblical theology. These terms have developed in Christian history and assumed a place of ascendency in articulating the church's place and role in the world. Stroope argues for the more biblical expression "witness" or, more fully, "pilgrim witness." The work of proclamation focuses on declaring the reign of God, not the fulfillment of a mission. Stroope says, "When discovered and embraced, God's reign forms us into pilgrim witnesses, who, though weak and afflicted, are liberated to live alongside and love those we encounter along the way." *Transcending Mission: The Eclipse of a Modern Tradition* (Downers Grove, IL: IVP Academic, 2017), 358. Although James McClendon devotes a chapter in the second volume of his systematic theology to "Holy Spirit and Mission," he titles the third volume *Witness*. That volume addresses the question, "What stance vis-à-vis the world must the church maintain in order to truly be the church?" *Systematic Theology*, vol. 1, *Ethics* (Nashville: Abingdon, 2002), 43.

2. I am using the unusual word "sentness" to describe a consciousness of being authoritatively dispatched for a purpose. Jesus demonstrates his "sentness" repeatedly in how he refers to himself and the Father. The same "sentness" applies to his disciples, both ancient and modern.

3. John uses the verbs *pempō* and *apostellō* interchangeably in these passages. John frequently uses words as synonyms that other writers might use more distinctively. See C. C. Tarelli, "Johannine Synonyms," *Journal of Theological Studies* 47, no. 187/188 (1946): 175–77.

4. God sent John the Baptist as well (John 1:6; 3:28) and, like Jesus, the Baptist describes God as "the one who sent me" (1:33).

of John's story, these elements come together as the risen Christ meets his disciples in an upper room, shows them his wounds, breathes on them the Spirit's power, and says, "As the Father has sent me, so I send you" (20:21).

The Synoptic Gospels, to a lesser degree than the Fourth Gospel, also emphasize the sentness of Jesus and his sending the disciples. Jesus calls God "the one who sent me" (Matt. 10:40 // Mark 9:37 // Luke 9:48 // 10:16) and refers to his sentness (Matt. 15:24). The parable of the wicked tenants (Matt. 21:33–41) speaks of a landowner who "sent his son" to face the violence of those who had taken over his vineyard (Matt. 21:37 // Mark 12:6). Jesus speaks of Jerusalem as a people who kill the prophets and stone "those who are sent to it" (Matt. 23:37 // Luke 13:34).

In Luke, Jesus speaks of his purpose in being among us ("For the Son of Man came to seek out and to save the lost" [19:10]) but not so often about being sent. At his inaugural sermon in Nazareth, Jesus reads from Isaiah 42:

> The Spirit of the Lord is upon me,
>   because he has anointed me
>   to bring good news to the poor.
> He has *sent* me to proclaim release to the captives
>   and recovery of sight to the blind,
>   to let the oppressed go free,
> to proclaim the year of the Lord's favor." (Luke 4:18–19; cf. Isa. 42:1–9)

Following the Scripture reading, Jesus declares, "Today this scripture has been fulfilled in your hearing" (4:21). Jesus claims to have been sent to preach the kingdom of God (4:43).

The Synoptics affirm that Jesus, sent by God, now sends his disciples to continue his witness to the kingdom (cf. John 4:37). He sends the Twelve out to bear witness to "the lost sheep of the house of Israel" (Matt. 10:5–15 // Mark 6:6–13 // Luke 9:1–6). Also, in Luke 10:1–12 Jesus sends out a group of seventy to bear witness in the cities where he himself would soon minister.

The risen Christ commissions his disciples to continue to bear witness to the world, in the Spirit's power, until the end of the age. As he dispatches them in the Spirit's power in John 20:21, so in Matthew he sends them with his full authority as Lord (28:18–20). In Luke he admonishes them to await the arrival of the Holy Spirit patiently so that they might bear witness to all nations (24:46–48), a promise repeated in Acts 1:8 and fulfilled in Acts 2.[5]

5. The conundrum of the ending of Mark's Gospel bears witness to the early church's sense of having been sent by Jesus. According to the manuscript evidence, the Gospel ends at 16:8,

As the story of the earliest church unfolds in the book of Acts, God's people bear witness to Christ's love and kingdom "in Jerusalem, in all Judea and Samaria, and to the ends of the earth" (1:8). The theme of sending pervades the church's story. Peter is sent to Cornelius's home to bear witness to the household of a God-fearing Roman centurion (Acts 10–11). The Spirit and the church send Paul and his companions to bear witness to gentiles in Asia Minor and Greece (Acts 13–14, 16–18, 18–21). Paul describes this work as being tied intrinsically to his call on the Damascus Road (Acts 22:21; 26:17–18). Even his arrest and journey to Rome for trial is an experience of being sent by Christ, who stands near him one night in a Jerusalem holding cell and says, "For just as you have testified for me in Jerusalem, so you must bear witness also in Rome" (Acts 23:11).

Being sent by Christ provides the authorization of one's ministry (Matt. 28:18–20). Sentness also implies the nature of the task. Those whom God sends are to demonstrate and proclaim the kingdom of God (Matt. 10:7), to witness to God's love (Acts 1:8; John 20:21), and to invite hungry people to the heavenly banquet (Matt. 22:1–10). Paul understands the importance of sending witnesses; otherwise, the world will not hear the gospel (Rom. 10:14–15). Christ himself had sent Paul to proclaim this good news (1 Cor. 1:17). He instructs Timothy to "do the work of an evangelist," fully carrying out his ministry (2 Tim. 4:5).

Although no single biblical passage addresses *pastors* and urges them to live with a sense of sentness, the models of Jesus and the apostles reinforce that aspect of the pastor's call. To be called by God is to be called for a purpose. Isaiah's response to God's call echoes in the hearts of those who have heard such a call themselves: "Here I am; send me!" (Isa. 6:8). One who has responded to God's call to bear witness to the kingdom will repeatedly hear echoed in Scripture that inner sense of having been sent to those "having no hope and without God in the world" (Eph. 2:12). In this sense, Baptists have regarded pastoral ministry as a kind of apostolic, missional, evangelistic task. The pastoral ministry of evangelism is the "this" echoing the "that" of the ministry of reconciliation exercised by Jesus and the apostles.

---

with the women being sent to bear witness to Jesus's disciples that the risen Christ would meet them in Galilee. Mark records no resurrection appearance of Jesus. The later alternative endings to Mark, however, include not just a reference to the appearances of the risen Christ but also his sending the disciples to bear witness in the world. The shorter ending reads, "And afterward Jesus himself sent out through them, from east to west, the sacred and imperishable proclamation of eternal salvation." In the longer ending Jesus says, "Go into all the world and proclaim the good news to the whole creation" (Mark 16:15). Jesus as "sender" and the church as "sent" were ingrained in the early church's faith and practice.

Historical Bypaths

Baptist pastors and churches have long valued both missions (usually thought of as bearing witness to people in other cultures) and evangelism (commonly understood as sharing the gospel with those like themselves). A hundred years ago, B. H. Carroll regarded the distinction as a merely semantic difference. He wrote, "Evangelization extended to the whole world becomes world-wide missions. Missionary endeavor is the highest development of the evangelistic spirit. There is no difference in the nature of evangelization and missions; the only difference is one of degree. The Spirit that leads a saved father to labor for the salvation of his boy, if cultivated to the proper degree, leads him to give his money to missions and even that boy as a missionary to the heathen."[6] In a world as cosmopolitan as ours, the distinction between evangelism and missions no longer obtains. Most of us are only minutes away from people of other cultures and languages at any given time.[7] Additionally, the conjecture that those who look like us and who speak our language also have the same theological or religious beliefs and values as we do is no longer a safe assumption.[8]

For decades, we have been living on a mission field in the West, although we may not have acknowledged that reality.[9] Our task in a post-Christian, postmodern world is to bear witness to a culture that no longer has even the slightest Christian assumptions to which we may appeal. Responding to the Baptist vision, pastors will see themselves as missionaries, witnesses sent to such a world and time. Pastoral example and leadership will in this century, as in centuries past, guide the church in the fulfillment of its calling to bear witness in Jerusalem, Judea, and Samaria and to ends of the earth (Acts 1:8). Our efforts to bear witness to our culture are grounded both in the biblical witness and the riches of our Baptist heritage.[10] The Great Commission (Matt. 28:18–20; Mark 16:15; Luke 24:46–49; John 20:21–22; Acts 1:8) provides the connection between contemporary pastoral ministry and the apostolic witness of the earliest church, as it has for generations. "This is that."

6. B. H. Carroll, "The Twentieth-Century Pastor; or, Lectures on Pastoral Theology," *Southwestern Journal of Theology* 58, no. 2 (2016): 257.

7. Bobby Ross, "Evangelism vs. Missions? Southern Baptists Contemplate Unleashing the IMB [International Mission Board] at Home," *Christianity Today* 54, no. 7 (July 2010): 10–11.

8. Robert P. Sellers, "A Baptist View of Missions for Postmodernity," *Review & Expositor* 100, no. 4 (2003): 641–84.

9. George G. Hunter, *How to Reach Secular People* (Nashville: Abingdon, 1992); Kennon L. Callahan, *The Future That Has Come: New Possibilities for Reaching and Growing the Grass Roots* (San Francisco: Jossey-Bass, 2002).

10. Melody Maxwell summarizes the historical role of missions in Baptist life; see "Baptists and Modern Missions: Historical Movement and Contemporary Reflections," *Baptistic Theologies* 10, no. 1 (2018): 18–32.

Baptist Confession of Missions and Evangelism

Proclaiming the gospel and gathering converts into the church has been a part of the Baptist experience from the beginning. According to Gerald Borchert, William Carey's *Enquiry into the Obligation of Christians to Use Means for the Conversion of the Heathens*, written in 1792, solidified a Baptist commitment to take the gospel across cultural borders.[11] These eighteenth-century Baptists labored at the forefront of the modern mission movement. However, Baptists did not immediately formulate their commitment to bear the gospel to the world as part of their confessions of faith.[12]

As with other matters, when it came to world missions, Baptists were more immersed in the practice of their faith than in the theological articulation of it. Baptist theologian and historian James Leo Garrett states, "Up to World War II, the Baptist systematic theologies seem with perhaps a single exception to have been totally silent about missions. One searches in vain for such in the systems of John Leadley Dagg, Augustus Hopkins Strong, Alvah Hovey, James Madison Pendleton, James Petigru Boyce, William Newton Clarke, Ezekiel Gilman Robinson, Edgar Young Mullins, Walter Rauschenbusch, and John Alexis Edgren, even though some of these authors were personally quite active in the support of foreign and home missions."[13] Garrett notes gradual changes to this situation that begin with Thomas Pohill Stafford in 1936, Walter Thomas Conner in 1945, and Herschel Harold Hobbs in 1960. Garrett traces the subject in Baptist theological writings through the end of the twentieth century, expressing his hope that twenty-first-century Baptist systematic theologies will give proper attention to our witness in the world.[14]

Statements on the church's mission to the world do not regularly appear in confessions of faith until the twentieth century. The Baptist Faith and Message (1925), built on the New Hampshire Confession (1833), modified the earlier

---

11. Gerald L. Borchert, "The Nature and Mission of the Church: A Baptist Perspective," *Perspectives in Religious Studies* 20, no. 1 (1993): 38.

12. Historian David Bebbington regards the modern mission movement as "the most important development" in all of Baptist history. *Baptists through the Centuries: A History of a Global People* (Waco: Baylor University Press, 2010), 215.

13. James Leo Garrett Jr., "Missions and Baptist Systematic Theologies," *Baptist History and Heritage* 35, no. 2 (2000): 67.

14. Garrett, "Missions and Baptist Systematic Theologies," 71. Garrett oddly omits the work of James McClendon, who devotes one of his three volumes of systematic theology to the subject of witness. McClendon also includes a chapter in his second volume devoted to the Holy Spirit and mission, writing, "Here the surprise is that systematic theologians have rarely listed mission among the essential theological doctrines, leaving it aside as only a study of effective methods. (Thus this volume displays some originality in treating *mission* as an essential part of doctrinal theology.)" *Systematic Theology*, vol. 2, *Doctrine* (Nashville: Abingdon, 1994), 417–18.

document in several ways. One modification was the addition of a statement on "Evangelism and Missions" (article 23). It reads,

> It is the duty of every Christian man and woman, and the duty of every church of Christ to seek to extend the gospel to the ends of the earth. The new birth of man's spirit by God's Holy Spirit means the birth of love for others. Missionary effort on the part of all rests thus upon a spiritual necessity of the regenerate life. It is also expressly and repeatedly commanded in the teachings of Christ. It is the duty of every child of God to seek constantly to win the lost to Christ by personal effort and by all other methods sanctioned by the gospel of Christ. Matt. 10:5; 13:18–23; 22:9–10; 28:19–20; Mark 16:15–16; 16:19–20; Luke 24:46–53; Acts 1:5–8; 2:1–2, 21, 39; 8:26–40; 10:42–48; 13:2, 30–33; 1 Thess. 1–8.[15]

This confession laid responsibility for the propagation of the gospel on every church and every follower of Jesus.

When Southern Baptists revised the Baptist Faith and Message in 1963, they allowed the statement on evangelism and missions to stand. In the revision of 2000, however, they made a few changes. They added a sentence near the end of the paragraph: "The Lord Jesus Christ has commanded the preaching of the gospel to all nations." Further, they revised the final sentence to read, "It is the duty of every child of God to seek constantly to win the lost to Christ by verbal witness undergirded by a Christian lifestyle, and by other methods in harmony with the gospel of Christ." These revisions did not change the tenor or content of the confession. At the heart of Baptist life lies a commitment to declare the gospel of Jesus Christ to the world. Other Baptist groups have adapted the Southern Baptist Convention's confession of faith along the way, such as the National Baptist Convention, including the article on missions and evangelism.[16]

Twentieth-century confessions of faith, whether denominational or the articles of faith of various Baptist institutions, regularly affirm the conviction that God intends for Christ's followers to share the gospel. Baptist faith does not single out pastors for this task. But as with other aspects of the Christian life, Baptists expect their pastors to model the behavior as part of their calling.[17]

---

15. H. Leon McBeth, *A Sourcebook for Baptist Heritage* (Nashville: B&H Academic, 1990), 514. The misprint of 1 Thess. 1:8 as 1 Thess. 1–8 is retained from the original document.

16. William L. Lumpkin, *Baptist Confessions of Faith*, 2nd rev. ed. (Valley Forge, PA: Judson, 2011), 409.

17. For a survey of Southern Baptist Convention programmatic efforts in evangelism, see John F. Havlik, "Evangelism: The Cutting Edge," *Baptist History and Heritage* 9, no. 1 (January 1974): 30.

Baptist Practice of Pastoral Evangelism

Paul reminds Timothy that "fulfilling" his ministry requires his "do[ing] the work of an evangelist [*euangelistēs*]" (2 Tim. 4:5). Paul includes evangelists alongside pastors and teachers in the list of offices Christ has given to the church to equip the saints.[18] Commentators usually assume that this describes itinerant preachers who travel about proclaiming the good news.[19] In Acts 21:8 the word *euangelistēs* describes Philip, one of the seven the church in Jerusalem set apart for ministry to their widows (Acts 6:1–6). Philip had a reputation for bearing witness to the good news of Jesus Christ wherever he traveled (Acts 8:12, 35, 40). Although the responsibility to bear witness belongs to all, it becomes part of pastoral ministry as the shepherd seeks the lost sheep (Matt. 18:10–14 // Luke 15:1–7).

Gaines S. Dobbins once wrote, "The pastor is by virtue of his calling an evangelist. The question by which he might test every phase of his pastoral responsibility and activity is: What does it contribute to evangelism?"[20] Dobbins's observation is in line with the conviction of Baptist pastors before him. Spurgeon called evangelism (or "soul-winning") "the chief business of the Christian minister."[21] Carroll made evangelism one of the pillars of his outline of pastoral theology. He said, "The pastor's duties are only begun when he has cared for all the sheep of his own fold. He is Christ's special representative on earth to entreat men to be reconciled to God. He is the ambassador of the King to show the world His glory and lead men to be His subjects (2 Cor. 5:18–20)."[22] L. R. Scarborough outlined the imperative of pastoral evangelism:

> [The pastor] must be a soul-winner if the church is to be soul-winning. The passion for lost men must absolutely master his ministry if he leads his church out into continuous and constructive evangelism. This passion must manifest itself in his *study, prayers, preaching, pastoral visitation, personal work, plans,* and entire church *programs.* He will carry a constant "heaviness and a great sorrow in his heart" for unsaved men going to hell about him. He ought

18. Gaines Dobbins writes, "True, one of these functions may well take the primacy in the work of the typical Christian minister, but his service will not be full-rounded unless all of these functions find a place in his service. As missionary he is to be an evangelist; as preacher he is to be an evangelist; as pastor he is to be an evangelist; as teacher he is to be an evangelist. Conversely, as evangelist he will be missionary, preacher, pastor, teacher." "Pastoral Evangelism," *Review & Expositor* 42, no.1 (January 1945): 48.

19. Robert G. Bratcher and Eugene Albert Nida, *A Handbook on Paul's Letter to the Ephesians*, UBS Handbook Series (New York: United Bible Societies, 1993), 101.

20. Dobbins, "Pastoral Evangelism," 48.

21. C. H. Spurgeon, *The Soul-Winner: Or How to Lead Sinners to the Saviour* (New York: Fleming H. Revell, 1895), 9.

22. Carroll, "Twentieth-Century Pastor," 247.

to make soul-winning the master note in his life. He will preach at least one evangelistic sermon each Sunday, hold at least one revival period in his church each year, hold other evangelistic services in other churches and communities and constantly seek to win men to Christ in public and private.[23]

George W. Truett observed that, in his opinion, pastors did not preach often enough. By that, however, he was not referring to sermons proclaimed in a pulpit. Truett meant that pastors often missed the opportunity to preach the gospel to those whose paths intersected with theirs each day. In a message to fellow pastors, he said, "Has the preacher one soul for an audience? Then let him there give his most faithful testimony for Christ, for issues are bound up with the preacher's audience and message, both for time and for eternity. Let Jesus teach us all by his suggestive, unceasing, wayside ministry."[24] Truett regarded the charge that a church lacked passion and compassion for the lost as "the supreme indictment" that Christ could bring against it. "A church," he preached, "is nothing better than an ethical club if its sympathies for lost souls do not overflow, and if it does not go out to seek to point lost souls to the knowledge of Jesus."[25]

Baptist Leaders in Missions or Evangelism

Andrew Fuller (1754–1815) and William Carey (1761–1834)

In the eighteenth century, Particular Baptists in England held to the high Calvinism that supposed God to have predestined people to salvation or damnation. Consequently, they placed little emphasis on taking the gospel to the world around them. One of their lot, a pastor named Andrew Fuller, read the works of David Brainerd and Puritan missionary John Eliot, who had been working among Native Americans. Through a study of Scripture, Fuller became convinced of the imperative to take the gospel to the world. In 1785 he published his convictions.[26] Historians regard Fuller as the theologian of the Baptist mission movement. The undergirding affirmations in Fuller's theology of missions are these: (1) God has uniquely and finally revealed

23. L. R. Scarborough, *With Christ after the Lost: A Search for Souls* (Nashville: Sunday School Board of the Southern Baptist Convention, 1919), 149.
24. George W. Truett, *Follow Thou Me* (New York: Harper, 1932), 237.
25. George W. Truett, *A Quest for Souls*, ed. J. B. Cranfill (Dallas: Texas Baptist Book House, 1917), 67.
26. Andrew Fuller, *The Gospel of Christ Worthy of All Acceptation: Or, the Obligations of Men Fully to Credit, and Cordially to Approve, Whatever God Makes Known. Wherein Is Considered the Nature of Faith in Christ, and the Duty of Those Where the Gospel Comes in That Matter* (Northampton, UK: Dicey, 1785).

himself in Jesus Christ; (2) in the gospel God is freely offering Christ to the world; (3) only those means that are consistent with the nature of the gospel are worthy of a Christian missionary; and (4) the final triumph of Christ and his cause is assured.[27]

Fuller became acquainted with a young man named William Carey, who became a convinced Baptist and was baptized in 1783. Carey became pastor of the Harvey Lane Baptist Church in Leicester in 1789. Influenced by Fuller, by his own reading of Eliot and Brainerd, and by his study of Scripture, Carey published a manifesto in 1792: *An Enquiry into the Obligations of Christians to Use Means for the Conversion of the Heathens*. Carey argued that Jesus's commission in Matthew 28:18–20 remains binding on all Christians. He called for Particular Baptists to establish a missionary society to send missionaries to the world in obedience to the Great Commission. Having overcome resistance within his denomination, in October 1792 he, along with Andrew Fuller, John Ryland, and John Sutcliff, founded the Particular Baptist Society for the Propagation of the Gospel amongst the Heathen (later renamed the Baptist Missionary Society and, since 2000, BMS World Mission). Carey himself became the first missionary supported by the society, sailing off to a sacrificial ministry in India that would last more than four decades. At his death in 1834, he was one of India's most widely respected and honored citizens.[28] Historians generally identify Carey's work as the beginning of the modern missionary movement.[29]

Adoniram (1788–1850) and Ann Judson (1789–1826) and Luther Rice (1783–1836)

On February 19, 1812, Adoniram Judson, his wife, Ann, whom he had married two weeks earlier, Luther Rice, and Samuel and Harriet Newell set sail for India on the *Caravan*. In 1810 Judson and others had convinced the Congregationalist General Association to form the first missionary board in America, the American Board of Commissioners for Foreign Missions, and to sponsor their effort in Asia. While sailing to Calcutta, Judson completed

27. Ernest F. Clipsham, "Andrew Fuller and the Baptist Mission," *Foundations* 10, no. 1 (January 1967): 6–7.

28. Rosalie Beck provides a concise account of William Carey's life and accomplishments; see "Baptist Missions and the Turn toward Global Responsibility: 1792," in *Turning Points in Baptist History: A Festschrift in Honor of Harry Leon McBeth*, ed. Michael E. Williams and Walter B. Shurden (Macon, GA: Mercer University Press, 2008), 102–27. For a more thorough account, see Timothy George, *Faithful Witness: The Life and Mission of William Carey* (Birmingham, AL: New Hope, 1991).

29. For a summary of Fuller's contribution to this movement, see Clipsham, "Andrew Fuller," 4–18.

a study of the subject of baptism, knowing he would face William Carey and that he might need to defend his views. By the time they arrived in June, Judson had adopted the Baptist position of believer's baptism by immersion. Ann was not convinced at first and several times told her new husband, "If you become a Baptist, I will not."[30] Later, she too became convinced. He and Ann were baptized in September by an associate of Carey. Luther Rice, arriving on another ship, also became a Baptist. The British East India Company would not permit them to pursue their calling in India, and so the Judsons moved to Burma, where they spent the remainder of their lives.

Accused of spying for the British in the Anglo-Burmese War of 1824–1826, Judson was violently arrested, bound with torture thongs, and taken away to the confines of the infamous death prison in Ava. After a year of deprivation in that prison, Judson, along with his colleague Dr. Jonathan Price and a small group of other Western prisoners, was marched overland, barefoot and sick, for six more months of misery in a primitive village in Mandalay. Judson wrote of this experience almost objectively:

> I was seized on the 8th of June, 1824, in consequence of the war with Bengal, and in company with Dr. Price, three Englishmen, one American, and one Greek, and was thrown into the death prison at Ava, where we lay eleven months—nine months in three pairs, and two months in five pairs of fetters. The scenes we witnessed and the sufferings we underwent during that period I would fain consign to oblivion. From the death prison at Ava we were removed to a country prison at Oung-pen-la, ten miles distant, under circumstances of such severe treatment, that one of our number, the Greek, expired on the road; and some of the rest, among whom was myself, were scarcely able to move for several days. . . . I remained in the Oung-pen-la prison six months in one pair of fetters.[31]

All but one of the British prisoners of war who were with them died. Edward Judson, Adoniram's son and biographer, recounts the brutal suffering of those months as a prisoner of war in far greater detail.[32] Ann died of smallpox in 1826, two years after Adoniram's release.

Meanwhile, Luther Rice returned to the United States to raise support for the Burma mission from among Baptist congregations. In 1814 Rice's efforts resulted in establishing the General Missionary Convention of the Baptist Denomination in the United States of America for Foreign Missions, also

---

30. Steven R. Harmon, "Adoniram Judson, Baptists, the Whole Church, and God's Mission," *Criswell Theological Review* 14, no. 2 (2017): 36.

31. Edward Judson, *Adoniram Judson: A Biography* (Philadelphia: American Baptist Publication Society, 1894), 90.

32. Judson, *Adoniram Judson*, 89–100.

known as the Triennial Convention. This organization was the first Baptist denomination in the United States. It emerged from a conviction about the missionary work of the churches.[33] During Rice's life, the Triennial Convention grew from eight thousand Baptists to more than six hundred thousand. The convention supported 25 missions and 112 missionaries. Additionally, Baptists established 15 institutions of higher education.[34]

Lottie Moon (1840–1912)

In 1872 the Southern Baptist Convention appointed Charlotte Digges "Lottie" Moon as a missionary to China, where she served forty years. Her passion was direct evangelism, telling the good news to Chinese women in the villages she visited. Since she was a single woman, however, her supervisors often relegated her to teaching a few children. Finally, in 1885 she began a ministry in China's interior, where her converts soon numbered in the hundreds. She worked tirelessly, not only among the people of P'ingtu and Hwangshien, where she lived, but in extensive correspondence. Moon made two visits to America, where she urged the cause of mission support in prayer, in generosity, and in calling out young people to serve. Her time in China included plagues, famine, war, and severe personal sacrifice for the people she loved. Lottie Moon became a sort of patron saint of missions for Southern Baptists.[35]

William Franklin Graham (1918–2018)

What Carey, the Judsons, Rice, and Moon were to Baptist missions, William Franklin "Billy" Graham Jr. was to evangelism. Following in the footsteps of the figures of Charles Finney, Billy Sunday, and D. L. Moody, Graham was known for his evangelistic crusades, preaching to large crowds in city arenas and ultimately over television during the second half of the twentieth century. He preached to more than 210 million people in 185 countries during his sixty years of ministry. The ministry expanded to publications, radio and television broadcasts, motion pictures, and training in personal evangelism and discipleship. The heart of Graham's ministry was the gospel of a cruci-

33. In 1845 Baptists in the South withdrew from the Triennial Convention over its slavery and missions policy and formed the Southern Baptist Convention. The Triennial Convention reorganized in 1907 as the Northern Baptist Convention and in 1972 took the name American Baptist Churches USA.

34. Karen Bullock, "Luther Rice and a Lasting Legacy in Baptist Missions," IMB, October 31, 2017, https://www.imb.org/2017/10/31/luther-rice-legacy/.

35. For details of Lottie Moon's life and ministry, see Catherine B. Allen, *The New Lottie Moon Story* (Nashville: Broadman, 1980); and Cathy Butler, *The Story of Lottie Moon*, WMU Heritage Series (Birmingham, AL: Woman's Missionary Union, 2004).

fied and risen Savior proclaimed to a lost world, which was separated from a relationship with God. Graham briefly served as a pastor for the First Baptist Church of Western Springs, Illinois, while a Wheaton student. However, the preponderance of his ministry was as an itinerant evangelist. Preaching during the tumultuous period of the 1960s and 1970s, Graham dealt with civil rights issues, the Vietnam War, Watergate, and other social movements. He provided spiritual guidance for every American president from Truman to Obama. Billy Graham had a reputation as "America's Pastor." He was also instrumental, along with John Stott, in inaugurating the Lausanne Movement. In July 1974, some 2,700 evangelical Christians from 150 nations gathered for the International Congress on World Evangelization to discuss the progress, resources, and methods of evangelizing the world. These few facts of Graham's life only begin to scratch the surface of his powerful influence on Baptists and evangelism.[36]

Less Visible Baptist Lights

For every well-known, venerated figure like those named above, thousands of other Baptists have responded sacrificially to the call to take the gospel to the ends of the earth. Although the modern mission movement's story is often a narrative of White European and American men, the full account includes others. Black missionaries carried the gospel and planted churches across the early frontier in the eighteenth and nineteenth centuries; these included Peter Durrett and London Ferrill in Kentucky, plus John Berry Meachum and John Richard Anderson in Missouri.[37] They preached and planted churches in Oklahoma, Arkansas, Texas, Kansas, Colorado, Wyoming, Arizona, New Mexico, California, Oregon, and Washington.[38] Black Baptists in America were also instrumental in Africa's evangelization in the late nineteenth and early twentieth centuries.[39] Ten years before Carey went to India, George Liele, a freed slave, left America to preach in Jamaica, becoming the first American Baptist missionary,

---

36. William C. Martin, Rice University professor of sociology of religion, offers a well-rounded, relatively objective biography of Graham, *A Prophet with Honor: The Billy Graham Story* (New York: Quill, 1991).

37. Sandy Dwayne Martin, "Black Baptists and the Frontier: Missions and Church Establishment, 1790–1925," *American Baptist Quarterly* 35, no. 3–4 (2016): 299–304. See also Hang Zou and Warren Hope, "Black Missionary Baptist Ministers and the Burden of the Great Commission," *Baptist History and Heritage* 50, no. 3 (2015): 27–42.

38. S. Martin, "Black Baptists and the Frontier," 304–9.

39. Sandy Dwayne Martin, *Black Baptists and African Missions: The Origins of a Movement, 1880–1915* (Macon, GA: Mercer University Press, 1989). Ferron Okewole narrates the role Black women have played as foreign missionaries as well; see "'Send Me Too': African American Baptist Women in Early Foreign Missions," *American Baptist Quarterly* 24, no. 3 (September 2005): 256–63.

three decades before Judson.[40] Baptist women, both Black and White, also played significant roles in the mission movement.[41] Increasingly today, those countries to whom American and British churches once sent missionaries are now sending hundreds of their own—some to the United Kingdom and the United States.[42] Not all of these will have their biographies recorded. But their contribution and faithfulness to this Baptist conviction remain.

Theological Reflection

A biblical sense of "sentness" accompanies the call to ministry that leads to becoming a pastor. A pastor's work entails personally sharing the good news of Jesus Christ with those who do not yet know him and equipping the congregation to do the same.

Pastor as Cultural Anthropologist

Pastoral ministry is inherently contextual. It takes place in a specific location, amid a particular culture, among people who speak a certain language and share common values and practices. As one whom God *sent* to this place, the pastor seeks to understand the culture of the world where they intend to bear witness. Part of comprehending the culture is to be like the two hundred chiefs of Issachar under David, "who understood the times and knew what Israel should do" (1 Chron. 12:32 NIV). The age in which we live, not just the place, is also the context to which God has sent us.

James McClendon's volume on Christian witness explores the church's relationship to the world, calling his effort a "theology of culture."[43] We understand that "missionaries" sent to some distant destination must learn the language, customs, beliefs, and traditions of those they go to serve. Over the past half century, changes in Western society have required the same kind of

40. Lesley Hildreth, "Missionaries You Should Know: George Liele," IMB, June 26, 2018, https://www.imb.org/2018/06/26/missionaries-you-should-know-george-liele. See also David T. Shannon, Julia Frazier White, and Deborah Van Broekhoven, *George Liele's Life and Legacy: An Unsung Hero* (Macon, GA: Mercer University Press, 2013).

41. See Carolyn Weatherford Crumpler, "The Role of Women in Baptist Missions," *Baptist History and Heritage* 27, no. 3 (July 1992): 25–33.

42. Israel Olofinjana, "Reverse Mission: African Presence and Mission within Baptists Together in the United Kingdom," *Journal of European Baptist Studies* 19, no. 2 (2019): 100–116. The World Christian Database reports that 450,000 missionaries were sent by churches around the world. About 150,000 are from the US and the UK. The database does not distinguish missionaries by their denominational affiliation. See "Missionaries and Christian Workers—World Christian Database," https://worldchristiandatabase-org.ezproxy.baylor.edu/wcd/#/results/1956.

43. McClendon, *Witness*, 20–24.

devotion to understanding the culture in which we minister. The church in the West can no longer assume even a basic understanding of the Christian story among those we are attempting to evangelize. George Hunter says that we, like the ancient church, are up against "ignositics": people who simply do not know the biblical story.[44] Moral assumptions that once made sense of sin no longer resonate with this audience with whom a profound moral relativism has taken hold. The gospel now contends with what researchers Christian Smith and Melinda Lundquist Denton term "moralistic therapeutic deism" rather than first-century idolatry.[45] This cultural shift ought to impact the theological education in which men and women engage as they prepare for ministry.

Pastors who minister with a sense of having been *called* and having been *sent* respond compassionately to their world. They come to their work with a holy curiosity about these people to whom God has sent them. Who are they? What do they believe? What are their chief concerns in life? What are their fears? How do they communicate? The pastor has endless questions to ask of the place. Listening becomes a primary skill for evangelism. Asking, listening, observing, and adapting, the missionary pastor and congregation learn to bring the gospel to the unique culture of the time and place to which God has sent them.

McClendon says that the church is a pilgrim people, not entirely at home in the culture surrounding us. But membership in the people of God remains an open invitation: "Whosoever will may come." This openness of the church to all human beings creates, McClendon says, both a policy and a problem. "The policy is evangelism, or more broadly, *witness*: authentic Christian existence is always missionary, possessed only to be imparted to others. Yet the policy can be restated as a problem: How shall present sharers of the journey be related to the human world in which they take the journey? What ties cement the people of the journey to the old, broken peoplehood in which they once did and now in a new way they still do have a part?"[46] From an evangelical

44. Hunter, *How to Reach Secular People*, 41. Hunter argues that, like those proclaiming the gospel in the first century, twenty-first-century witnesses in the Western world face a culture ignorant of the basic stories of Israel and Jesus. The task of witness becomes in part an educational and informative work.

45. Christian Smith and Melinda Lundquist Denton, *Soul Searching: The Religious and Spiritual Lives of American Teenagers* (Oxford: Oxford University Press, 2005). Smith and Denton list the following basic beliefs as part of this pervasive religious outlook: "1. A God exists who created and orders the world and watches over human life on earth. 2. God wants people to be good, nice, and fair to each other, as taught in the Bible and by most world religions. 3. The central goal of life is to be happy and to feel good about oneself. 4. God does not need to be particularly involved in one's life except when God is needed to resolve a problem. 5. Good people go to heaven when they die" (162–63).

46. McClendon, *Witness*, 20.

position, he argues, what is needed is a theology of evangelism, which he then equates with a theology of culture. Our sentness implies not only a place but also a time. We must learn to communicate the never-changing good news of God's love and redemption in Christ to an ever-changing world, whose categories shift, not only from place to place, but also from era to era.

Creating an Atmosphere of "Sentness"

Pastors take responsibility for igniting the congregation's passion for missions and evangelism. In the twenty-first century, they will handle this role differently than in the past. Carroll and Scarborough exhorted pastors to instruct their congregations about missions. They encouraged pastors to teach the church to support missions financially, pray for missionaries, and recruit men and women to devote their lives to missionary careers.[47] A hundred years later, these responsibilities have shifted significantly. The overall goal of igniting a passion for evangelism remains, but the means have changed.

Career missionaries are no longer the primary expression of the Great Commission among Baptists. Inexpensive air travel has made it possible for ordinary people to participate in short-term mission projects themselves. In reaction to colonialism and other economic factors, countries often do not welcome Christian missionaries. Instead, Baptist men and women respond to the call of God by taking their training in education, medicine, engineering, agriculture, and other fields across international borders for a time or a lifetime, bearing witness to Christ as they have the opportunity. Increasingly, local congregations, not mission agencies, are doing the sending. Older, retired disciples have time, experience, health, and resources available to them for many years beyond their first career. Many of them will consider investing those years in the church's witness in the world.[48] Pastors will clearly express their leadership in witness and evangelism in preaching, teaching, congregational planning, and personal example.

The goal of pastoral leadership in witness and evangelism is to create and sustain a culture of "sentness," in which all believers identify as priests and as ministers sent into the world to serve. Clyde Fant argues that biblical preaching does not encourage a church toward protective isolation but toward "existing in the world for the world."[49] He writes, "What can preach-

---

47. Carroll, "Twentieth-Century Pastor," 258–65; L. R. Scarborough, *My Conception of the Gospel Ministry* (Nashville: Sunday School Board of the Southern Baptist Convention, 1935), 94–98.

48. For other trends in modern missions, see Michael W. Stroope, "The Future of Baptists and Missions," *Baptist History and Heritage* 41, no. 2 (2006): 30–40; and Robert P. Sellers, "A Baptist View of Missions for Postmodernity," *Review & Expositor* 100, no. 4 (2003): 641–84.

49. Clyde E. Fant, *Preaching for Today*, rev. ed. (Cambridge: Harper & Row, 1987), 19.

ing do? It can send the church into a real world, a world of starving children and murderous competition, of lonely rooms and smug clubs, of shattered dreams and burned-out hopes. This is the final mark of true preaching, to send the church into the world. That is where the Christ of the church is: 'He goes before you into Galilee: there you shall see him' (Mark 16:7)."[50] In such a culture, Baptist believers understand that their baptism ordained them to the reconciliation ministry.[51]

To live with a sense of sentness does not require a passport and a plane ticket. Christ's disciples take that pervasive sense of bearing witness to the reign of God into every encounter in everyday life. Both pastors and congregants learn to act, speak, and love in the name of Jesus as a way of life. Just before Jesus says, "As the Father has sent me, so I send you" (John 20:21), John recalls that he extended his hands and exposed his side where the messianic wounds were still visible. Those wounds defined the "as" in Jesus's words of commission. The sending was into a broken world, a traumatized world that inflicts trauma on those sent to it. His disciples would face such a world as they bore witness to Christ's wounds, which bring healing and reconciliation. Pastors who seek to nurture and sustain a culture of sentness will equip disciples for such a ministry in their world, a ministry of witness to the kingdom that often necessitates sacrifice and sometimes requires suffering.

CONCLUSIONS ···

When Baptist historian David Bebbington offered his "quadrilateral" characterizing evangelicalism in Britain, he included not only *biblicism* (high regard for Scripture) and *crucicentrism* (stress on Christ's sacrifice on the cross) but also *conversionism* (belief in the need for lives to be changed by the gospel) and *activism* (the expression of the gospel in effort).[52] All four qualities define Baptists over the last four centuries. Our commitment to Scripture, our loyalty to the message of the cross, our belief in human lostness apart from Christ, and our activist spirit have driven us to engage the world as witnesses to the kingdom of God. Pastoral leadership by both word and example has often

50. Fant, *Preaching for Today*, 20.

51. Bent Hylleberg, "Baptism as Commitment to Ministry and Mission: A Consideration of the Rites for Baptism and Ordination in the Nordic Baptist Churches," in *Rites of Ordination and Commitment in the Churches of the Nordic Countries: Theology and Terminology* (Copenhagen: Museum Tusculanum, 2006), 355–76.

52. David Bebbington, *Evangelicalism in Modern Britain: A History from the 1730s to the 1980s* (Grand Rapids: Baker, 1992), 2–3.

been at the heart of these efforts and movements. As the world continues to change—as culture shifts, as technology evolves, as climate transforms, as immigrants flow from one part of the world to another—so will the methods that Baptist pastors employ to engage their world change. But the call to ministry and a sense of sentness to that world will continue to actively shape compassionate responses to the world in its lostness and brokenness.

FOR FURTHER REFLECTION

1. How do you understand the pastor's role in the church's work of witness and evangelism as in any way distinct from that of other church members?

2. Has the word "evangelism" lost its meaning in the contemporary setting? If you think so, how might it be reclaimed or replaced? What does "evangelism" mean for the twenty-first-century church in North America?

3. What do you believe to be the implications of the Great Commission for your pastoral ministry? For your congregation? How is the Great Commission expressed in your life and your church?

4. What role do the lives of Baptist "saints" such as William Carey, Adoniram and Ann Judson, Lottie Moon, and Billy Graham play in motivating your engagement with the Great Commission? What other lives inspire you to bear witness to Christ faithfully?

5. If you were to write your own confession of faith, what would you say about bearing witness and evangelism?

PART THREE

CARE

Pastor as Priest

7

Worship and the Ordinances

Directing Attention to God

We affirm baptism, preaching, and the Lord's table as powerful signs that seal God's faithfulness in Christ and express our response of awed gratitude rather than as mechanical rituals or mere symbols.

—"Re-envisioning Baptist Identity: A Manifesto for Baptist Communities in North America"

For as often as you eat this bread and drink the cup, you proclaim the Lord's death until he comes.

—Paul (1 Cor. 11:26)

The priesthood of all believers is a core Baptist principle frequently identified as a distinctive of this tradition. By declaring this conviction, Baptists are not claiming to have no priests. On the contrary, Baptists affirm that all of us are priests (1 Pet. 2:9; Rev. 1:6; 5:10; 20:6). All believers have both priestly privileges, such as access to God through Jesus Christ, and priestly responsibilities, such as intercession for one another. Despite the truth that all believers are priests and that we do not refer to our ministers as priests, pastoral ministry bears a noticeable resemblance to sacerdotal ministry. Pastors rightly share priestly ministry with others in the congregation. Still, a priestly sort of light shines on the work that we do as we minister in the congregation's stead in worship, in the waters of baptism, and at the Lord's Table.

Biblical Foundations

Priesthood in the Old Testament

In the Old Testament, God sets apart the tribe of Levi as the priestly tribe and apportions them no land (Deut. 18:1; Josh. 18:7). Instead, the Levites live in specified cities among the other tribes (Josh. 21:1–45). Initially, "Levites" referred to all those descended from Levi and was synonymous with the Levitical priesthood (Deut. 18:1). Later, Israel distinguished "priests and Levites" from each other, but they considered all the cultic personnel to be Levi's descendants.[1] Among the duties and privileges of the Levites were bearing the sacred ark of the covenant (1 Chron. 15:11–15), providing music for the temple services (1 Chron. 16:4–37), and administering and teaching the Torah (1 Chron. 23:4; 2 Chron. 17:7–9; 19:8–11; 35:3). Several psalms are attributed to Asaph (50, 70–83) and Korah (42–49), the Levites' two main divisions.

The priests performed the ritual services of the Torah and offered the required sacrifices at the altar. Deuteronomy affirms that all of Levi's descendants held the right to serve as priests (10:8–9). Aaron and his descendants served as high priests, wearing distinctive vestments (Exod. 28–29) and overseeing the rituals surrounding sin offerings and the Day of Atonement. The priests pronounced God's blessings on the people (Num. 6:22–26), sounded trumpets at various festivals and holy days, and blew the shofar announcing the Day of Atonement. They were also responsible for maintaining the temple, conducting regular inspections of the temple grounds, and soliciting funds to carry out the work.[2] The priests examined people stricken with specific diseases and declared them to be clean or unclean ritually (Lev. 13–14). The people also relied on priests to judge matters of the law (Deut. 17:9).

Priesthood in the New Testament

Priests are mentioned often in the Gospels and Acts. They performed an influential role in Jewish society during the Second Temple period, so they

---

1. Joshua R. Porter, "Levi," in *Harper's Bible Dictionary*, ed. Paul J. Achtemeier (San Francisco: Harper & Row, 1985), 557.
2. Lawrence H. Schiffman, "Priests," in Achtemeier, *Harper's Bible Dictionary*, 822.

consequently played a significant part in the story of Jesus and the early church in Jerusalem.[3] Paul never mentions priests in his epistles, but he does refer to his own ministry to the gentiles once as "priestly service" (*hierougeō*) (Rom. 15:16). When Peter and John refer to priests, they have in mind the priesthood of all believers (1 Pet. 2:4–5, 9; Rev. 1:5–6; 5:10). Church leaders are never called "priests" in the New Testament writings, and the early church certainly did not see its leaders stepping into the role of the Jewish priesthood. On the contrary, the scribes as teachers of the Torah served as more of a model for those who made disciples among the early Christians (Matt. 13:51–53).[4]

The priesthood is a central theme in the book of Hebrews. The writer mentions it thirty-three times. The heart of the argument is that the Levitical and Aaronic priestly functions are now obsolete since a new priesthood in Jesus Christ, after the order of Melchizedek, has replaced them.[5] The "once for all" (*hapax*) sacrifice of Jesus on the cross has fulfilled and replaced the temple's sacrificial system (9:26, 28; 10:2). Like Leviticus and Chronicles, Hebrews describes the priestly role of offering sacrifices, administering the cultic ritual, and interceding on behalf of God's people. The idea of the priesthood of all believers or a priestly role for Christian leaders is not in view in Hebrews. However, the only remaining sacrifices are to be offered by all believers—namely, the praise of God, good works, and generosity (Heb. 13:15–16).

3. Levites and the Jewish priesthood play a prominent role in the New Testament narratives: Matt. 2:4; 8:4; 12:4–5; 16:21; 20:18; 21:15, 23, 45; 26:3, 14, 47, 51, 57–59, 62–63, 65; 27:1, 3, 6, 12, 20, 41, 62; 28:11–12; Mark 1:44; 2:26; 8:31; 10:33; 11:18, 27; 14:1, 10, 43, 47, 53–55, 60–61, 63, 66; 15:1, 3, 10–11, 31; Luke 1:5, 8; 5:15; 6:4; 9:22; 10:31–32; 17:14; 19:47; 20:1, 19; 22:2, 4, 50, 52, 66; 23:4, 10, 13; 24:20; John 1:19, 22; 7:32, 45; 11:47, 49, 51, 57; 12:10; 18:3, 13, 15–16, 19, 22, 24, 26, 35; 19:6, 15, 21; Acts 4:1, 6, 23, 36; 5:17, 21, 24, 27; 6:7; 7:1; 9:1, 14, 21; 19:14; 22:30; 23:2, 4–5, 14; 24:1; 25:2, 15; 26:10, 12, 14.

4. Derek Tidball, *Ministry by the Book: New Testament Patterns for Pastoral Leadership* (Downers Grove, IL: IVP Academic, 2008), 18–37.

5. Melchizedek is a shadowy figure appearing briefly in Gen. 14, where he is referred to as both a king and a priest. He greets Abraham following the patriarch's victory over the kings who had taken his nephew Lot captive. Melchizedek brings out bread and wine and blesses Abraham in the name of God Most High. Psalm 110, a messianic psalm, refers to the Messiah (king) as "a priest forever according to the order of Melchizedek" (110:4). Allusions to Ps. 110 appear both on the lips of Jesus in the New Testament and in the words of the apostles, always with reference to Jesus, the Messiah, sitting at the right hand of God (Matt. 22:42–46 // Mark 12:35–37 // Luke 20:41–44; Acts 2:34; Eph. 1:20–22; 1 Cor. 15:25; Heb. 1:3, 13; 10:12–13; 12:2; 1 Pet. 3:22). Only the writer of Hebrews takes up the sacerdotal aspect of Melchizedek, arguing that Jesus's status as "a priest forever according to the order of Melchizedek" is greater than that of any priest descended from Aaron (Heb. 5:5–10; 6:13–20; 7:1–28).

Baptism as a Priestly Act

Although we most commonly identify John the Baptist as a prophet, he also had a priestly heritage, like Jeremiah and Ezekiel. His father, Zechariah, belonged to the priestly order of Abijah (Luke 1:5; 1 Chron. 24:10). While he was exercising his priestly responsibilities in the sanctuary in Jerusalem, he received the angelic annunciation of the birth of a son, who would be the Messiah's forerunner (Luke 1:5–23). Given John's background, it is reasonable to inquire about the priestly nature of the baptism he offered. In the Fourth Gospel, Jewish authorities dispatched ritual purification experts, "priests and Levites," to investigate John's baptismal practice (John 1:19). Scholars have long debated the background of John's use of this rite. They often suggest a connection with the Essenes at Qumran, a sect who likely seceded from the Zadokite priesthood. The Essenes practiced water purification rites in their community, as evidenced by their texts, the presence of ritual baths, and the testimony of Josephus. At the least, the Essenes' presence in the region near John's ministry may have led the Jerusalem authorities to send emissaries to investigate.[6] John's baptism represented a kind of ritual cleansing akin to the Jewish mikveh.[7]

G. R. Beasley-Murray, however, associates John's baptism with the Jewish practice of proselyte baptism rather than with the Essenes' ritual.[8] Connecting John's practice with proselyte baptism implies that he considered even the people of Israel to be outsiders to the kingdom. A claim to be Abraham's descendant was insufficient for kingdom citizenship (Luke 3:8). Even Israelites entered the kingdom of God on the basis of repentance as they prepared themselves to receive the Messiah.

Christian baptism differs in significance from the baptism of John. John's baptism signified repentance and cleansing in preparation for the coming of the Messiah (Matt. 3:11). Christian baptism, however, looks back on the death and resurrection of Jesus and portrays the believer's participation in Jesus's death and resurrection by faith (Rom. 6:1–4). In Acts 19:1–7, Paul encounters some who had been baptized by John but had not heard that Jesus had fulfilled John's message. Having instructed them, he baptizes them in the name of Jesus.

6. Raymond E. Brown, *The Gospel According to John*, Anchor Bible 29 (Garden City, NY: Doubleday, 1966), 46.

7. Geoffrey Wigoder, Fred Skolnik, and Shmuel Himelstein, eds., *The New Encyclopedia of Judaism*, 2nd ed. (New York: New York University Press, 2002), s.v. "mikveh."

8. G. R. Beasley-Murray, *Baptism in the New Testament* (Grand Rapids: Eerdmans, 1973), 1–44. See also Wigoder, Skolnik, and Himelstien, *New Encyclopedia of Judaism*, s.v. "conversion to Judaism."

The preceding paragraph in Acts tells of Apollos, who seems to have been in much the same state as those Paul encountered. However, Acts does not record that Apollos received an additional baptism after Priscilla and Aquila instructed him. He left them and went out as a Christian evangelist (Acts 18:24–28).

Although Christian baptism differs from John's, it retains a priestly association. Peter J. Leithart understands Hebrews 10:19–22 to refer to Christian baptism. He claims that "from Tertullian's second-century treatise *De baptismo*, it has been a truism of liturgical commentary that Christian baptism fulfills the priestly ordination rite of the Old Testament (Exod. 29; Lev. 8–9) and thus initiates [new believers] into the New Covenant priesthood."[9] Our baptism is our priestly ordination. Consequently, baptizing is itself a priestly act. When the apostles and others baptized new believers, they were themselves believer-priests performing a sacerdotal act.

Lord's Supper as a Priestly Act

Jesus himself performed a priestly act when he took bread and wine at the Last Supper and offered it to his disciples as his broken body and shed blood (Matt. 26:26–29 // Mark 14:22–26 // Luke 22:14–23 // 1 Cor. 11:23–26; cf. Gen. 14:18). Jesus gave these physical elements to the church to remind us of his sacrifice on the cross. Early Christians interpreted his death as the sacrifice of the Passover lamb, "the Lamb of God who takes away the sin of the world" (John 1:29; cf. 1 Cor. 5:7; 1 Pet. 1:18–19; Rev. 5:6).[10] In John's Gospel, even the chronology of Jesus's death underscores a connection with the paschal lamb, since Jesus dies on the cross as the priests slaughter the lambs in the temple.[11] The breaking of bread and the pouring out of wine in celebration of

9. Peter J. Leithart, "Womb of the World: Baptism and the Priesthood of the New Covenant in Hebrews 10.19–22," *Journal for the Study of the New Testament* 22, no. 78 (October 2000): 49.

10. R. Robert Creech, "Christology and Conflict: A Comparative Study of Two Central Themes in the Johannine Literature and the Apocalypse" (PhD diss., Baylor University, 1984), 115–55.

11. Brown comments on John 19:14,

> The time when this fatal renunciation of the Messiah takes place is noon on Passover Eve, the very hour when the priests have begun to slaughter the paschal lambs in the temple precincts. It is an ironical touch of the Johannine writer to have "the Jews" renounce the covenant at the moment when their priests are beginning the preparations for the feast that annually recalls God's deliverance of His people. By the blood of the lamb He marked them off to be spared as His own, and now they know no king but the Roman Emperor. As they recite the Passover *Haggadah*, how hollow will ring the frequent praise of the kingly reign of God! They think of Passover as a traditional time for God's judgment of the world (Mishnah *Rosh Hashanah* 1:2), and on Passover Eve they have judged

the Lord's Supper memorializes the sacrificial death of Jesus on our behalf. Just as the Passover meal for Jewish participants is "a day of remembrance" of their deliverance from Egypt (Exod. 12:14), so Jesus's disciples celebrate the supper "in remembrance" of him (Luke 22:19). In breaking the bread and sharing the cup, believers handle the elements representing the sacrificial Lamb of God (1 Cor. 10:16). The pastor represents the church in this priestly act. The members of the congregation, as believer-priests, then pass the elements to each other.

Historical Bypaths

The degree to which Baptists understand pastoral ministry as partaking of priestly roles is affected by how we interpret the authority conveyed in ordination and by our theology of the ordinances of baptism and the Lord's Supper.

The Priesthood of All Believers and Ordained Ministry

Arising as it did out of the Radical Reformation, rather early the Baptist movement attempted to distance itself from Roman Catholicism. In particular, the affirmation of the priesthood of all believers made explicit that priesthood was not a category applying only to the ordained clergy. Nevertheless, Baptists continued, for the most part, to ordain their pastors. The tension between doctrine and practice remains. What role does ordination play in our understanding and practice of pastoral leadership in worship, particularly regarding presiding over the ordinances?

Baptists, like other groups rooted in the Reformation era, sometimes described ordination as being "to the Word and the Sacraments."[12] The Waterland Confession (1580) affirms that those who are called and elected to the teaching office are authorized to administer the "sacraments" of Holy Baptism and Holy Supper (articles 30–34).[13] John Smyth's Short Confession (1610) affirms that "in this holy church hath God ordained the ministers of the Gospel, the doctrines of the holy Word, the use of the holy sacraments, the oversight of the poor, and the ministers of the same office."[14] In his *Twenty*

---

themselves by condemning the one whom God has sent into the world, not to judge it but to save it (3:17). (*Gospel According to John*, 895)

12. Brian C. Brewer, "A Baptist View of Ordained Ministry: A Function or a Way of Being? Part 2," *Baptist Quarterly* 43, no. 4 (October 1, 2009): 222.

13. William L. Lumpkin, *Baptist Confessions of Faith*, 2nd rev. ed. (Valley Forge, PA: Judson, 2011), 58–62.

14. Lumpkin, *Baptist Confessions of Faith*, 101.

Articles, written earlier that year, Smyth had declared that it was the bishops "to whom power is given of dispensing both the word and the sacraments."[15] The Dordrecht Confession (1632) assigns authority for administering "the Lord's ordinances" to the congregation's ordained leaders.[16] Some British Baptists continued to affirm this position.[17] Others, like Charles Spurgeon, who rejected ordination altogether, disagreed. He wrote,

> The small matter we have mentioned leads on to another which is by no means small, namely, the notion in some churches that *only an ordained or recognized minister should preside at the Lord's table*. Small is our patience with this unmitigated Popery, and yet it is by no means uncommon. Pulpits which are most efficiently supplied on other Sundays by men who are without pastoral charge must be vacated by them on the first Sunday of the month because the friends like a stated minister to *administer the sacrament*. This may not always be the language employed, but it often is, and it is an unsanctified jargon, revealing the influence of priestcraft. Whence comes it? By what Scripture can it be justified? "Breaking bread from house to house" does not read very like it. We suppose that the idea of a deacon leading the communion would horrify a great many, but why? If the church should request a venerable brother to conduct the service, a brother of eminent grace and prayerfulness, would the ordinance be any the less instructive or consoling because he was not in the ministry?[18]

Spurgeon also took issue with baptism, weddings, funerals, and visitation of the sick, which most Baptists saw as tasks belonging especially if not exclusively to the pastor.

During most of the nineteenth century, Baptists in the United States assumed that ordination bestowed some authority regarding the ordinances.[19] J. R. Graves, the Landmark movement's leading voice, insisted that proper ordination was essential for a person to officiate at the Lord's Table. Without an ordained minister, a congregation could not observe the ordinances.[20] Theologian J. L. Dagg's argument about authority to baptize supported a Baptist version of apostolic succession. Dagg did not make the same case

15. Lumpkin, *Baptist Confessions of Faith*, 95.

16. Lumpkin, *Baptist Confessions of Faith*, 73.

17. J. Ithel Jones, "British Baptist Views of Ordination," *Southwestern Journal of Theology* 11, no. 2 (1969): 47–48.

18. Charles H. Spurgeon, "Fragments of Popery among Nonconformists," *The Friend* 14, no. 165 (August 1, 1874): 195.

19. G. Thomas Halbrooks, "The Meaning and Significance of Ordination among Southern Baptists, 1845–1945," *Baptist History and Heritage* 23, no. 3 (July 1988): 28.

20. Halbrooks, "Meaning and Significance," 28.

regarding the Lord's Supper, however.[21] Extreme positions such as these evoked reactions from others, such as E. C. Dargan, who argued,

> It is the privilege of the church to appoint any of its members to preside and direct the observance of the Supper. It does not require the presence and action of an ordained minister in all cases. It was one of the common statements of our Baptist fathers that the administration of the ordinances "was not tied to any office." It is to be regretted that custom has bound us hard and fast in this respect so that many churches fail for long periods to observe the Supper because of the absence of an ordained minister. So rigid has this custom become that it may seem startling at first to state a contrary view.[22]

Over time, and with reflection, the more sacerdotal position regarding ordination moderated among Baptists.

By the twentieth century, Baptists were clear that ordination conferred no "grace, spiritual gifts, abilities, power, priestly authority, special rights or privileges, mysterious virtues, or magic 'fluid.'"[23] Among Southern Baptists, none of the three twentieth-century iterations of the Baptist Faith and Message requires that an ordained pastor perform either of the ordinances. The article on "The Church," which names pastors as one of the two church officers, ascribes no privilege to them in this matter. Although pastors *ordinarily* preside over baptism and the Lord's Supper, Southern Baptists never claimed that they are uniquely qualified to do so. In their policy statement on ordination, the American Baptists Churches USA specify that "the New Testament gives no explicit indication that these persons were especially responsible for leadership in the observance of baptism or the Lord's Supper."[24] Any believer-priest authorized by the congregation may perform these two priestly acts.

Sacraments or Ordinances?

Just as Baptists have positioned ourselves along a continuum regarding ordination, from purely functional to somewhat sacerdotal, so it is with our understanding of the Lord's Supper and baptism. Early Baptists quickly differentiated their view of the Supper from transubstantiation or from viewing

21. J. L. Dagg, *Manual of Theology* (Charleston, SC: Southern Baptist Publication Society, 1859), 2:230, 257, 357.

22. Edwin Charles Dargan, *Ecclesiology: A Study of the Churches* (Louisville: Dearing, 1897), 201–2.

23. Halbrooks, "Meaning and Significance," 28.

24. American Baptist Churches USA, "American Baptist Policy Statement on Ordained Ministry," adopted December 1989, modified September 1992, 1997, 2002, https://www.abc-usa.org/wp-content/uploads/2019/02/ordain.pdf.

it as a sacrifice; they nevertheless continued for a time to refer to it as a "sacrament." In his *Eighteen Dissertations* (printed pamphlet, 1524), Balthasar Hübmaier insisted that "the Mass is not a sacrifice but a memorial of the death of Christ."[25] The Waterland Confession refers to "the holy sacraments," Holy Baptism and the Holy Supper, describing them as "external and visible actions, and signs of the immense goodness of God toward us." The Holy Supper proclaims Christ's death and bitter sufferings. Likewise, Holy Baptism is a sign of the internal work of Christ in the life of the believer.[26] John Smyth's Short Confession and the Dordrecht Confession continued to use sacramental language.[27]

By 1677, in the Second London Confession, Particular Baptists had begun to use the term "ordinances"; meanwhile, the Orthodox Creed (1679) of General Baptists continued with the word "sacrament."[28] In America, the New Hampshire Confession (1833), the Treatise on the Faith and Practices of Freewill Baptists (1834), and subsequent confessions of faith by Baptist groups, following the Second London Confession, took up the language of ordinances to describe these acts of worship. This practice holds among Baptist confessions around the world in the twentieth century. Where confessions of faith describe the two signs at all, they designate them as ordinances.[29] Beginning in the latter half of the twentieth century, some Baptists in North America have returned to sacramental language, acknowledging that God works through the physical elements of creation to accomplish redemptive purposes of grace, as in the incarnation itself.[30] One confession of faith that has emerged from this movement speaks to the issue:

> Baptist reflections on "the sacraments" have for too long been fixed on late medieval and early modern theories. As modernity draws to its close, it is a fitting time to revisit afresh these practices and their significance for the people of God. We reject all accounts of these practices that would limit the presence of the risen Lord to the performance of the enacted signs as we also reject all accounts that deny the reality of his presence in their enactment. The Lord is

25. Lumpkin, *Baptist Confessions of Faith*, 21.
26. Lumpkin, *Baptist Confessions of Faith*, 57–58.
27. Lumpkin, *Baptist Confessions of Faith*, 69, 95.
28. Lumpkin, *Baptist Confessions of Faith*, 291, 324.
29. One exception might be the Confession of Faith of the Baptist Union of Romania (1951), in which they are described as "the two communal symbols" of the New Testament church. See Lumpkin, *Baptist Confessions of Faith*, 489.
30. See the collection of essays in Anthony R. Cross and Philip E. Thompson, *Baptist Sacramentalism*, Studies in Baptist History and Thought 5 (Carlisle, UK: Paternoster, 2003); and Anthony R. Cross and Philip E. Thompson, *Baptist Sacramentalism 2*, Studies in Baptist History and Thought 25 (Milton Keynes, UK: Paternoster, 2008).

present and active both in the performance of these remembering signs and with the community that performs them. . . . *We call others to the freedom of the faithful enactment of the Lord's remembering signs.*[31]

Preferring the term "remembering signs" and wanting to grasp both the symbolism and the reality of God's presence in them, these Baptists seek to reframe their thinking about baptism and the Lord's Supper in a no longer modern world.[32]

Theological Reflection

Pastors and Worship Leadership

The pastor bears responsibility for leading the congregation in worship. B. H. Carroll writes that the pastor "must be conscious of his responsibility as the Divinely appointed leader in bringing the congregation into this adoring fellowship with God."[33] The degree of pastoral responsibility taken in this role, beyond preaching, varies significantly among Baptists. Some have engaged, either as the congregation's only staff member or as part of a team of pastors, in carefully crafting worship, aligning Scripture, music, prayers, and other components with the message proclaimed in the moment of preaching. Others have often taken responsibility only for preaching, leaving it to others to structure a service that may have little to do with the day's sermon. Baptist pastors can be located at either extreme and everywhere along the continuum.

This observation remains valid for the ordinances as well. On the one hand, some pastors intentionally shape the worship service around the celebration of baptism or the Lord's Supper. They want to ensure that these elements contribute to congregational worship, directing attention to the gospel proclaimed

31. Mikael Broadway et al., "Re-envisioning Baptist Identity: A Manifesto for Baptist Communities in North America," May 1997, section 4, https://www.nobts.edu/baptist-center -theology/confessions/Re-envisioning_Baptist_Identity.pdf (emphasis added).

32. These theologians see much of the earlier Baptist opposition to the sacramental language as reactionary. In Great Britain, Baptists reacted against the Oxford Movement; see Michael J. Walker, *Baptists at the Table: The Theology of the Lord's Supper amongst English Baptists in the Nineteenth Century* (Didcot, UK: Baptist Historical Society, 1992), 91–97. In America, the reactivity focused on Landmarkism and the Campbellites, as well as the emphasis on personal faith and experience in the frontier revivalism; see Curtis W. Freeman, *Contesting Catholicity: A Theology for Other Baptists* (Waco: Baylor University Press, 2014), chap. 8. See also James William McClendon Jr., *Systematic Theology*, vol. 2, *Doctrine* (Nashville: Abingdon, 1994), 386.

33. B. H. Carroll, "The Twentieth-Century Pastor; or, Lectures on Pastoral Theology," *Southwestern Journal of Theology* 58, no. 2 (2016): 240.

by these actions and the preaching of the Word. On the other hand, many Baptist pastors treat the ordinances as an addendum to the service, inserted or tacked on to the beginning or the end of the hour.

The Significance of the Ordinances

Since Baptists take our name from one of the two nearly universal practices of Christian churches, we might expect that we would have reflected seriously on the practice of baptism, at least. What is the meaning of baptism? How necessary is it? Who is a candidate for baptism? Who can administer baptism? What of the baptism of small children? What does it mean to be a baptized person? Do we accept as members those baptized by other means? Do we receive as members those baptized in other traditions, with different modes or meanings? Or must they receive baptism from us? We could raise the same sort of questions regarding our practice of the Lord's Supper.

Most Baptists regard baptism and the Lord's Supper as symbolic acts, but we must never allow them to become "mere symbols," as if we might somehow take or leave them. Over time, however, they have sometimes been treated as such. On the frontier, Baptists often argued with the Campbellites over the necessity of baptism for salvation. Consequently, Baptists, who derive our name from the act, found ourselves implying that baptism was somehow optional. "Can a person be saved without being baptized?" became the question. The thief on the cross became the answer (Luke 23:39–43). Lest we give the impression that the rite is somehow sacramental, we unintentionally diminished its importance to the Christian life by asking a question that would never have arisen in the earliest church.

Baptists may consistently aver that the ordinances are symbolic acts, but we ought never to speak of them as *merely* symbolic. Does one have to wear a wedding ring to be married? Certainly not. No state law or biblical commandment requires such a thing. A wedding ring is a symbol. One can be married without one. Wearing one does not make one married. However, it is not a *mere* symbol. The ring is a public declaration that one has committed one's life, in love, to one other person in an exclusive relationship of fidelity. The ring states that the wearer's body and soul are no longer available to anyone else. The band reminds both the wearer and others that they are living life as a married person. As Wendell Berry observes, "The forsaking of all others is a keeping of faith, not just with the chosen one, but with the ones forsaken. The marriage vow unites not just a woman and a man with each other; it unites each of them with the community in a vow of sexual responsibility toward all others. The whole community is married, realizes its essential unity, in each of its marriages."[34] One would find it disconcerting at the least to have their groom or bride withdraw their hand at the wedding ceremony and refuse to accept a wedding ring, as if to say, "I want to be married to you, but I just don't want anyone to know it."

Paul links marriage and baptism in Romans 6 and 7. He argues in Romans 6 that becoming a follower of Jesus means a change as radical as dying and rising again: "What then are we to say? Should we continue in sin in order that grace may abound? By no means! How can we who died to sin go on living in it? Do you not know that all of us who have been baptized into Christ Jesus were baptized into his death? Therefore we have been buried with him by baptism into death, so that, just as Christ was raised from the dead by the glory of the Father, so we too might walk in newness of life" (6:1–4). Interpreters often gloss over Paul's words as a simple metaphor. Dallas Willard, however, asserts that Paul uses language "realistically" in Romans 6 and elsewhere as he speaks of our dying and being raised.[35]

In Romans 7:1–4, Paul engages the metaphor of marriage to express the change we have experienced. Just as the law permits a woman whose husband has died to remarry without being considered unfaithful, so we have died to the life under the law and have now remarried, as it were, Christ: "In the same way, my friends, you have died to the law through the body of Christ, so that you may belong to another, to him who has been raised from the dead in order that we may bear fruit for God" (7:4). We died to that old life, and baptism is the act that demonstrates the transformation from one realm to another, from death to life.

Paul does not regard baptism as a "mere" symbol. Instead, the church and the new believer reenact the Christian faith: the mystery of Good Friday and Easter ("Christ died for our sins . . . [and] he was raised on the third day" [1 Cor. 15:3–4]), the marvel of new life in Christ ("If anyone is in Christ, there

---

34. Wendell Berry, "The Body and the Earth," in *The Art of the Commonplace: The Agrarian Essays of Wendell Berry*, ed. Norman Wirzba (Emeryville, CA: Shoemaker & Hoard, 2003), 117. To complete his idea, Berry includes the following in a footnote attached to the words cited above:

> Marital fidelity, that is, involves the public or institutional as well as the private aspect of marriage. One is married to marriage as well as to one's spouse. But one is married also to something vital of one's own that does not exist before the marriage: one's given word. It now seems to me that the modern misunderstanding of marriage involves a gross misunderstanding and underestimation of the seriousness of giving one's word, and of the dangers of breaking it once it is given. Adultery and divorce now must be looked upon as instances of that disease of word-breaking, which our age justifies as "realistic" or "practical" or "necessary," but which is tattering the invariably single fabric of speech and trust.

35. Dallas Willard, *The Spirit of the Disciplines: Understanding How God Changes Lives* (San Francisco: HarperSanFrancisco, 1990), 108–9.

is a new creation" [2 Cor. 5:17]), and our mighty hope ("The dead will be raised imperishable, and we will be changed" [1 Cor. 15:52]). The church's past, present, and future are in view as the pastor lowers new believers into the waters of baptism and lifts them again.

Jesus *commanded* the church to make disciples and *baptize* them (Matt. 28:18–20), just as he instructed his disciples in the upper room, "Do this in remembrance of me" (Luke 22:19). Baptists have regarded these statements as imperatives—hence, as *ordinances* of the Lord.[36] We practice these to obey Jesus. To fail to practice them would be disobedience. "Does one have to be baptized to be a Christian?" is a nonsensical question biblically. How does one begin life as a follower of Jesus as Lord by refusing to obey his instruction? The early church would never have considered the question. They assumed baptism. That act becomes a way of identifying publicly as a follower of Jesus. How is it that so many Baptist churches have lists naming people "awaiting baptism" who claim to have publicly professed faith in him?

Our teaching on the significance of baptism has been dramatically watered down over the years. The evangelical invitation at the close of the sermon subtly replaced baptism as the designated way to profess faith in Christ. To "walk the aisle" and "take the preacher's hand" supplanted the waters of baptism. When a person has done the former, the latter becomes optional. Our failure to catechize new believers adequately left us with a diminished perspective on the meaning of baptism. We have often engaged what some refer to as an "undisciplined" practice of baptism.[37] The earliest Christian disciples and believers in many parts of our world today might not recognize our practice.

Baptism is anything but optional for Jesus's followers. It is the public declaration of our faith in Christ, our hope in Christ, and our love for Christ. Like the wedding ring and marriage, it may not be necessary for salvation, but it is no mere symbol.[38] G. R. Beasley-Murray calls on us to highly value

36. Some Baptists have historically added a third ordinance: foot washing. Jesus just as clearly, they argue, commanded his disciples, "So if I, your Lord and Teacher, have washed your feet, you also ought to wash one another's feet. For I have set you an example, that you also should do as I have done to you" (John 13:14–15). See, for example, the Dordrecht Confession, article 11; and the Treatise of the Faith and Practices of Free Will Baptists, article 18.

37. Broadway et al., "Re-envisioning Baptist Identity," section 3.

38. In his magisterial treatment of baptism, Baptist theologian G. R. Beasley-Murray avoids the word "necessary" when speaking of baptism because of the misunderstanding the word engenders. He says,

> But is it not better to recognize positively that God has graciously given us sacraments for our good and that it is our part to receive them gratefully? It is not customary for us to argue whether it was "necessary," or in what sense, that Christ should have become incarnate of the Virgin Mary, that He should have been born a Jew, that He should have died on a cross and risen from the dead, that He should have united humanity to Himself

the act of baptism in the church and Christian life. He says, "It behoves us accordingly to make much of baptism. It is given as the trysting place of the sinner with his Saviour; he who has met Him there will not despise it. But in the last resort it is only a *place*: the Lord Himself is its glory, as He is its grace. Let the glory then be given to whom it belongs!"[39]

Similarly, our attempt to avoid association with the Roman Catholic doctrine of transubstantiation pushed Baptists to lean heavily on the symbolic or memorial interpretation of the ordinance. From a reactive position, consequently, we have often devalued the significance of the Lord's Supper for the Christian life. We may see this diminishment in the frequency (or infrequency) with which Baptists observe the ordinance: Baptists in America commonly partake of the Lord's Supper only quarterly. They often contend, ironically, that to celebrate too frequently dilutes its significance. We should revisit that argument. Church members unable to attend worship on the specific Sunday the congregation celebrates the Supper might go as long as six months before sharing the bread and cup with their community. If that is of no consequence to the congregation or the individual, then perhaps it is the infrequency of celebration that has diluted its importance.

Other congregations schedule the Supper as frequently as every month or every other month. Some independent Baptist churches celebrate the Supper weekly, but usually on Sunday evenings, appended to a regular worship service. The Baptist congregation that includes the Lord's Supper as an integral part of every worship service is rare.

We can celebrate the Supper more frequently without turning it into an empty ritual. Baptist pastors can enrich worshipers' experience of the Lord's Supper by attending more carefully to its meaning in Scripture. Paul calls the practice the Lord's Supper (*kyriakon deipnon*) in 1 Corinthians 11:20. When we understand the meal in these terms, the memorial aspect comes into focus. In this worship act, we "proclaim the Lord's death until he comes" (1 Cor. 11:26). We remember his words, and we recall his sacrifice. The practice can mean more than this, however.

Paul also refers to this meal as "communion" (KJV) or "sharing" (*koinōnia*) in the body and blood of Christ (1 Cor. 10:16). Paul's statement is somewhat ambiguous—literally, "sharing *of* the body of Christ" and "sharing *of* the

---

in the one Body by the Spirit, that He should bestow on us the Kingdom prepared for us from the foundation of the world; in these events we perceive the unspeakable grace, love, wisdom and power of God, and we adore Him for it. And I see in baptism a gift of grace, at which I wonder the more as I ponder it the more. The sacramental principle is rooted in life as God has created it. (*Baptism in the New Testament*, 304–5)

39. Beasley-Murray, *Baptism in the New Testament*, 305.

blood of Christ." The genitive here may be objective, meaning that we share these elements with one another; the body and the blood are what we share. Or the genitive may be subjective, implying that we participate in the body and blood of Christ as we eat and drink together. The equivocal nature of Paul's language may be intentional. The celebration is an act of communion with each other and with Christ as we share the bread and cup.

When celebrated as "communion," the meal focuses on intimacy with Christ and the church, not merely remembering his death. We often associate Jesus's words in John 6, in which he declares himself to be "the bread of life" (vv. 35, 41, 50, 51), with this aspect of the ordinance: "Those who eat my flesh and drink my blood have eternal life, and I will raise them up on the last day" (v. 54). By eating and drinking, we incorporate the bread and the wine into our bodies physically. That act is a sign of the spiritual intimacy of receiving Christ into our lives and being sustained by him. That we do this together is a sign of the church's unity as the body of Christ.

Luke's account of the Last Supper includes a series of verbs: Jesus "took" the bread, he "gave thanks" (*eucharisteō*), he "broke" it, and he "gave" it to his disciples (22:19).[40] Matthew and Mark include this same sequence but use "blessed" (*eulogeō*) instead of "gave thanks" (Matt. 26:26; Mark 14:22).[41] The change in verb does not change the meaning since Jesus would likely have recited a traditional prayer of thanksgiving for God's gift of bread and the fruit of the vine brought forth from the earth. Like Luke, Paul recounts the Supper's establishment with Jesus's giving thanks for the bread (1 Cor. 11:23–24). From Jesus's grateful prayer comes yet another facet of the ordinance, "Eucharist"—a time to thank God for the gift of Christ's redemption. We not only remember what he suffered but also express gratitude for what he accomplished on our behalf. "Christ died for our sins" (1 Cor. 15:3).

Additionally, Luke occasionally uses the expression "the breaking of bread" to refer to the Supper. He says that the early church in Jerusalem devoted themselves to the apostle's teaching, sharing life, and the breaking of bread (Acts 2:42). This phrase refers to the early church's celebration of the Lord's Supper, perhaps following a fellowship meal (Acts 2:46; 20:7; cf. 1 Cor. 10:16–17).[42]

40. Dom Gregory Dix observes the way these four verbs have served to structure Roman Catholic liturgy in the Eucharist. See *The Shape of the Liturgy*, 2nd rev. ed. (London: Bloomsbury T&T Clark, 2015), 48–50.

41. These same four verbs occur in the accounts of Jesus's feeding the multitudes: Matt. 14:19 ("blessed"); 15:36 ("gave thanks"); Mark 6:41 ("blessed"); 8:6 ("gave thanks"); Luke 9:16 ("blessed"); John 6:11 ("gave thanks"; omits "broke").

42. F. F. Bruce, *The Book of the Acts*, rev. ed., New International Commentary on the New Testament (Grand Rapids: Eerdmans, 1988), 79; Barclay Moon Newman, *A Translator's Handbook on the Acts of the Apostles*, Helps for Translators 12 (London: United Bible

The association of this phrase with the resurrection of Jesus, rather than his death, is significant. Luke records the story of Cleopas and his companion (his wife?) in Luke 24:13–35. As they walked back from Jerusalem to their home in Emmaus on the day of Jesus's resurrection, the risen Christ joined them incognito. He instructed them along the road: "beginning with Moses and all the prophets, he interpreted to them the things about himself in all the scriptures" (v. 27). Still, they did not recognize him. When they reached their destination, the two disciples invited Jesus to join them for a meal. Luke says that the risen Christ "took" bread, "blessed" it, "broke" it, and "gave" it to them (v. 30), and then they recognized him, just before he vanished from their presence. They hurried back to Jerusalem to report their experience to the other disciples. "They told what had happened on the road," Luke says, "and how he had been made known to them in the breaking of the bread" (v. 35). Celebrating the Lord's Table as the breaking of the bread has a distinct resurrection facet to it.

As with baptism, we observe the Lord's Supper from a temporal perspective. We look back, remembering Christ's death on the cross and giving thanks for what he did in the past. The celebration also contains a present aspect. We seek communion with him and with each other as we gather and give thanks for his daily blessings in our lives. We look forward, celebrating and remembering the resurrected Christ, who will one day come again and spread for us the messianic feast (Rev. 19:7–10). Paul said that when we celebrate the Supper, we "proclaim the Lord's death until he comes" (1 Cor. 11:26). Christian hope of the fulfillment of the kingdom is declared by the Supper just as Jews express their hope the Passover prayer, "Next year in Jerusalem."

Standing in for the whole congregation, the pastor baptizes those who have confessed faith in Jesus as their Savior and who desire to follow him as Lord. The "this" of the moment of baptism is a direct response to the "that" of Jesus's Great Commission. Hearing the candidate's profession of faith in Jesus, the pastor lowers the believer into the water and then raises the one being baptized, calling on the name of the Father, Son, and Holy Spirit. The pastor often pronounces, "We are buried with Christ in baptism and raised to walk in newness of life," or some other formula or passage of Scripture. This enactment of baptism is a priestly kind of act. Converts do not baptize themselves, and not everyone in the congregation can participate. So the pastor mediates between the candidate and the congregation, between the candidate and Jesus Christ. The authenticity of the candidate's faith in

Societies, 1972), 63; John B. Polhill, *Acts*, New American Commentary 26 (Nashville: Broadman, 1992), 119.

Christ is what makes the baptism truly a baptism, not the status of the one administering the act.[43] The one enacting the sign of baptism need not be an ordained pastor. Anyone authorized by the congregation may represent them in this moment of worship. Most commonly, however, the privilege falls to the pastor.

Pastors stand in front of the worshiping congregation with unleavened bread and a cup of grape juice or wine and recount the story of Jesus's final meal with his disciples. The "this" of the Lord's Table is a direct response to the "that" of Jesus's instruction: "Do this in remembrance of me." They encourage the church to remember Jesus's sacrifice, to give thanks for his love and salvation, to enter into communion with him and with one another, and to celebrate the presence of the risen Christ. The participants break the bread and distribute it. They offer the cup to the congregation. The pastor says, "The Lord Jesus on the night when he was betrayed took a loaf of bread, and when he had given thanks, he broke it. . . . In the same way he took the cup also, after supper." Then deacons take the elements to the congregation, who pass them along to one another, also serving as priests at this moment. At the pastor's direction, all eat the bread and drink the juice in the small cups simultaneously.

In some Baptist congregations, worshipers will line up and walk to the front, where the pastor and others hold chalices of grape juice and pieces of bread. Servers offer the pieces of bread ("the body of Christ broken for you") to dip in the cup ("the blood of Christ shed for you"). Worshipers eat the now reddened bread, like the blood-soaked flesh it portrays, as they return to their place in the pew. The shepherd presides over this holy moment as prayer, memory, repentance, faith, joy, gratitude, and hope nourish the flock's life once more.

In the enactment of this sign given by Jesus, pastors once more occupy a priestly role. At that moment the pastor represents Christ, breaking the bread and sharing the cup. The pastor stands in for the entire congregation of believer-priests, any one of whom might just as well be narrating the story and sharing the elements with the rest. Most commonly, however, the privilege falls to the pastor.

Speaking of the pastor's responsibility here as "a priestly role" is not to diminish the priesthood of the believers or imply that the pastor has received superior power or privilege at ordination. The pastor, chosen by the congregation to stand in for them in these moments of worship, ought to assume that role with humility and awe.

---

43. Augustus H. Strong, *Systematic Theology* (New York: Armstrong & Son, 1889), 532.

The word "sacraments" gave way to "ordinances" among Baptists. As we found theological language of our own, our words shaped our practices. The journey between seeing them as commandments or instructions to be obeyed and ultimately seeing them as mere boxes to be checked was a short one. The challenge for Baptist pastors is to help our congregations hold a high view of these acts of worship, seeing them as more than "mere symbols," as deeply significant signs that Christ has graciously given to us for our spiritual nourishment. No one else in the congregation is in a position to magnify the role of these signs. The pastor engages the priestly work of leading the flock to fully celebrate the waters of baptism and the bread and the cup in a way that leads to a more faithful expression of discipleship.

CONCLUSIONS

For a Baptist pastor to plan worship, to lead in public worship, to see to the care of the worship facilities of the church, to administer baptism, to offer the communion bread and cup, to pray for the sick, and to intercede with those seeking God's guidance or forgiveness—all this is acting in a priestly light. All believers may be priests, but the biblical model of priestly ministry continues to inform and shape the work of pastoral ministry. The New Testament writers never designate church leaders as priests. However, we can affirm that many essential pastoral tasks seem to reflect the service of ancient, devoted Hebrew priests.

FOR FURTHER REFLECTION

1. How would you explain to someone who is not a Baptist how our pastors are and are not priests?
2. How do you distinguish between baptism and the Lord's Supper as sacraments, ordinances, signs, and symbols? How does your view of them affect the way you practice them in your congregation?
3. How does baptizing a very young child in a Baptist church differ from infant baptism? What steps ought the church take to assure that we are baptizing a disciple of Jesus as he commanded (Matt. 28:18–20)?
4. Who in the congregation is authorized to baptize or preside at the Lord's Supper? Why?

5. In your experience, do Baptists consider baptism and the Lord's Supper as mere symbols or as meaningful signs? Which are they to you? What makes them so?

6. What might pastors do to magnify these practices in worship in their congregations?

8

Pastoral Care

Tending the Flock

> Doing pastoral care for the sick, grieving, and troubled members—
> beyond being your pastoral duty—is a means of maintaining a pastoral
> heart.
>
> —H. B. Charles Jr., *On Pastoring*

> He then asked a second time, "Simon, son of John, do you love
> me?"
> "Yes, Master, you know I love you."
> Jesus said, "Shepherd my sheep."
>
> —Jesus and Simon Peter (John 21:16 Message)

Shepherd imagery is at the heart of the concept of pastoral care. Jesus's restorative words to Peter in John 21:15–17 were themselves an act of pastoral care for one of his sheep that had wandered. They are also a call for pastors to engage such care with God's people: "Feed my lambs, . . . tend my sheep, . . . feed my sheep." Human beings face a variety of challenges as we make our way through this life. Being people of faith in Jesus does not exempt us from those trials. We are lonely. We live with fears and worries. We face disease and death. We fail God, others, and ourselves. We do not know which way to turn and need guidance. We are frail and sometimes falter in doing what is ours to do. The list goes on and on. Immense joy also marks our lives. We love, we marry, we bear children. We succeed and celebrate. We persevere and grow stronger. This list, too, is potentially quite long. In all of this, sorrow and joy, people want to know God's presence, grace, and love, so they often welcome pastors into their lives in these moments.

Pastoral care is the act of saying "God" to people in the most ordinary and sometimes most difficult moments of their lives.[1] This aspect of our work is more than "meeting people's needs." It is shepherding work done in the name of Jesus, the Chief Shepherd. Stepping pastorally into people's lives during their pain and confusion is, as Wayne Oates describes it, to serve as "the functional representative of God the Father, God the Son, and God the Holy Spirit—of God at work in the world through the church."[2] Pastoral care is priestly work, done in the name of Jesus, the Great High Priest. Pastoral care is kingdom work, done in the name of Jesus the Messiah. The roots of such ministry reach deep into the story of God's people in Scripture.

Biblical Foundations

Pastoral Care and the Old Testament

God established the priesthood and gave Israel instructions about worship during their journey through the wilderness (Exod. 25–30). Aaron and his sons exercised the priestly ministry among God's people. Part of that responsibility entailed overseeing the worship of God, tending the sanctuary, and offering sacrifices. Another aspect of the priestly role, however, involved caring and interceding for Israel.

Exodus 28 provides the details of the elaborate vestments the priests would wear. A couple of details stand out. The high priest's ephod, or garment, was held in place at the shoulder by two carved stones:

> You shall take two onyx stones, and engrave on them the names of the sons of Israel, six of their names on the one stone, and the names of the remaining six on the other stone, in the order of their birth. As a gem-cutter engraves signets, so you shall engrave the two stones with the names of the sons of Israel; you shall mount them in settings of gold filigree. You shall set the two stones on the shoulder-pieces of the ephod, as stones of remembrance for the sons of

1. Wayne E. Oates, *The Christian Pastor*, rev. ed. (Philadelphia: Westminster, 1982), 21.
2. Oates, *Christian Pastor*, 9.

Israel; and Aaron shall bear their names before the LORD on his two shoulders for remembrance. (Exod. 28:9–12)

The high priest carried on his shoulders the names of the twelve tribes, symbolic of his bearing responsibility for their well-being and life with God. Additionally, the high priest wore a "breastpiece of judgment" (Exod. 28:15–30). Twelve precious gemstones representing the twelve tribes of Israel adorned this garment: "So Aaron shall bear the names of the sons of Israel in the breastpiece of judgment on his heart when he goes into the holy place, for a continual remembrance before the LORD" (Exod. 28:29). The high priest carried responsibility for his people on his shoulders, and he also bore them compassionately near his heart.

In the ordinary course of life, these priests had practical responsibilities that expressed this care for Israel. Not only did they oversee the offering of sacrifices for sin or thanksgiving, but they also tended to a variety of physical illnesses or conditions that could render a person ritually impure and required cleansing. In many ways, God had called them to care for the people. Priests did not always engage their office with integrity, however. During the judges' time, Eli's sons corrupted the role, treating the people and their offerings with contempt (1 Sam. 2:12–17), resulting in God's judgment (1 Sam. 2:22–36). In the sixth century BC, Ezekiel, himself a priest, portrayed Israel's religious and political leaders as false shepherds who did not care for the flock of God (Ezek. 34:1–10). This condemnation may well have included the priests, given the description of their failure to care for the people.

Against this background, the description of Jesus as both the Good Shepherd (John 10; cf. Ezek. 34:23–24) and the Great High Priest (Heb. 4:14; cf. Exod. 28:29) stands in stark relief: "For we do not have a high priest who is unable to sympathize with our weaknesses, but we have one who in every respect has been tested as we are, yet without sin. Let us therefore approach the throne of grace with boldness, so that we may receive mercy and find grace to help in time of need" (Heb. 4:15–16). The Great High Priest sympathizes with their weakness and intercedes for them.

Pastoral Care in the New Testament

Jesus the Good Shepherd

The life and service of the Good Shepherd, Jesus, provides the primary scriptural model for understanding pastoral care. His ministry to the hurts and hopes of people in his story offers a biblical path for Baptist pastors.

The "this" of yesterday's hospital visit is the "that" of Jesus's compassionate interactions with sick people in his day.

The Gospel writers summarize Jesus's ministry in various ways, but they nearly always include encountering and caring for hurting people. He preached the kingdom of God, and he demonstrated that kingdom's power. Matthew describes such work: "Jesus went throughout Galilee, teaching in their synagogues and proclaiming the good news of the kingdom and curing every disease and every sickness among the people. So his fame spread throughout all Syria, and they brought to him all the sick, those who were afflicted with various diseases and pains, demoniacs, epileptics, and paralytics, and he cured them" (Matt. 4:23–24). The Gospels contain several of these summary statements (Mark 1:35–39; Luke 6:17–19).

Jesus tells the disciples of John the Baptist that these acts of power and compassion are evidence of the kingdom's presence in his ministry (Matt. 11:2–6 // Luke 7:18–23). Jesus's mighty acts (*dynameis*) are acts of hope. They summon into the present moment that time in the future when the kingdom will come in its fullness, when "he will wipe every tear from their eyes" and "death will be no more; / mourning and crying and pain will be no more" (Rev. 21:4). Addressing human hurts does not merely supplement Jesus's ministry; it is also central to it. Peter summarizes the compassionate works of Jesus in his sermon to the household of Cornelius: anointed by God with the Holy Spirit and with power, Jesus of Nazareth "went about doing good and healing all who were oppressed by the devil, for God was with him" (Acts 10:38).

Besides the summary statements, the Gospels report many specific encounters and conversations between Jesus and suffering people. He engaged people who, in their lostness, were failing to find meaning in religion (John 3:1–21) or relationships (John 4:1–42). He compassionately confronted some whose lives were infested with evil that was destroying them physically, socially, and inwardly (Mark 5:1–20). Jesus took time to talk and listen. He responded to requests from families facing death (Matt. 8:5–13; Mark 5:21–24, 35–43; John 4:46–54) and to people dealing with chronic suffering (Mark 5:25–34; John 5:1–9). He engaged those whose choices had left them lonely (Luke 19:1–10) and those who were separated and lonely through no fault of their own (Luke 17:11–19). He served the poor and fed the hungry (Mark 6:30–44), and he spoke with the rich who were hungry for more than they had accumulated (Mark 10:17–31). He ate with sinners and outcasts (Matt. 9:9–13) as well as the pious and respected (Luke 7:36; 14:1). He attended weddings (John 2:1–11) and funerals (Luke 7:11–17), bringing the kingdom's power to bear on each.

One of humanity's deepest desires is to be heard. We long to have someone listen to us. In the Psalter the cry to God is often "Hear me!" (5:1; 17:6; 31:2;

61:1; 71:2; 86:1; 88:2; 102:2), and the greatest confession of confidence is that God will hear (5:3; 6:8; 10:17; 18:6; 40:1; 55:17; 94:9; 116:2). God is the God who hears, who listens. In the same way, Jesus demonstrates the heart of the Father, who hears even our prayers offered in secret (Matt. 6:6). He does so by listening to people.

A prime example is the story of Jesus's conversation with an unnamed woman who had suffered chronic illness for twelve years (Matt. 9:18–21 // Mark 5:21–34 // Luke 8:40–48). She interrupts Jesus as he is on his way to the home of Jairus, a synagogue leader in Capernaum, whose adolescent daughter is dying. The woman's faith in Jesus's ability to heal her has drawn her to him. She comes out of the crowd and attempts to unobtrusively gain healing by merely touching Jesus's clothing. When she does so, Jesus senses that something has happened, that "power [has] gone forth from him" (Mark 5:30). Although he is responding to an emergency, he stops and asks, "Who touched me?" Given the size of the bustling crowd, his disciples consider that a pointless question. But Jesus scans the crowd until he sees her. She comes forward, falls at his feet, and "[tells] him the whole truth" (Mark 5:33). Jesus hears her out before pronouncing her whole.

Consider this: the woman had been chronically ill for twelve years. Mark says, "She had endured much under many physicians, and had spent all that she had; and she was no better, but rather grew worse" (5:26). Luke (the physician [Col. 4:14]?) gives those physicians the benefit of the doubt: "though she had spent all she had on physicians, no one could cure her" (8:43). The point is that the woman had a considerable case history and a long story to tell. Jesus listened to her tale as she told him the whole truth. Then he announced her healing. He did this while his disciples and Jairus stood anxiously by, eager to get on to the home where a girl's life hung in the balance.

The Gospels offer other examples of Jesus's patient listening: his conversation with Nicodemus (John 3:1–21), his dialogue with the Samaritan woman (John 4:1–42), his exchange with the Canaanite woman (Matt. 15:21–28 // Mark 7:24–30), and his encouragement of a father who brought his demon-possessed son for healing (Mark 9:14–29). Jesus asks questions, listens, and responds thoughtfully.

In the Gospel of John, Jesus identifies himself as the Good Shepherd (pastor) who, like Yahweh in Psalm 23, cares for his flock, even laying down his life for them (10:11). He knows his sheep (10:14, 27) and calls them by name (10:3). He protects them (10:12–13). Ezekiel promised Israel that on a future day God would come to shepherd (pastor) the people whose false shepherds had so neglected them (Ezek. 34:11–40). "The LORD God" says, "I will seek the lost, and I will bring back the strayed, and I will bind up the injured, and I will strengthen the weak, but the fat and the strong I will destroy. I will feed them with justice" (Ezek. 34:16). This series of verbs describes pastoral care well: seek, bring back, bind up, strengthen, and feed. Jesus, the Good Shepherd, fulfills this promise. In the Synoptic Gospels, Jesus compares the kingdom of God to a compassionate shepherd who leaves ninety-nine sheep safe in the fold to search for the one who is lost (Matt. 18:10–14 // Luke 15:1–7).

Pastoral Care in the Early Church

This care and concern for people in their everyday struggles continued in the earliest church. Jesus taught his disciples that he took their acts of caring ministry personally, whether feeding the hungry, giving water to the thirsty, offering hospitality to the stranger, providing clothing for the cold and naked, caring for the sick, or extending a comforting presence to those isolated in prison cells (Matt. 25:31–46). The apostles continued such care for the sick (Acts 3:1–10; 28:7–9). James urged believers to express concern for one another when healing is needed (James 5:16). He specifically encouraged them to call on their elders, or pastors, during times of illness (James 5:14). The "soul care" assigned to congregational leaders certainly included those times of sickness and other experiences of suffering (Heb. 13:17).

James's instruction in 5:14 raises the issue of pastoral intercession on behalf of the flock. Although Scripture does not explicitly enjoin intercession as a pastoral responsibility, it undoubtedly implies it. Jesus tells Peter, "Simon, Simon, listen! Satan has demanded to sift all of you like wheat, but I have prayed for you that your own faith may not fail; and you, when once you have turned back, strengthen your brothers" (Luke 22:31–32). Interpreters sometimes refer to John 17 as Jesus's high-priestly prayer. As he prays, Jesus intercedes not only for his disciples but also for those who would eventually believe in him because of their testimony (v. 20). The early church lived with a confidence that the risen Jesus continues to offer intercession on our behalf (Rom. 8:34; Heb. 7:25). Paul's intercessory prayers for his churches and friends occupy a vital part of his ministry, especially when circumstances separate them. He offers model prayers for pastors to follow (Rom. 1:8–10; 1 Cor. 1:4–9; Eph. 1:15–23; 3:14–21; Phil. 1:3–11; Col. 1:3–8; 1 Thess. 1:2–10; 2 Thess. 1:3–6; Philem. 4–7).

When Baptist pastors engage in caring for human hurts and hopes, in listening to human hearts, in ministry to human brokenness, in taking the compassion of Christ into the ordinary events of human life, they follow the example of the Good Pastor, Jesus, and of his apostles. The "this" of their pastoral care is the "that" of the biblical examples of Jesus and the earliest church.

Historical Bypaths

Pastoral Care after the Apostles

"I was sick," Jesus said, "and you took care of me" (Matt. 25:36). The church of Jesus Christ has often cared for the weak, the sick, the infirm, and the dying. By doing so, it expresses a distinctive mode of witness to the world. This kind of pastoral care predates the Baptist movement by many centuries. Sociologist of religion Rodney Stark describes early Christians' response to an epidemic, perhaps smallpox, that began in AD 165 during the reign of Marcus Aurelius. Stark argues that their compassionate reaction was a factor in the rapid growth of the "Jesus movement."[3] The epidemic lasted for fifteen years (plus later outbreaks), and as much as one-third of the population died. Marcus Aurelius, who eventually died of the disease, wrote about caravans of oxcarts bearing victims' corpses out of the cities. A century later, another plague struck.

No one knew how to respond. Bishop Dionysius wrote a pastoral letter during the second epidemic (ca. AD 251) describing the situation among the pagans in Alexandria: "For they thrust aside any who began to be sick, and kept aloof even from their dearest friends, and cast the sufferers out upon the public roads half dead, and left them unburied, and treated them with utter contempt when they died, steadily avoiding any kind of communication and intercourse with death; which, however, it was not easy for them altogether to escape, in spite of the many precautions they employed."[4] The bishop contrasts that behavior with the compassionate actions of his fellow Christians:

> Certainly very many of our brethren, while, in their exceeding love and brotherly-kindness, they did not spare themselves, but kept by each other, and visited the sick without thought of their own peril, and ministered to them assiduously, and treated them for their healing in Christ, died from time to time most joyfully along with them, lading themselves with pains derived from others, and drawing upon themselves their neighbours' diseases, and willingly taking over to their own persons the burden of the sufferings of those around them. And many who had thus cured others of their sicknesses, and restored them to strength, died themselves, having transferred to their own bodies the death that lay upon

3. Rodney Stark, *The Triumph of Christianity: How the Jesus Movement Became the World's Largest Religion* (New York: HarperOne, 2011), 114–19.

4. Dionysius of Alexandria, "Epistle XII—To the Alexandrians," trans. S. D. F. Salmond, in *Fathers of the Third Century: Gregory Thaumaturgus, Dionysius the Great, Julius Africanus, Anatolius and Minor Writers, Methodius, Arnobius*, ed. Alexander Roberts, James Donaldson, and A. Cleveland Coxe, vol. 6 of *The Ante-Nicene Fathers* (Buffalo: Christian Literature Co., 1886), 109.

these. . . . Yea, the very best of our brethren have departed this life in this manner, including some presbyters and some deacons, and among the people those who were in highest reputation: so that this very form of death, in virtue of the distinguished piety and the steadfast faith which were exhibited in it, appeared to come in nothing beneath martyrdom itself.[5]

During this epidemic, the church bore witness with compassionate, sacrificial pastoral care that included laying down their own lives.

Charles Haddon Spurgeon and the Cholera Pandemic

Sixteen centuries later, a cholera pandemic struck the world. London experienced waves of the disease in 1832 and 1849. In 1854, when Charles Haddon Spurgeon, a twenty-year-old Baptist pastor, had just taken up ministry in the city, the Broad Street Outbreak struck, and more than six hundred people died in one section of the city. Spurgeon devotes a chapter of his autobiography to "The Cholera Year." Pastoral care for both his congregants and people outside the church occupied a central role for months. He remembers,

> In the year 1854, when I had scarcely been in London twelve months, the neighbourhood in which I laboured was visited by Asiatic cholera, and my congregation suffered from its inroads. Family after family summoned me to the bedside of the smitten, and almost every day I was called to visit the grave. At first, I gave myself up with youthful ardour to the visitation of the sick and was sent for from all corners of the district by persons of all ranks and religions; but soon, I became weary in body, and sick at heart. My friends seemed falling one by one, and I felt or fancied that I was sickening like those around me. A little more work and weeping would have laid me low among the rest; I felt that my burden was heavier than I could bear, and I was ready to sink under it.[6]

Spurgeon tells of how, walking home from a funeral, he passed a bill posted in a store window on which someone had written the words of Psalm 91:9–10 (KJV): "Because thou hast made the LORD, which is my refuge, even the most High, thy habitation; There shall no evil befall thee, neither shall any plague come nigh thy dwelling." Reading those verses encouraged him to continue faithfully in the work of pastoral care with the sick and dying. He writes, "The effect upon my heart was immediate. Faith appropriated the passage as her own. I felt secure, refreshed, girt with immortality. I went on with my

---

5. Dionysius of Alexandria, "Epistle XII," 108–9.
6. C. H. Spurgeon, *The Autobiography of Charles H. Spurgeon*, vol. 1, *1834–1854* (Chicago: Fleming H. Revell, 1898), 371.

visitation of the dying, in a calm and peaceful spirit; I felt no fear of evil, and I suffered no harm."[7]

Engaging the gospel of Jesus Christ with human hurts and hopes, even when it requires risk and sacrifice, is essential to pastoral ministry. In 1866 cholera hit London for the fourth time, killing more than four thousand people from the end of July to the beginning of November.[8] Spurgeon, preaching in the Metropolitan Tabernacle at the beginning of this new plague, recounted his experience from a dozen years earlier: "I recollect when first I came to London how anxiously people listened to the gospel, for the cholera was raging terribly. There was little scoffing then. All day and sometimes all night long I went about from house to house, and saw men and women dying, and oh! how glad they were to see one's face, and when many were afraid to enter their houses for fear of disease, we who had no fear about such things found ourselves most gladly listened to when we spoke of Christ and of divine things."[9] He urged those who ministered during that time to bear the gospel of Christ into the midst of human fear, suffering, and death: "And now, again, is the minister's time; now is the time for all of you that love souls. You may see men more alarmed than now, I hope they may not be; I pray to God that they may not be; but if they should, avail yourselves of it. You have the balm of Gilead; when their wounds smart, pour it in. You know of him who died to save, tell them of him. Lift high the cross before their eyes."[10]

Baptist Preachers and Pastoral Care

Baptist pastors have multiplied Spurgeon's example thousands of times as they have cared for their flock during wars, famines, economic depressions, and pandemics and through the personal crises of illness, fear, loss, and grief. This ministry imitates the love and compassion of the great shepherd of the sheep, Jesus Christ (Heb. 13:20).

While Spurgeon was dealing with the London crisis, Francis Wayland, president of Brown University in Providence, Rhode Island, was instructing young students preparing for ministry. He insisted on engaging in the work of pastoral care, which he called "parochial visitation." He wrote in 1853,

7. Spurgeon, *Autobiography*, 1:372.

8. W. Luckin, "The Final Catastrophe—Cholera in London, 1866," *Medical History* 21 (1977): 32.

9. Spurgeon in a sermon on John 4:35, "Fields White for Harvest," preached on Sunday evening, July 29, 1866, at the Metropolitan Tabernacle. Charles Haddon Spurgeon, *Spurgeon's Sermons*, vol. 12, *1866*, ed. Anthony Uyl (Woodstock, ON: Devoted Publishing, 2017), 299.

10. Spurgeon, *Spurgeon's Sermons*, 12:299.

But the gospel is to be preached not only publicly, but from house to house. . . . The sick are to be visited, the mourner consoled, the thoughtless aroused, the secure alarmed, the convicted urged to decision, the penitent pointed to Christ, the wandering reclaimed, the feeble encouraged. Until a minister has learned not only to perform but to love this part of his labor, he cannot hope to be a workman that needeth not be ashamed. I do not know of a more common or a more just ground of complaint against the ministry, than that of the neglect of parochial visitation.[11]

Baptist figures most well known for their public preaching commend by word and example the personal, intimate work of pastoral care.

One's performance in the pulpit cannot replace the pastor's engagement in the ordinary events of the lives of those they serve. John Broadus, writing about preaching, underscores the role that competent, caring pastoral ministry plays in that work. He says, "*Pastoral work* is of immense importance, and all preachers should be diligent in performing it. But it cannot take the place of preaching, nor fully compensate for lack of power in the pulpit. The two help each other, and neither of them is able, unless supported by the other, to achieve the largest and most blessed results."[12]

B. H. Carroll reminded pastors that "the pastor has not completed his work when he has finished his sermon on the Lord's day. Preaching the word is but the broadcast sowing of the truth, while pastoral visitation tills the soil of the heart and brings to fruitage the seed sown on the Lord's day."[13] Carroll recommended that pastors use their mornings for study and put in at least four solid afternoons in pastoral visitation, including the bereaved, the calamity stricken, the indifferent, the backslider, the skeptic, those under conviction, new converts, and the poor.[14]

George W. Truett, best known for his preaching ministry and leadership in various Baptist organizations, was careful to shepherd his large congregation. When he was home in Dallas, he was available for personal pastoral conversations. Truett regularly recorded these conferences in his diary but, constrained by confidentiality, omitted details. In 1937 he wrote one day, "Serious conferences with troubled souls were had in the Church Office today. One often wonders how God can bear the sorrows of humanity."[15] He wrote

11. Francis Wayland, *The Apostolic Ministry* (Rochester: Sage & Brother, 1853), 73–74.

12. John Albert Broadus, *A Treatise on the Preparation and Delivery of Sermons*, 17th ed. (New York: Armstrong & Son, 1891), 22.

13. B. H. Carroll, "The Twentieth-Century Pastor; or, Lectures on Pastoral Theology," *Southwestern Journal of Theology* 58, no. 2 (2016): 237.

14. Carroll, "Twentieth-Century Pastor," 238–39.

15. Keith E. Durso, *Thy Will Be Done: A Biography of George W. Truett* (Macon, GA: Mercer University Press, 2009), 251.

thousands of letters in response to people's needs, often spending several hours dictating them in the afternoon.[16] He conducted many weddings, often in his office or home and sometimes several during a day.[17] Truett also frequently preached funeral sermons for those who were members of his congregation and some who were not.[18] Keith Durso records that in 1942, the year Truett turned seventy-five, he preached 251 sermons, officiated at 28 funerals and 47 weddings, delivered 50 addresses, and was away from Dallas for 153 days.[19] Preaching and leadership alone did not constitute Truett's pastoral ministry.

Baptists and the Twentieth-Century Pastoral Care Movement

Social sciences, such as sociology and psychology, took root in Western culture in the early twentieth century. Baptist educators were among those who took an interest in these newly developing disciplines. In the 1920s, Gaines Dobbins, professor of religious education and church efficiency at the Southern Baptist Theological Seminary, pioneered integrating psychology into ministry training. Having studied with both John Dewey and George Albert Coe, Dobbins sought to "capture psychology for Christ." He argued that apart from the study of Scripture, psychology is "the most important single subject which should be mastered by one who all his life must deal firsthand with people."[20] His teaching in religious education introduced a new version of pastoral theology into the conservative Southern churches.

By the mid-twentieth century, a movement in pastoral care and counseling formed across denominational lines, employing psychiatric and psychological models in clergy training. Anton Boisen introduced a methodology of training pastors in a hospital setting, where one could study "living human documents." Clinical pastoral education (CPE) became a movement of its own. At Andover Newton Theological School, an institution with American Baptist roots, Phil Guiles, director of clinical training, began the Andover Newton Project, developing CPE training centers in general hospitals in New England.[21] During the latter half of the twentieth century, CPE became a more standardized

16. Durso, *Thy Will Be Done*, 251.

17. On March 29, 1941, Truett recorded in his diary, "Today has been the busiest day of my life for weddings—I have officiated at the marriages of six couples today. This is the record so far." Durso, *Thy Will Be Done*, 250.

18. Durso, *Thy Will Be Done*, 251.

19. Durso, *Thy Will Be Done*, 247.

20. E. Brooks Holifield, *A History of Pastoral Care in America: From Salvation to Self-Realization* (Eugene, OR: Wipf & Stock, 2005), 227.

21. Homer L. Jernigan, "Clinical Pastoral Education: Reflections on the Past and Future of a Movement," *Journal of Pastoral Care & Counseling* 56, no. 4 (December 1, 2002): 382.

process, providing chaplaincy training and certification and supplementing theological education for students in many denominations, including Baptists.

Wayne Oates, who had trained under Boisen at Elgin State Hospital in Chicago, was a professor of pastoral care and psychology of religion at the Southern Baptist Theological Seminary. Like Dobbins before him, Oates attempted to combine the language of traditional Protestant theology with psychological insights derived from theories of psychosocial role behavior. Oates became one of the four pastoral theologians who provided intellectual leadership to the pastoral care and counseling movement following World War II.[22] Raymond Lawrence argues that Oates was "among the most influential of American clerics in the 20th century."[23] Despite his prominent role in the pastoral care and counseling movement, Oates, like many prophets in their hometown, was not widely received among Southern Baptists.[24] Other Baptist pastoral theologians, such as Franklin M. Segler and C. W. Brister, contributed their thinking and experience to bring the care of souls into conversation with the clinical insights of psychology, psychiatry, and sociology.[25]

Early in the twenty-first century, following the so-called Conservative Resurgence among Southern Baptists, some have questioned the use of insights from the social sciences in pastoral ministry. In 2002 the Southern Baptist Convention, meeting in St. Louis, ratified a resolution titled "On the Sufficiency of Scripture in a Therapeutic Culture." The document laments the neglect of "our God-ordained responsibility for the care and cure of souls," which is becoming "practically ineffective, both marginalizing ourselves from the culture and being marginalized by the mental health establishment."[26] Eleven years later, meeting in Houston, however, messengers ratified a resolution "On Mental Health Concerns and the Heart of God." This resolution affirms "the wise use of medical intervention for mental health concerns when appropriate" and expresses support for "research and treatment of mental health concerns when undertaken in a manner consistent with a biblical worldview."[27]

22. Holifield, *History of Pastoral Care*, 275.
23. Raymond J. Lawrence, *Recovery of Soul: A History and Memoir of the Clinical Pastoral Movement* (New York: CPSP, 2017), 1.
24. Lawrence, *Recovery of Soul*, 147.
25. C. W. Brister, *Pastoral Care in the Church* (New York: Harper & Row, 1964); Franklin M. Segler, *A Theology of Church and Ministry: The Christian Pastor; His Call, His Life, His Work in and through the Church* (Nashville: Broadman, 1960).
26. "On the Sufficiency of Scripture in a Therapeutic Culture," SBC, June 1, 2002, https://www.sbc.net/resource-library/resolutions/on-the-sufficiency-of-scripture-in-a-therapeutic-culture/.
27. "On Mental Health Concerns and the Heart of God," SBC, June 1, 2013, https://www.sbc.net/resource-library/resolutions/on-mental-health-concerns-and-the-heart-of-god/.

T. Dale Johnson Jr. published his 2014 PhD dissertation criticizing the approach of Dobbins, Oates, and others. He argues that "secular therapeutic explanation of mental health reverberates from the pulpits and pews of many Southern Baptist churches. There are divided responses to issues of soul care that create confusion and doubt concerning the authority and validity of Scripture as competent for modern concerns."[28] He cites the 2013 resolution on mental health concerns as evidence that Baptists continue to receive confusing messages regarding psychology and Scripture.

In this debate, it is easy to hear the never-ending struggle of Baptists to "get it right biblically." The Baptist vision requires it. The effort to relate biblical teachings to various theories in the physical or social sciences is real. Baptists continue to work out our own salvation with fear and trembling in this matter. We are not therapists, yet we want to understand the human condition as fully as possible in order to minister in Jesus's name as fully as possible. Finding an adequate hermeneutic to bring science and Scripture into conversation affects something as practical as the pastoral care offered in Jesus's name in the face of human suffering. We want the "this" of our ministries to human hurts and hopes to match the "that" of the biblical witness.

Theological Reflection

C. W. Brister regarded pastoral care, in the broadest perspective, as "the mutual concern of Christians for each other and for those in the world for whom Christ died."[29] That definition includes more than the work of that person in the congregation designated "the pastor." And that description certainly embraces more than the members of any given church. It extends to the entire world. If, however, we want to understand the biblical and theological undergirding of our work, considering what it means for a *pastor* to offer pastoral care, then perhaps a narrower description is necessary. What is it about our ministry of pastoral care that differs significantly from the good and essential work those in the helping professions provide?[30]

28. T. Dale Johnson Jr., *The Professionalization of Pastoral Care: The SBC's Journey from Pastoral Theology to Counseling Psychology* (Eugene, OR: Wipf & Stock, 2020), 162.

29. Brister, *Pastoral Care in the Church*, xxiii.

30. The American Psychological Association defines helping professions as "occupations that provide health and education services to individuals and groups, including occupations in the fields of psychology, psychiatry, counseling, medicine, nursing, social work, physical and occupational therapy, teaching, and education." Gary R. VandenBos, ed., *APA Dictionary of Psychology*, 2nd ed. (Washington, DC: American Psychological Association, 2015), 489. Some definitions of this field include ministry as one of these professions, which I resist. Grouping ministry with these others signals a secularizing of the work of Christian ministry in order to

Pastoral care differs from other efforts to support people in their crises in several ways. In the first place, pastors offer care with a distinctive goal in mind. The people in our congregations are not problems for us to solve. They are people who need to know and experience God's love for them in the ordinary events of their lives. That goal distinguishes pastoral care from merely "helping people" or "meeting people's needs"; pastors seek to transcend suffering, not simply to explain or eliminate it.

Pastoral care seeks to consider with people about their lives in the light of the gospel. The goal is to help them connect the ordinariness of life, particularly the experiences of suffering, with God's work in their lives. Pastoral care contributes to the work of making disciples, of seeing followers of Jesus formed spiritually. Our goal in pastoral care is not to alleviate pain or provide therapeutic solutions. Instead, we intend to help people discern God's loving presence and activity in their lives in all situations. When pastors forget this, we too quickly become "a combination minister and masseur," as Flannery O'Conner once described a Protestant pastor in Atlanta.[31]

Second, pastoral care is offered "in the name of Jesus." That is, we step into people's lives in times of joy or crisis, representing not ourselves but the one who sent us. Our education, training, degrees, and years of experience are not on display. The young pastor, newly minted from theological training, and the pastor who has served faithfully for decades are on equal footing in this. We enter an intensive care unit not merely as ourselves, with whatever credentials we might have accumulated, but as persons authorized to represent Christ to suffering people and their anxious family members. When we walk into the presence of human suffering, we do so in the name of Jesus, representing him and his love. Pastors are present not to find solutions, necessarily, but by our own words and presence to remind those who are suffering that God loves them and is present with them.

Third, pastoral care has a genuine priestly responsibility attached to it. Like Aaron wearing a garment with the names of the tribes on his shoulders, we are responsible to God for the welfare of our flock (Heb. 13:17). We do not merely give an account to the congregation for their care, but we answer to God as well. We are "overseers," attending to the physical, emotional, relational, and spiritual welfare of those we serve. The burden of their life with God during their pain lies on our shoulders.

---

justify itself to a modern therapeutically oriented culture. See William H. Willimon, *Pastor: The Theology and Practice of Ordained Ministry*, rev. ed. (Nashville: Abingdon, 2016), 59–61.

31. Flannery O'Connor, *The Habit of Being: Letters of Flannery O'Connor*, ed. Sally Fitzgerald (New York: Farrar, Straus & Giroux, 1988), 81.

Fourth, we give pastoral care with the authority of the one who sent us. A secular counselor or therapist has no business knocking on a client's door and asking how they are doing with the issues discussed at last Thursday's session. They cannot encounter a client in a grocery store aisle and pick up the conversation about the client's marriage. A licensed counselor cannot phone a person they suspect to be struggling and invite them for coffee and conversation. We can. As long as we are working within our flock, pastors can take the initiative in extending care in ways our secular counterparts cannot ethically do. Pastors engage this work as a part of our legitimate pastoral authority to "tend the flock of God" in our charge (1 Pet. 5:2).

Finally, pastoral care has a distinctive communal dimension to it. Whether we are officiating a wedding ceremony, conducting a funeral, visiting a hospital or nursing home, or sitting with fellow Christians in our study, we are doing so on behalf of the entire congregation. We represent Christ, of course. But we also represent his church. We are expressing the church's care, concern, and compassion, not merely our own. In pastoral care, we offer the body of Christ, not by sharing bread and cup, but by providing care on behalf of the church itself. Professional counselors or social workers may be Christians. Still, when acting in their professional role, they do not deliver care as representatives of the church in the way that pastors do. We understand ourselves to be representing more than our professional training or our certification. We represent Christ and his church in those moments of intervention.

Pastoral Care in Ordinary Events

Pastoral care is often and appropriately associated with being present to people during crises. That is only part of the story, however. Ordinary events of life deserve a pastoral presence and ministry as well. One contribution of the pastoral care movement in the twentieth century was the attention it gave to human development's spiritual significance. These junctures are *kairoi*, decisive moments when pastors and churches can step into people's lives and help them make space for God's work. Birth, adolescence, conversion, graduation, vocation, marriage, and retirement are times when people may not think to call on their pastor or church, yet which are ripe with opportunity for care. Pastoral conversations around the regular stuff of life—education, employment, parenting, being married, finances, and many others—are expressions of pastoral care as appropriate as visiting a hospital room. Good shepherds bring intentionality to pastoral care that assures a connection between God's love and the ordinary events in the lives of those they serve.

Pastoral Care and Crises

Although we may think of life's crises as somehow out of the ordinary, they are not. As intense and painful as many of these experiences may prove to be, they are ordinary by any human measure. All humans face such times. As Paul put it, "No testing has overtaken you that is not common to everyone" (1 Cor. 10:13). Disease, family conflicts, marital struggles, parental pain, congenital disabilities, miscarriages and stillbirths, accidents and injuries, job losses, war, natural disasters, untimely deaths—the list could go on for pages—are ordinary events of human experience. These events qualify as crises because they are moments of emotional upheaval that call the future into question.[32] These are times when people are often more open to a pastor's presence, even as they long for the presence of God. Seeing the pain or confusion of parishioners we hold in affection can derail our efforts to offer pastoral care. We can too quickly move toward palliative efforts to make the hurting stop rather than being willing to be with them in their pain. Our aversion to the sight of "emotional blood" can cause us to faint rather than to do the difficult work of saying "God" to them in their confusion and discomfort. Our theology of pastoral care will hold us to the task so that we will not abandon them to mere human "helpfulness" when they need the compassionate presence of God and the church, whom we represent.

Pastoral Care and the Social Sciences

That some among Baptists would react negatively to the pastoral care and counseling movement is unsurprising. The Baptist vision calls for a connection between our beliefs and practices and what we read in Scripture. Since the nineteenth century, Baptists have struggled to reconcile their understanding of the Bible with the claims and conclusions of modern science. This difficulty has affected the wide acceptance of the results of the physical sciences until now. Many Baptists are among those evangelicals who deny scientific findings regarding the causes and effects of our changing climate, for example. The high regard in which Baptists hold the Bible has also made it a challenge to engage the social sciences, such as psychology and sociology. Many simply ignore the insights those disciplines offer because they regard the Bible as the only source of information about human life.[33] However, to affirm the

---

32. I am indebted to Dr. Gene Klann for this definition of a crisis. See *Crisis Leadership: Using Military Lessons, Organizational Experiences, and the Power of Influence to Lessen the Impact of Chaos on the People You Lead* (Greensboro, NC: Center for Creative Leadership, 2003), 4.

33. Elsewhere I have attempted to describe a hermeneutic allowing for a biblical theology to interact legitimately with one psychological approach, Bowen Family Systems Theory. See

salvific truth of Scripture does not preclude us from learning the truth that God has written into creation as well.[34] We risk greatly misusing Scripture by demanding that it answer questions it does not address. In the fourth century, Augustine warned that our doing so may damage the witness of Scripture to unbelievers. His admonition still obtains:

> Whenever, you see, they [uneducated believers] catch some members of the Christian community making mistakes on a subject which they know inside out, and defending their hollow opinions on the authority of our books, on what grounds are they going to trust those books on the resurrection of the dead and the hope of eternal life and the kingdom of heaven, when they suppose they include any number of mistakes and fallacies on matters which they themselves have been able to master either by experiment or the surest of calculations?[35]

Our very testimony to the truth of the gospel requires us to be wary of making claims for the Bible that it does not make of itself.

Pastors who use sources other than Scripture in the work of pastoral care must do so thoughtfully. Sin, repentance, love, forgiveness, suffering, and perseverance are not scientific categories, yet these and other essential theological concepts are central to the work of pastoral care. Nevertheless, the pastor who understands how God has created the human brain and body to function during times when anxiety is high, such as life's crises, can minister with insights and options that make ministry more effective. Comprehending human development issues at various life stages can teach the pastor the value of spiritual intervention during those transitions. Knowing something about the process of grief and mourning can equip the pastor to be a more useful resource to people working through their losses. One of the challenges of a Baptist theology of pastoral care in the twenty-first century will be to

R. Robert Creech, *Family Systems and Congregational Life: A Map for Ministry* (Grand Rapids: Baker Academic, 2019), 117–84; and Jim Herrington, Trisha Taylor, and R. Robert Creech, *The Leader's Journey: Accepting the Call to Personal and Congregational Transformation*, 2nd ed. (Grand Rapids: Baker Academic, 2020), 177–88.

34. In his magisterial *Systematic Theology*, Baptist pastor and theologian Augustus Hopkins Strong defines inspiration as "that influence of the Spirit of God upon the minds of the Scripture writers which made their writings the record of a progressive divine revelation, sufficient, when taken together and interpreted by the same Spirit who inspired them, to lead every honest inquirer to Christ and to salvation." *Systematic Theology* (New York: Armstrong & Son, 1907), 197. This emphasis on the infallibly salvific focus of Scripture set aside the debate about turning to the Bible for answers to scientific questions.

35. Saint Augustine, *On Genesis*, trans. Edmund Hill, ed. John E. Rotelle, The Works of Saint Augustine I/13 (Hyde Park, NY: New City, 2004), 187. Alister E. McGrath reports that John Calvin later issued similar warnings; see *The Foundations of Dialogue in Science and Religion* (Malden, MA: Wiley-Blackwell, 1991), 124–25.

continue to refine our understanding of Scripture and of the contributions to be found in the sciences of human behavior.

Pastoral Care and Intercession

One other aspect of pastoral care not always included in discussions of either the theology or the practice of it is the role of prayer and intercession. Baptist writers frequently discuss pastoral prayer when they address preaching and often include it as part of worship leadership. However, they often ignore the significance of a pastor's faithful ministry of regularly praying for the people, the shepherd interceding for the sheep. Yet this is an inherently priestly act on the part of the pastor.

If the ministry of the Good Shepherd and Great High Priest is a model for our pastoral work, then intercessory prayer is not optional. Despite knowing that, we pastors sometimes too glibly respond to people with "I'll be praying for you." Apart from some intentional practice on the part of the pastor, however, such words can become dismissive. The pastor who takes these priestly aspects of the work seriously will develop a prayer practice in which individual congregational members are regularly the subject of prayer. Additionally, pastors must become comfortable saying, not "I'll be praying for you," but "Let us pray," and interceding for people in the moment they share their need.

All believers are priests before God. All can and should intercede for one another. Yet, like other pastoral responsibilities, such a practice cannot be optional for the pastor. Even as Aaron bore the names of Israel's tribes on his shoulders, indicating responsibility, he also bore their names on the breastpiece, near his heart, symbolizing his affection and care for them as he ministered before the Lord. Intercessory prayer is one way that pastors can reflect that priestly role. Samuel DeWitt Proctor writes, "[Intercession] remains one of the pastor's most vital ministries and it intersects with every other aspect of the office."[36]

CONCLUSIONS ●

Any contemporary ministry model that excludes the pastor from participation in the care of the flock is suspect, biblically and theologically. Pastoral

---

36. Samuel D. Proctor and Gardner C. Taylor, *We Have This Ministry: The Heart of the Pastor's Vocation* (Valley Forge, PA: Judson, 1996), 38.

care is integral to the pastor's call, the work of preaching, and the exercise of leadership. A CEO model of ministry that leaves the pastor running a religious business ("shopkeeping," according to Eugene Peterson) falls short of the models of ministry offered by Jesus and the early church.[37] For the Baptist vision to flourish in pastoral ministry, pastoral conversations in the ordinary and crisis events of people's lives are nonnegotiable. Biblically, historically, and theologically, shepherding calls for pastors to care for the sheep, for we will answer to the Chief Shepherd, who loves them.

FOR FURTHER REFLECTION ·

1. How would you define pastoral care? What does it include? What does it not include?
2. How does the work of pastoral care enhance the ministries of preaching and leadership? How might those ministries improve pastoral care?
3. Is all pastoral care to be done by the pastor? What work can the pastor share with other staff members? What can lay ministers take on? What needs require the pastor's attention and presence?
4. What is the relationship between the insights offered by modern social sciences and the guidance found in Scripture? Can a biblically based ministry of pastoral care make use of those disciplines as well?
5. Where do the pastor and the pastor's family receive pastoral care when needed?

---

37. Eugene H. Peterson, *Working the Angles: The Shape of Pastoral Integrity* (Grand Rapids: Eerdmans, 1987), 2.

9

Spiritual Formation

Teaching Them to Obey All That I Have Commanded

God bless the pastors whose images bear faithful witness to the leadership of our Lord, and whose discipleship, abilities, and opportunities have prepared him or her to teach with effectiveness.

—Samuel DeWitt Proctor, *We Have This Ministry*

I will give you shepherds after my own heart,
who will feed you with knowledge and understanding.

—The LORD (Jer. 3:15)

Dallas Willard famously describes the work of spiritual formation and discipleship as "the great omission from the Great Commission."[1] From the beginning, those whom Jesus sent out were charged with the task of "making disciples" (*mathēteuō*), baptizing them, and teaching them to obey everything he had commanded (Matt. 28:18–20). This "Great Commission" of Jesus

1. Dallas Willard, *The Great Omission: Reclaiming Jesus's Essential Teachings on Discipleship* (New York: HarperOne, 2007), 5–6.

has been a fundamental text in Baptist life. However, we have not always focused on making genuine disciples and teaching them to live as Jesus taught.
Instead, we have often emphasized making converts to the faith, or saving
people from hell, and boasting in the number of our baptisms. Meanwhile we
may leave discipleship and obedience as options—thus, the great omission.
When Baptists have been at our best, we have, however, taken Jesus's words
with the utmost seriousness, seeing the Christian life in terms of *Nachfolge
Christi* (following Christ), as our Anabaptist ancestors would say.

Biblical Foundations

The Teaching Ministry in the Old Testament

In Old Testament times, God gave the priests the responsibility for teaching
the law to the people, beginning with Aaron (Lev. 10:8–11). Anticipating a
time when the people would settle in the land of promise, Moses instructed
the priests to gather the people to read the law and teach them to live in fear
of the Lord (Deut. 31:9–13). The judge-prophet Samuel, although not a priest
himself, had served alongside Eli the priest. Samuel committed himself to the
priestly tasks of intercession for the people in their disobedience and promised, "I will instruct you in the good and the right way" (1 Sam. 12:23). Azariah
the prophet addressed Asa the king and described the time of Israel's rebellion
under his father, Rehoboam: "In those times it was not safe for anyone to
go or come, for great disturbances afflicted all the inhabitants of the lands.
They were broken in pieces, nation against nation and city against city, for
God troubled them with every sort of distress" (2 Chron. 15:5–6). Asa said
of that time, "For a long time Israel was without the true God, and without
a teaching priest, and without law" (2 Chron. 15:3). Ignorant of the law and
the life God had called them to, the people had wandered from the truth.

When Judah's people returned from exile in Babylon, Ezra, a scribe and
priest, gathered the people to listen to the reading of the law from morning
until noon. The Levites helped the people understand the meaning of what
they had heard:

> So they read from the book, from the law of God, with interpretation. They
> gave the sense, so that the people understood the reading.
>
> And Nehemiah, who was the governor, and Ezra the priest and scribe, and
> the Levites who taught the people said to all the people, "This day is holy to
> the LORD your God; do not mourn or weep." For all the people wept when they
> heard the words of the law. (Neh. 8:8–9)

After the exile, there developed a class of sages in Israel whose teaching appears in Ecclesiastes, Job, Proverbs, Psalms, and some writings among the Apocrypha. Proverbs, in particular, has a keen interest in teaching the way of life called for by the fear of the Lord. Eventually, there developed a class of scribes in Judaism whose responsibilities included instructing others in the law. By Jesus's time, the synagogue had emerged as an institution in Judaism alongside the temple, and rabbis or teachers occupied a place in religious leadership with the priests and Levites.

The Teaching Ministry in the Life of Jesus

Jesus provides a model for the role of teacher. The verb *didaskein* (to teach) occurs fifty-nine times in fifty-five verses in the Gospels, nearly always referring to Jesus. Teaching about the kingdom of God was at the heart of his ministry. He taught in the synagogues (Matt. 4:23; 9:35; Luke 4:54), in the temple (Matt. 21:23; 26:55), in the open country (Matt. 5:1–2; Mark 10:1), and beside the sea (Mark 2:13; 4:1). He taught both his chosen disciples and the crowds that followed him. He used parables, examples, questions, biblical texts, and the example of his own life. He made it clear that his words and teachings were themselves the source of the eternal kind of life he came to offer (Matt. 7:24–27; John 6:63). Obedience to his teaching was the way to the life with God that he proclaimed. Following his resurrection, he commissioned his apostles to make disciples and teach them to obey what he had taught.

The crowds who followed him knew Jesus as a teacher (Matt. 7:28–29; John 7:14–15). His disciples, strangers, and even his opponents addressed him as "Teacher" or "Rabbi" (Mark 12:14; 13:1; 14:4; Luke 9:38; John 1:38). Those who followed him were his "disciples, "learners," or "apprentices" (*mathētai*). Like a rabbinical teacher, he invited disciples to "take [his] yoke . . . and learn from [him]" (Matt. 11:28–30).[2] His teaching amazed the crowds because of its distinctive difference from what they had heard from their scribes (Mark 1:22; Matt. 7:29). Jesus also warned of false teachers whose instruction would lead people away from the life God offers in the kingdom (Matt. 7:15–20). Jesus's ministry focused on teaching to transform the lives of his followers (Matt. 7:24–26), so accounts of his teaching ministry occupy a good portion of the Gospel story.[3]

2. The rabbis spoke of "the yoke of the law," which many common people found burdensome. Jesus, by contrast, speaks of "my yoke" (his instructions, his teaching about living in the gospel of the kingdom), which is "easy," which fits and does not chafe.

3. The four Gospels contain roughly eighty-two thousand words, about half of which—thirty-nine thousand—are the words of Jesus. A precise number would depend on the version one used to count.

The Teaching Ministry in the Early Church

Making disciples and teaching them the life of Christ is a pastoral task. When Paul lists "pastor" as a gifted office in the church in Ephesians 4:11–13, he states this explicitly: "The gifts he gave were that some would be apostles, some prophets, some evangelists, some pastors and teachers, to equip the saints for the work of ministry, for building up the body of Christ, until all of us come to the unity of the faith and of the knowledge of the Son of God, to maturity, to the measure of the full stature of Christ." In verse 11, the phrase "pastors and teachers" emphasizes the teaching role of pastors.[4] Apostles, prophets, and evangelists are specific leadership roles. But when Paul comes to pastors, he does not say "some pastors and some teachers," but "some pastors and teachers." He uses one definite article with two nouns—literally, "the pastors and teachers." In Paul's language, that closely identifies the roles. God calls pastors both to proclaim the gospel as a preacher (*kēryx*) and to explain the way of Christ as a teacher (*didaskalos*).[5] These two aspects of ministry roughly parallel the Old Testament roles of prophet and priest. Among the character traits and skills listed in the qualifications for overseers in 1 Timothy 3:1–6 is the requirement to be an "apt teacher" (3:2; see also 2 Tim. 2:24; Titus 1:9; 2:1). Elders who labor in "preaching and teaching" are worthy of "double honor," Paul says (1 Tim. 5:17; cf. Gal. 6:6). He encourages Timothy to train faithful people who will then teach others (2 Tim. 2:2). In the church, pastors are teachers. It is a part of our calling.

These pastor-teachers pursue a goal (along with the apostles, prophets, and evangelists) of the saints' formation and growth and the increasing spiritual maturity of church, the body of Christ.[6] These servants are to "equip the saints for the work of ministry, for building up the body of Christ, until all

---

4. The phrase *tous de poimenos kai didaskalous* (some pastors and teachers) in Eph. 4:11 is often interpreted in light of a grammatical principle known as Granville Sharp's Rule of the Article. That rule would indicate that Paul, by using only one article (*tous*) to apply to two nouns (*poimenas kai didaskalous*) was referring to only one group—the pastor-teachers. However, Daniel B. Wallace has argued that Sharp's Rule applies only to singular words and so is not in play in this verse. Although that rule may not apply here, the context lends itself to identifying the two very closely. Later in 1 Tim. 3:2, an overseer is expected to be an "apt teacher." See Wallace, "Sharp Redivivus?—A Reexamination of the Granville Sharp Rule," Bible.Org, June 30, 2004, https://bible.org/article/sharp-redivivus-reexamination-granville-sharp-rule.

5. Darrell L. Bock, *Ephesians: An Introduction and Commentary* (Downers Grove, IL: InterVarsity, 2019), 126.

6. Gaines Stanley Dobbins, an early voice among twentieth-century Baptist educators, believed that these various roles overlapped in the pastor's ministry. He wrote, "True, one of these functions may well take the primacy in the work of the typical Christian minister, but his service will not be full-rounded unless all of these functions find a place in his service. As missionary he is to be an evangelist; as preacher he is to be an evangelist; as pastor he is to be an evangelist;

of us come to the unity of the faith and of the knowledge of the Son of God, to maturity, to the measure of the full stature of Christ" (Eph. 4:12–13). The gifts, in this case, are gifted persons given to the church to develop its capacity to carry out its ministry with Christlike maturity and love.

The content of pastoral teaching is not a set of abstract creedal affirmations but a way of life. Disciples are learning "to obey everything" Jesus commanded them. They are learning how to follow Christ, turn the other cheek, love their enemies, pray, worship, engage in spiritual practices, be generous, and share their faith. This teaching is transformative. People who hear and learn and practice are changed by it.

In the story of the earliest church in Acts, teaching plays a central role. The first summary of life in the Jerusalem church affirms that these disciples "devoted themselves to the apostles' teaching" (Acts 2:42). The admonition given to Peter and John by the local authorities trying to squelch the new messianic movement in Jerusalem was that they must desist from speaking or teaching in the name of Jesus (Acts 4:18). Despite their arrest, however, Peter and the others "went on with their teaching" (Acts 5:21; cf. 5:25, 42). According to the high priest's accusation, their teaching "filled Jerusalem" (Acts 5:28). Peter's rationale for advising the selection of seven men to oversee the needs of the Hellenistic Jewish Christian widows in the Jerusalem church was so that he and the other apostles might devote themselves "to prayer and to serving the word" (Acts 6:4).

Teaching is also at the core of Paul's ministry described in Acts (11:26; 15:35; 18:11; 20:20; 28:31). Paul himself claims that teaching about Jesus Christ is at the heart of his mission. He writes, "It is he whom we proclaim, warning everyone and teaching everyone in all wisdom, so that we may present everyone mature in Christ" (Col. 1:28). The Pastoral Epistles include advice and encouragement about the importance of teaching in the church (1 Tim. 4:11; 6:2–3; 2 Tim. 2:2). Much of what Paul writes, both to his churches and to individuals, is also intended to teach them. The work of spiritual formation and discipleship shaped Paul's vision for his ministry.

Pastoral teaching is necessary for the health and formation of the flock as well as its protection. Paul warns Timothy and Titus of false teachers (1 Tim. 1:3; 6:3; 2 Tim. 4:3; Titus 1:11), as he had warned the elders in Ephesus in his last visit with them: "Keep watch over yourselves and over all the flock, of which the Holy Spirit has made you overseers, to shepherd the church of God that he obtained with the blood of his own Son. I know that after I have gone,

---

as teacher he is to be an evangelist. Conversely, as evangelist he will be missionary, preacher, pastor, teacher." "Pastoral Evangelism," *Review & Expositor* 42, no. 1 (January 1945): 48.

savage wolves will come in among you, not sparing the flock" (Acts 20:28–29). Much of his teaching in his epistles is offered to counter those who would twist the truth of the gospel he preached and taught (for examples, see Galatians; 2 Cor. 10–11; Phil. 3; Colossians; and 2 Thessalonians). Sound teaching both prevents wandering from the truth and summons wanderers back.

The pastor who opens a Bible to teach the contents of one of Paul's letters at a midweek Bible study, or who sits with a church member over coffee, talking about growing in the life of prayer, or who explains baptism to a new believer—such a pastor is stepping into the ancient role of pastoral teacher. Those acts are the "this" corresponding to the "that" of the teaching ministries of Jesus and the apostles. Pastors may not be the only teachers in the congregation, but teaching is one of the indispensable roles belonging to our calling. Feeding the sheep is part of the shepherd's task.

Historical Bypaths

Baptist pastors have engaged in teaching Scripture and theology from the earliest days of the movement. Our Anabaptist ancestors primarily focused on teaching for changed lives, learning to become followers of Jesus. This focus on teaching occasionally appears in the early creeds and discussions of pastoral ministry. In 1524 Hübmaier urged congregations to support and protect "those who teach them the Word of God in its purity."[7] The 1527 Schleitheim Confession defines the role of the pastor in this way: "This office shall be to read, to admonish and teach, to warn, to discipline, to ban in the church, to lead out in prayer for the advancement of all the brethren and sisters, to lift up the bread when it is to be broken, and in all things to see to the care of the body of Christ, in order that it may be built up and developed, and the mouth of the slanderer be stopped."[8] Article 25 of the Waterland Confession (1580) affirms that in Christ's holy church he has "ordained an evangelical ministry, namely, teaching of the divine word (a), use of the holy sacraments, and the care of the poor (b), as also ministers for performing these ministries."[9] For example, Hutterite Peter Riedemann describes the office of pastor as "that of teaching and baptizing."[10] Teaching rather than preaching is specified as a

---

7. William L. Lumpkin, *Baptist Confessions of Faith*, 2nd rev. ed. (Valley Forge, PA: Judson, 2011), 21.

8. Lumpkin, *Baptist Confessions of Faith*, 27–28.

9. Lumpkin, *Baptist Confessions of Faith*, 55.

10. Peter Riedemann, "The Manner of Baptizing," in *Account* (1542), 79–81; cited in Walter Klaassen, *Anabaptism in Outline: Selected Primary Sources*, Classics of the Radical Reformation 3 (Kitchener, ON: Herald Press, 1981), 129–30.

task among these early Anabaptists, although a distinction between the two would be difficult to tease out.

Over the next four centuries, Baptist pastors continued to underscore the capacity of pastors to teach effectively. C. H. Spurgeon listed one's ability to teach as a "public instructor" among the evidence that one might gather in discerning a call to ministry.[11] J. B. Tidwell offered pastors a criterion to examine their preaching: "What is the teaching or subject matter of my preaching? Is it the Holy Scripture? Can the preacher answer that all his teaching is found in that Book, and does he ring true to all of its messages, and does he preach the whole Gospel of God or leave out any part?"[12] Given the Baptist vision, the teaching ministry of the pastor is the "this" corresponding to the "that" of the examples of Jesus and the early church. Even as that first Jerusalem church "devoted themselves to the apostles' teaching" (Acts 2:42), so the church now gathers to hear its pastor expound the truth of Scripture.

Two twentieth-century Baptist voices that emphasized the role of teaching in their ministries and in training others deserve our attention. Their approaches to the teaching role are not contradictory, but neither are they identical. Samuel Proctor addressed himself to the context of the Black churches he served and the role the pastor played in that community. Teaching occupied a prominent place in that work and ranged from Scripture and theology to practical life skills. Dallas Willard focused on the practical teaching of preparing women and men to follow Christ effectively in their daily life at work and home so that the reign of Christ's kingdom might extend ever further. He understood pastors to play an indispensable role in the formation of such disciples of Jesus.

Samuel DeWitt Proctor (1919–2005): Pastors as Teachers of the Church

Samuel DeWitt Proctor was a Black pastor, educator, and civil rights activist. Dr. Martin Luther King Jr. considered him a mentor, and Proctor was himself the protégé of the Reverend Dr. BG Crawley, a prominent Baptist minister in Brooklyn, New York, and a New York State judge.[13] Proctor learned the value of education from his grandparents and diligently pursued his training, earning degrees from Virginia Union University (BA, 1942),

---

11. C. H. Spurgeon, *Lectures to My Students* (Grand Rapids: Zondervan, 1955), 28.

12. J. B. Tidwell, *Concerning Preachers: What All Preachers Should Know* (New York: Fleming H. Revell, 1937), 18.

13. For details of Proctor's life, see his autobiography, *The Substance of Things Hoped For* (New York: Putnam Adult, 1996).

Crozer Theological Seminary (BD, 1945), and Boston University (PhD, 1950). His career comprised teaching and administration in institutions of higher learning, government service, and pastoral leadership in congregations, including the prestigious Abyssinian Baptist Church of Harlem. Regardless of his assignment, Proctor focused on teaching, believing education was the key to freedom.

He viewed the pastorate as a teaching position. In a book for pastors coauthored with Gardner Taylor, Proctor devotes an entire chapter to "The Pastor as Teacher."[14] He advocates for the education of pastors and celebrates the privilege of growing up in churches with well-trained ministers. The pastor, he argues, should be a resource to the congregation, not only in matters of religion, but also in other areas of life (14). Proctor lists seven areas in which a pastor needs to be prepared to serve as a teacher: personal behavior, civic orientation, political choices, stewardship, healthcare and management, intercultural relations, and worldview (16). The pastor must address those practical aspects of life from the solid ground of a well-thought-out theology, teaching the congregation who God is and what our relationship with God should be. Sound theology, he believes, is where the pastor's teaching role becomes most crucial (17).

The pastor should teach theology knowledgeably in the context of contemporary scientific claims and should bring the best critical tools to the study and teaching of the Scriptures. "A good pastor," Proctor asserts, "will teach the Bible with all the tools of scholarship available and will show the people how these sixty-six books are a compendium of inspired writings that cover a long period of divine-human encounters, culminating in God's revelation in Jesus Christ, the ultimate act of God's love for us" (19). Proctor understands that teaching theology or biblical truth is not about intellectual knowledge but about teaching the church how to live as God's children. Part of that practical instruction is the pastor's own life lived as an example to the flock, as Paul boldly says, "Be imitators of me, as I am of Christ" (1 Cor. 11:1). Pastoral teaching by example includes both character and actions. So Proctor calls on pastors to model the life and character of Jesus Christ in the most ordinary aspects of our lives (23).

The pastor also bears responsibility for teaching the church about the church (24–30). The church's long history and valued traditions and its identity, mission, and purpose are on the teaching pastor's syllabus. The pastor

14. Samuel DeWitt Proctor and Gardner C. Taylor, *We Have This Ministry: The Heart of the Pastor's Vocation* (Valley Forge, PA: Judson, 1996), 13–30. Subsequent page references appear in the text.

trains men and women to care for the church, taking responsibility for its growth and well-being.

Proctor claims that the pastor who understands the importance of the teaching role would seize opportunities to exercise it constantly. Pastoral conversations, sermons, classroom settings, committee meetings, song selection in worship, planning meetings, and many other ordinary responsibilities of the pastor hold out possibilities for the pastor-teacher to point fellow believers to a more faithful and effective life in Christ (24–30).

Dallas Willard (1935–2013): Pastors as Teachers of the Nations

Few Baptists have influenced evangelical believers' appreciation of spiritual formation as much as Dallas Willard, a Baptist professor of philosophy at the University of Southern California. Willard's writing and speaking have contributed to the understanding of spiritual life well outside Baptist circles.[15] Willard grew up in a conservative Baptist setting, which continued to influence his devotion to Scripture and his emphasis on an experiential (he called it "conversational") relationship with God. He received degrees from Tennessee Temple College (BA, 1956), Baylor University (BA, 1957), and the University of Wisconsin–Madison (PhD, 1964). Although his career was primarily in academia, Willard also served as a pastor and devoted himself to teaching pastors and church leaders so that they might teach others the life of Christian discipleship.

Willard understood teaching as essential to the role of pastor. He devotes an entire chapter to "Pastors as Teachers of the Nations" in his *Knowing Christ Today: Why We Can Trust Spiritual Knowledge*.[16] Willard, whose philosophical writings dealt with Edmund Husserl's phenomenology, focuses on the issue of epistemology, or how we know the things we know.[17] He argues that spiritual knowledge (not just "belief" or "commitment" or "profession")

15. For Dallas Willard's biography, see Gary W. Moon, *Becoming Dallas Willard: The Formation of a Philosopher, Teacher, and Christ Follower* (Downers Grove, IL: IVP Books, 2018). Some of Willard's most influential writings for the church are *Hearing God: Developing a Conversational Relationship with God* (Downers Grove, IL: InterVarsity, 1983); *The Spirit of the Disciplines: Understanding How God Changes Lives* (San Francisco: HarperSanFrancisco, 1990); *The Divine Conspiracy: Rediscovering Our Hidden Life in God* (San Francisco: HarperSanFrancisco, 1998); *Renovation of the Heart: Putting on the Character of Christ* (Colorado Springs: NavPress, 2002); and *Knowing Christ Today: Why We Can Trust Spiritual Knowledge* (New York: HarperOne, 2009).

16. Willard, *Knowing Christ Today*, 193–214. Subsequent page references appear in the text.

17. Dallas Willard, *The Disappearance of Moral Knowledge*, ed. Steven L. Porter, Aaron Preston, and Gregg A. Ten Elshof (New York: Routledge, 2018). This deeply philosophical work underlies Willard's more popularly written *Knowing Christ Today*.

is a real thing. We can *know* spiritual truth. We have knowledge of something when "we are representing it (thinking about it, speaking of it, treating it) as it actually is, on an appropriate basis of thought and experience" (15). We can *know* of God's existence, for example. We can know what is real, the nature of the good life, what it means to be a truly good person, and how one becomes a truly good person. We need not approach these matters as mere beliefs. Knowledge inherently connects to the truth, whereas beliefs may be either true or false. People with knowledge are responsible for sharing the truth with others. Willard says, "Knowledge, but not mere belief or commitment, confers on its possessor an authority or right—even a responsibility—to act, to direct action, to establish and supervise policy, and to teach" (17).

Willard's philosophy intersects with pastoral ministry at this point. Pastors should be people with authentic knowledge of spiritual truth. Their responsibility is to make disciples, apprentices of Jesus. Pastors are to teach Jesus's followers how to know him and how to acquire spiritual knowledge. Willard identifies four "basic questions of life": (1) What is real? (2) What is the good life? (3) What is the truly good person? and (4) How does one become a truly good person? Jesus's answers to these questions provide the "curriculum for Christlikeness" that the pastor is authorized to teach. Willard says, "The task of Christian pastors and leaders is to present Christ's answers to the basic questions of life and to bring those answers forward as knowledge—primarily to those who are seeking and are open to following him, but also to all who may happen to hear, in the public arenas of a world in desperate need of knowledge of what is real and what is good" (198). Willard believed that pastors occupy a strategic position that would allow such teaching to permeate a community or society.

The vision for such a widespread influence grows out of Willard's recognition that Christian discipleship is not for life in the church but for life in the world. Pastors are to prepare Christian men and women to live Christlike lives in their workplace. "Discipleship to Jesus, properly guided by pastors," he says, "enables individuals to find in their work a divine calling and see the hand of God in their efforts to create what is good and to serve others in love" (208). Pastors teach these apprentices of Jesus "how to be God's men and women in the places they work and live" (209). Pastors help people convert their "job," whether out in the marketplace or the home, into their "calling," the place where they express their discipleship (Col. 3:22–24). The kingdom's influence expands as these disciples reign with Christ in these ordinary places of their lives: "in the office, laboratory, farm, the schoolroom as well as in media, sports, the fine arts, and so forth. They reign for what is good in the home, the community, and in voluntary and involuntary associations of all kinds, even up to international organizations and relations. They effectively care for the goods of human life that come under their care and influence" (211).

Willard's understanding of spiritual knowledge, pastoral ministry, and the influence of God's kingdom among "the nations" connects directly to the pastor's role as a teacher. "The most important thing that is happening in your community," he writes, "is what is happening there under the administration of true pastors for Christ. If you, as a pastor, do not believe that, then you do not understand the dignity of what you are supposed to be doing. Whatever your situation, there is nothing more important on earth than to dwell in the knowledge of Christ and to bring that knowledge to others" (211). This describes the teaching ministry of the pastor.

Theological Reflection

Teaching versus Preaching

The fine line between teaching and preaching, especially as a public act, is challenging to draw. We sometimes hear a person say that their pastor "is more of a teacher than a preacher." That may have much more to do with the level of emotion displayed in delivering the message than with some rational distinction between the two roles. Some claim that teaching, not preaching, takes place in small groups or personal conversations. Yet pastors may find ourselves more of a *kēryx* (proclaimer of the message) than a *didaskalos* (teacher) as we share the gospel of the kingdom with an individual or a group. Some have tried to distinguish the two roles in terms of the audience. The teacher instructs the church to build up disciples in the faith, and the preacher addresses unbelievers with the gospel, calling them to faith. That distinction becomes tricky to maintain as well. How much teaching do people need to receive to respond in faith to the good news? And do those in the church not need to hear a call to faith on occasion?

Perhaps the best we can do is to recognize distinct but overlapping purposes in the two acts. Teaching imparts spiritual knowledge or develops practices and skills necessary for ministry or growth in Christlikeness. On the other hand, preaching declares the kingdom of God manifest in Jesus's death and resurrection and calls people to respond to that reality with their lives. Proclamation focuses more on the hearers' will, and teaching addresses the intellect. We may not be able ultimately to draw a sharp line between them. However, Scripture, as well as Baptist writings and confessions of faith, sometimes differentiate the two ministries, despite their frequent overlap in practice.

A Theology of Pastoral Teaching

Pastors face three essential questions when reflecting theologically on our role as teacher: (1) To what end do we teach? (2) What is it that we teach? and (3) How do we teach? Is the role of pastoral teaching like that of the college or seminary professor, where we take the knowledge we have acquired in our training and replicate it in our congregations? Is our teaching no more than lectures in biblical or theological subjects? Or is it more? What is implied by spiritual formation or making disciples?

Teaching for Transformation

Our initial task is gaining clarity on the purpose of our teaching. Teaching in the church seeks to renovate the hearts of Jesus's followers, seeing them formed progressively into Christlikeness. Jesus's instructions call for us to "disciple the nations," "teaching them to obey everything I have commanded you" (Matt. 28:18–20). Paul describes his ministry philosophy in terms of "teaching everyone in all wisdom, so that we may present everyone mature in Christ" (Col. 1:28). The purpose of pastor-teachers and the other offices described in Ephesians 4:12–13 is "to equip the saints for the work of ministry, for building up the body of Christ, until all of us come to the unity of the faith and of the knowledge of the Son of God, to maturity, to the measure of the full stature of Christ." This ministry develops spiritual maturity in the church that protects the church from the seduction of false teaching (Eph. 4:14–15).

Teaching for such transformation fosters a kingdom-centered view of the world in which disciples see the world as Jesus sees it, accept as real what Jesus accepts as real, and regard as true what Jesus regards as true. This teaching is not merely dumping content from one who knows into the empty head of one who does not. Instead, disciples engage kingdom truths to understand how to live in light of God's reign. The goal is that disciples might live more fully in this world as they learn to live in the kingdom that is among us, which Jesus introduced.

Teaching the Whole Gospel

The second task we face is becoming clear on what we teach. Indeed, a disciple needs to acquire specific skills to read and understand the Bible for themselves. This knowledge is not transformative on its own but contributes to people's ability to understand scriptural truth. Biblical surveys, classes on hermeneutics, biblical history, theology, and other such subjects can help. But this level of learning (knowing about) is not to be equated with the goal of experiential knowledge. Pastoral teaching involves more than delivering lectures.

Disciples need to learn *how* to live the life Jesus calls us to live. They need to learn how to discern God's voice in their lives. They must learn to pray, to listen to God, and to obey God. They will need to acquire a facility in those spiritual disciplines that help them give their attention to God, such as silence, solitude, prayer, fasting, worship, and study. They need to engage those practices that help shape them from the inside out. Disciplines of community, service, and generosity will certainly be part of the plan. A "curriculum for Christlikeness" will address living the abundant life that Christ offers, being capable of expressing such things as a love for our enemies and radical trust in God's provisions, just as Jesus taught. Willard says,

> When you teach children or adults to ride a bicycle or swim, they actually do ride bikes or swim on appropriate occasions. You don't just teach them that they *ought* to ride bicycles, or that it is *good* to ride bicycles, or that they should be ashamed if they don't. Similarly, when you teach people to bless those who curse them, they actually do bless those who curse them—even family members! They recognize the occasion as it arises for what it is and respond from the heart of Jesus, which has become their own. They do it and they do it well.[18]

Pastors, then, teach experiential knowledge, not mere content. Such teaching implies the opportunity for the learning to be tested, reported, and reflected on. Pastoral teaching aims for this outcome.

Pastors may find ourselves teaching many different things out of our love for God and the people we serve, as Proctor described above. We will desire to equip them with the knowledge and skills they need to live and serve effectively in the world. Our prime objective, however, is to teach them to know God and God's ways so that they might live the blessed life that Jesus offers and might take that life into their ordinary, everyday world.

Teaching Effectively

The third issue for us is the act of teaching itself. How do we best do it? The adage is true: Telling is not teaching; listening is not learning. Whatever else learning is, it involves change on the part of the learner. Learning is not something that happens to us. It is something we participate in with our whole being. Whether the change is simply from not knowing a fact to knowing it, it is still change. But the kind of change we have called "transformation"

---

18. Willard, *Divine Conspiracy*, 314.

implies more than the acquisition of facts. Transformation requires a shift in our way of thinking and living (Rom. 12:1–2). It is usually incremental and not instantaneous. The changes show up over time as we learn increasingly to see the world as Jesus sees it, to believe in the God in whom Jesus believed, and to relate to people in love as he does. How does one teach to that end?

Jesus's example as a teacher may offer guidance. He told stories (Mark 4:33–34). He asked questions (Luke 10:25–28, 36–37). He challenged false thinking (Matt. 5:21–48). He described the kind of life he was offering (Matt. 5–7). He spoke of current events (Luke 13:4). He used language imaginatively with hyperboles, metaphors, poetry, and proverbs. He acted and then debriefed those acts with his students (John 13:1–15). He modeled all that he taught. He referred to Scripture often. In other words, he creatively employed every tool at his disposal to communicate the vital truth of life in the kingdom of God, and people marveled at his teaching (Matt. 7:28–29; 13:54; Mark 1:22; 6:2; Luke 4:22, 32; 19:48; John 7:15, 46).

A pastor following Jesus's example will approach the task of teaching more intentionally than ever. It is not enough simply to lecture the congregation when so many other communication tools are at hand. Developing skills in effective pedagogy is not often required training in theological education. We learn to preach but not to teach. Pastors may need to supplement their training to learn (or change) teaching skills. What would Jesus do as a teacher in the twenty-first century? Some of his methods would indeed remain—especially his use of Scripture, stories, and modeling the truth. What might he do with an audience increasingly accustomed to learning in other ways, including print and digital media? Wise and competent pastors in this rapidly changing world will find ways to become the kind of teachers who contribute to the spiritual formation of those they lead.

Teaching Ministry in a Digital World

In the first century, fledgling congregations were susceptible to itinerant teachers who came with what Paul called "a different [*heteron*] gospel," in a "different [*heterov*] spirit," proclaiming "another [*allos*] Jesus" (2 Cor. 11:4). Some of the false teachers the early church faced, often labeled "Judaizers," taught a legalism that undermined the message of God's grace in Christ (Gal. 1:6–9; Phil. 3:2). Others seemed to have offered a teaching that syncretized Christian doctrine and Greek philosophies, such as Gnosticism (Col. 2:8–23; 1 John 2:18–26; 2 John 7–11; 3 John). Sometimes the exact nature of the false teaching is not evident, but the danger of false teachers is (Matt. 7:15–23;

Acts 20:28–29; 1 Tim. 1:3–7; 4:1–3; 6:3–5; 2 Pet. 2:1–3; Jude 5–16; Rev. 2:6, 14–15). Consequently, Paul urges Timothy to pay close attention to his pastoral teaching so that he might save himself and his hearers from such distortions of the truth (1 Tim. 4:16). "But as for you," Paul admonishes Titus, "teach what is consistent with sound doctrine" (Titus 2:1). The pastor's teaching ministry serves not only to feed and grow the flock but also to protect them from false teaching that will inevitably challenge their understanding of the truth. Along with the other offices, the pastor-teacher builds up the church toward a maturity in which they are no longer "tossed to and fro and blown about by every wind of doctrine, by people's trickery, by their craftiness in deceitful scheming" (Eph. 4:14).

Christians have faced false teaching from the beginning of the Jesus movement. Much of the New Testament and a fair bit of the early church fathers' writings exist because of the need to counter so many misleading doctrines. As media technology has advanced, the opportunity to spread the good news has also increased. But so has the prospect of spreading false teaching. Both truth and falsehood took advantage of the print media, as they had used the spoken and handwritten word before. When radio and television became available, both light and darkness took to the airwaves. With the advent of that new media, church members often gather with their fellow disciples while carrying the infection of dangerous teaching acquired in the past week. The number of channels available to communicate both the gospel and the many distortions of the Christian message multiplied with cable and satellite television. The chances of a heretical infection grew accordingly. And now, with the internet and the many devices available to access it, everyone on earth possessing a cell phone can become a "television preacher" with a potentially worldwide audience. The people in our pews face exposure to more distortions of Christian doctrine than ever before, from the prosperity gospel to Christian nationalism to various ancient heresies.[19] All this is taking place while biblical and theological literacy is perhaps at an all-time low in Western Christianity. We face a pandemic of false teaching, and our people have not developed antibodies to resist it.

The teaching ministry has always been an essential component of pastoral work. It has certainly not lost its importance in such times as these. More than ever, pastors need to devote themselves to "sound doctrine," to teaching Scripture and the knowledge of God. Pastors must think clearly about their

19. I served as interim pastor in a Baptist congregation in Texas where several prominent leaders in the church were caught up in the teachings of a "Christian rabbi" online who twisted the truth of Jesus's teaching, Paul's letters, and the book of Acts. They essentially were facing the very teachers Paul warned the Galatians about.

responsibility to teach and to engage a plan to develop those under their care. The church's well-being and our witness to the world depend on it.

CONCLUSIONS

The ancient prophet bore a responsibility to proclaim God's message to God's people, to summon them to repentance and obedience. The ancient priest carried the people on his shoulders and near his heart and bore the charge of teaching them God's law and God's ways. The pastor identifies with both of those traditions. God has called us to preach, to proclaim the good news of the kingdom of God, and to summon people to repent and believe the gospel (Mark 1:14–15). God has also entrusted us to care for the souls of the congregation by encouraging them and instructing them in God's ways. We have not fulfilled our teaching responsibility when church members can pass a Bible trivia quiz. When they begin to see the world as Jesus does, believe in the God Jesus believed in, value people the way Jesus values people, and know how to live conversationally with the God, in whose kingdom they now are citizens, we have done our job.

FOR FURTHER REFLECTION

1. Do you think that Dallas Willard's critique, exposing the church's "great omission" in obeying the Great Commission, is still valid? What about your congregation? Are people being taught how to follow Christ and to obey all the things he commanded?

2. How would you distinguish Samuel Proctor's description of the teaching role of the pastor from Dallas Willard's? How might they both describe essential aspects of the pastoral teaching role?

3. What advice or encouragement or correction do you think Samuel Proctor might give you concerning your approach to pastoral teaching? What about Dallas Willard?

4. How would you express your own "theology of teaching" as a pastor? What is your goal? How is that goal grounded in Scripture and Christian doctrine? What is the content that you have to teach? If you were to outline a "curriculum for Christlikeness," what would you include? What teaching methods are most effective in the context where you serve?

5. How dangerous do you think false teaching is to the church in the twenty-first century? What are some examples you have seen? How does a pastor teach to make the congregation less susceptible to deception by such modern heresies as the prosperity gospel or Christian nationalism?

PART FOUR

LEADERSHIP

Pastor as Servant

10

Pastoral Authority

Serving Something Larger

As a preacher of the gospel his authority is of another and a higher kind, in that he is an ambassador from the king, and speaks with an authority more than human.

—Edward Hiscox, *New Directory for Baptist Churches*

So if I, your Lord and Teacher, have washed your feet, you also ought to wash one another's feet. For I have set you an example, that you also should do as I have done to you.

—Jesus (John 13:14–15)

The scriptural foundations for understanding pastoral authority are more implicit than explicit. Biblical teachings about church leadership maintain a tension between authority and servanthood. Baptists wrestle with this tension as we attempt to connect the "this" of contemporary pastoral leadership to the "that" of the early church. Church leaders are "overseers" or "bishops" (*episkopoi*) (Acts 20:28; Phil. 1:1; 1 Tim. 3:1–7; Titus 1:5–9; 1 Pet. 5:1–5), implying a kind of supervisory role in the church; yet they are also "pastors" or "shepherds" (*poimenes*) (Acts 20:28; Eph. 4:11; 1 Pet. 5:1–5), implying a more caring and protective role. They are "elders" (*presbyteroi*), suggesting a ruling position (Acts 20:28; 1 Tim. 5:17; Titus 1:5); yet they are also "the Lord's servant[s]" (2 Tim. 2:24), implying a posture of gentleness toward the congregation. The writer of Hebrews charged readers to "obey" their leaders and "submit" to them (13:17); yet Jesus also taught that to exercise authority over those we lead is to wield power in a pagan manner (Mark 10:41–42). "It is not so among you," the Teacher said; "whoever wishes to become great among you must be your servant, and whoever wishes to be first among you must be slave of all" (Mark 10:43–44).

Biblical Foundations

To speak of authority is also to address the use of power. When one's "authority" arises from one's position of "power," a potentially dangerous situation is at hand. Like money, which when mixed with the sinful human heart often becomes an idol (Matt. 6:24; 1 Tim. 6:9–10), so also with power. Human beings' tendency to grasp power as a way of securing our lives rather than living in dependence on God has generated all sorts of evil in our history.[1]

So, at his baptism, Jesus hears the Voice from heaven speak: "You are my Son," an allusion to Psalms 2:7, a messianic psalm (Mark 1:11). This announcement affirms Jesus's eventual rule over all things. But the second part of the word that Jesus hears addresses the issue of power: "the Beloved; with you I am well pleased" (Mark 1:11b), echoing Isaiah 42:1:

> Here is my servant, whom I uphold,
>   my chosen, in whom my soul delights;
> I have put my spirit upon him;
>   he will bring forth justice to the nations.

This verse from Isaiah opens the first of four Servant Songs (42:1–4; 49:1–6; 50:4–7; 52:13–53:12). The fourth song (52:13–53:12) especially underscores the suffering experienced by the servant as in some way vicarious. We might paraphrase the message Jesus heard: "You are the Messiah, the Anointed One who will rule over the nations, but the route to your throne is through rejection and suffering as my servant."

---

1. Richard J. Foster argues that the three great issues of idolatry in human experience are money, sex, and power. Early monastic movements affirmed vows of poverty, chastity, and obedience as responses to those very temptations. He calls on Christians to learn to live in a disciplined manner in relation to these potentially good gifts of God. See *Money, Sex and Power: The Challenge of the Disciplined Life* (San Francisco: Harper & Row, 1985).

In the Synoptic Gospels, Jesus retreats to the Judean wilderness immediately after his baptism to spend forty days in solitude and silence (Matt. 4:1 // Mark 1:12–13 // Luke 4:1).[2] The close association of these two events in the Gospels implies that they are significantly related theologically. One way to understand the connection is to suppose that Jesus goes to the desert to wrestle with the meaning of what he has heard. How is it that the call to messiahship entails suffering? That was not the common Jewish understanding of the Messiah's experience, whose role was to overthrow the oppressors of God's people. The temptations narrated in Matthew and Luke imply that the evil one urged him to accept the first part of the message ("You are the Messiah") while avoiding the second part ("You are the suffering servant of the Lord"). Jesus's temptation was to accept the popular cultural understanding of messiahship, which would mean a throne (power) but no cross (suffering). Ultimately, he rejects this notion as satanic (Mark 8:31–33).

Henri Nouwen argues that in the wilderness Jesus faced the temptations to be relevant, to be spectacular, and to be powerful (Matt. 4:1–11 // Luke 4:1–13).[3] Satan offered him all the kingdoms of the world along with their glory and authority in exchange for Jesus's bowed knee (Matt. 4:8–9 // Luke 4:5–7). Jesus, however, refused the idolatry of political power, submitting his heart in worship only to God (Matt. 4:10 // Luke 4:8). God had destined him, as the Messiah, to rule over all the world's kingdoms (Ps. 2:7–9; Rev. 11:15), but the route to the throne was not raw political power. It was servanthood, suffering, and the cross.[4]

Jesus's teaching on leadership and authority consequently leaned heavily on a servant model. He understood his own role as the fulfillment of the suffering servant of the Lord whom Isaiah describes in the Servant Songs. Isaiah 52:13–53:12 was especially important to Jesus and the early church for interpreting Jesus's life and death and is frequently alluded to or cited by New Testament writers.[5] Jesus affirmed that he had not come among us

2. John's Gospel narrates neither Jesus's baptism nor the wilderness temptations. Raymond E. Brown notes, however, that Jesus faces the same temptations in the Fourth Gospel, but they are spread out in the story of his life. "Incidents That Are Units in the Synoptic Gospels but Dispersed in St John," *Catholic Biblical Quarterly* 23, no. 2 (April 1961): 152–55.

3. Henri J. M. Nouwen, *In the Name of Jesus: Reflections on Christian Leadership* (New York: Crossroad, 1992).

4. See Donald B. Kraybill's description of the political dimensions of Jesus's temptation to power in *The Upside-Down Kingdom*, 5th ed. (Harrisonburg, VA: Herald Press, 2011), 33–55.

5. Appendix 2 in the 26th edition of the Nestle-Aland *Novum Testamentum Graece* (Stuttgart: Deutsche Bibelgesellschaft, 1979) lists the following parallels: *Isa. 52:13* // John 3:14; Acts 3:13. *Isa. 52:15* // Matt. 13:16; Rom. 15:21; 1 Cor. 2:9. *Isa. 53:1* // John 12:38; Rom. 10:16. *Isa. 53:3* // Mark 9:12; Phil. 2:7. *Isa. 53:4* // Matt. 8:17; 1 John 3:5; 1 Pet. 2:24. *Isa. 53:5* // Rom. 4:25; 5:1; 1 Cor 15:3; 1 Pet. 2:24. *Isa. 53:6* // 1 Pet. 2:25. *Isa. 53:7* // Matt. 27:12; Mark 14:49,

to be served. Instead, he had come to serve and give his life for many (Mark 10:45). In John 10, Jesus, the Good Shepherd, speaks of laying down his life on behalf of his sheep (10:11–17). He declared to his disciples, "I am among you as one who serves" (Luke 22:27). Jesus's emphasis on servanthood was not a minor theme in his teaching (Matt. 20:20–28 // Mark 10:35–45; Matt. 23:8–12; Luke 9:48; 14:11; 18:14; 22:24–30). J. Nelson Kraybill writes,

> Jesus rejected the familiar power pyramid and patronage systems of his day: "The kings of the Gentiles lord it over them; and those in authority over them are called benefactors. But not so with you" (Luke 22:25–26). In other words, Jesus recognized that pagan society had a pyramid of power relationships, and he intended for his followers to avoid any striving for upward mobility. At banquets, where social position usually dictated seating position, Jesus instructed his followers to take the lowliest place at the table (Luke 14:7–11).[6]

Narry F. Santos has argued convincingly that the tension between authority and servanthood is a paradoxical theme central to Mark's Gospel.[7]

Most famously, Jesus demonstrated servant leadership at his last meal with his disciples when he washed their feet (John 13:1–11). After that parabolic act, Jesus questioned his followers about their understanding of the moment:[8]

> After he had washed their feet, had put on his robe, and had returned to the table, he said to them, "Do you know what I have done to you? You call me Teacher and Lord—and you are right, for that is what I am. So if I, your Lord and Teacher, have washed your feet, you also ought to wash one another's feet. For I have set you an example, that you also should do as I have done to you. Very truly, I tell you, servants are not greater than their master, nor are mes-

---

61; John 1:29; Acts 8:32–33; Rev. 5:6, 9. *Isa. 53:8* // 1 Cor. 15:3. *Isa. 53:9* // 1 Pet. 2:22; 1 John 3:5; Rev. 14:5. *Isa. 53:10* // Matt. 20:28; Mark 10:45. *Isa. 53:11* // Mark 14:24; Acts 3:13; Rom. 5:15, 19; Phil. 2:7; 1 John 3:5. *Isa. 53:12* // Matt. 12:29; 26:28; 27:38; Mark 15:27; Luke 11:22; 22:37; 23:34; Rom. 4:24; 1 Cor. 15:3; Heb. 9:28; 1 Pet. 2:24. See also Luke 24:25 as an allusion to all of Isa. 52:13–53:12.

6. J. Nelson Kraybill, "Power and Authority," in *The Heart of the Matter: Pastoral Ministry in Anabaptist Perspective*, ed. Erick Sawatzky (Telford, PA: Cascadia, 2004), 217.

7. Narry F. Santos, "The Paradox of Authority and Servanthood in the Gospel of Mark," *Bibliotheca Sacra* 154, no. 616 (October 1997): 452–60. See also his book-length study *Slave of All: The Paradox of Authority and Servanthood in the Gospel of Mark*, Journal for the Study of the New Testament Supplement Series 237 (London: Sheffield Academic, 2003).

8. The foot-washing episode is parabolic in the sense that Jesus is using the act to upend our understanding of power and authority. The "Teacher and Lord" performs an act of servanthood for those under his authority. The tendency of Jesus to turn our view of the world upside down is characteristic of his parables, which include not only his stories but also his deeds and his death on the cross. John Dominic Crossan calls Jesus "the parable of God." See *The Dark Interval: Towards a Theology of Story* (Sonoma, CA: Polebridge, 1994), 102.

sengers greater than the one who sent them. If you know these things, you are blessed if you do them." (John 13:12–17)

The image of Jesus as a servant profoundly shaped the early church's understanding of who he was and what he had done (Phil. 2:5–8; 1 Pet. 5:1–6).

Jesus delivered a direct commission to his disciples to carry on with his ministry. "All authority," said the risen Christ, "in heaven and on earth has been given to me. Go therefore and make disciples of all nations" (Matt. 28:18–19). He showed them his wounds while in the upper room and said, "As the Father has sent me, so I send you" (John 20:21). He breathed on them and said, "Receive the Holy Spirit" (John 20:22). He "authorized" them so that when they bore the message of the gospel and exercised leadership in the church, they did so not by their own authority but "in the name of Jesus Christ" (Acts 3:6).

The early church recognized their leaders' authority, but those leaders exercised their authority with care. Peter's confrontation of Ananias and Sapphira was an authoritative act (Acts 5:1–11), as was his engagement with Simon Magus (Acts 8:14–24). These examples reveal an apostle acting authoritatively, not to establish himself or his agenda, but to protect the church (cf. Paul's warning to the elders in Ephesus in Acts 20:25–31). We might understand the passages in Paul's letters that sound "authoritarian" in the same way (such as 1 Cor. 4:14–20; Gal. 1:6–10; 4:2–12). However, when Paul describes his relationship to the churches, he resorts to servant images (2 Cor. 4:1–15). Servant leaders are committed to a project larger than their personal agendas and are willing to do what is necessary to see it succeed. In the case of these first-century pastoral leaders, their dedication to the kingdom of God and the well-being of Christ's church emboldened them to exercise authority when needed.

Authoritative servant leadership takes various forms in the early church. The story in Acts demonstrates a decision-making act that delegates responsibility to others more appropriately placed to make decisions. For example, the apostles ask the Hellenistic Jewish Christians to determine whom they should charge with overseeing the ministry to their widows (Acts 6:1–7). The people most affected by the decision selected seven men they trusted to take on that responsibility. Apostolic authority did not translate into an authoritarian decision.

Sometimes leaders reach decisions by consulting with others. A conflict developed over admitting gentiles into the church who had not converted to Judaism. Some argued that they must receive circumcision to become Christians. Others declared that God accepted them because of their faith in Christ alone. In a decisive moment for the future of the church's witness to gentiles, James, the leader, listened to all sides of the matter and then offered his wisdom (Acts 15:13–20). With the whole church's approval, the apostles and the elders chose emissaries to go to Antioch, bearing the news of the decision the church had reached (Acts 15:21). The letter they delivered introduces the critical decision of the Jerusalem Council in these words: "For it has seemed good to the Holy Spirit and to us" (Acts 15:28). This event demonstrates the interplay of authorized servant leadership in the pastoral ministry of James, the apostles, and the elders of the Jerusalem church.

New Testament writers offer a few instructions to the church about responding to their leaders. Paul writes to the believers in Thessalonica with this exhortation: "But we appeal to you, brothers and sisters, to respect those who labor among you, and have charge of you in the Lord and admonish you; esteem them very highly in love because of their work. Be at peace among yourselves" (1 Thess. 5:12–13). Paul describes church leaders as "those who labor among you" and "have charge of you in the Lord." The verb translated "have charge of you" is *proistēmi* (literally, "to stand before"), a word that implies leadership, direction, or rule. Additionally, these leaders are responsible for "admonishing" (*noutheteō*) the believers, indicating authoritative instruction about conduct or behavior.

At the same time, Paul speaks of church leaders as those who "labor" or work hard among the disciples on Christ's behalf. The writer of Hebrews describes church leaders with the verb *hēgeomai*, which means to lead or guide, and encourages his readers to follow their example (Heb. 13:7). The words to the church are a bit stronger a few sentences later: "Obey your leaders and submit to them, for they are keeping watch over your souls and will give an account. Let them do this with joy and not with sighing—for that would be harmful to you" (Heb. 13:17).

"Obey" and "submit" indicate some degree of authority on the part of church leaders. But this authority does not originate from their personal power or position. These people are Christ's servants. They will answer to him for their work and the well-being of those in their charge. Paul also emphasizes church leaders' accountability in his letters (1 Cor. 3:5–14; 4:1–5). In the church, the leader's accountability to Christ tempers and guides the exercise of power and authority.

The "authority" that pastors wield is not dictatorial power but loving, sacrificial servanthood. The shepherd imagery speaks of both service and sacrifice, since "the good shepherd lays down his life for the sheep" (John 10:11). Jesus, "the great shepherd of the sheep," was also the sacrificial lamb who offered the "blood of the eternal covenant" (Heb. 13:20–21).

Authority to act "in Jesus's name" extends beyond the church's governance to acts of ministry as well. Peter and John minister to a lame man "in the name of Jesus" (Acts 3:6; cf. 3:16; 4:10). Similarly, Jesus authorized our pastoral ministry: "Feed my lambs. . . . Tend my sheep. . . . Feed my sheep" (John 21:15–17). The promised power of the Holy Spirit is for ministry (Acts 1:8), not for governance. Those who minister or lead "in Jesus's name" must reject the temptation to use their position as a way of exercising personal power.

Historical Bypaths

Over the centuries, Baptists have debated pastoral power and authority primarily around the meaning of ordination. The question at stake in that discussion is whether ordination bestows any specific spiritual authority for presiding over the ordinances or participating in the laying on of hands in an ordination service. Except for J. R. Graves and J. L. Dagg, Baptist theologians tended to support the congregation's authority to designate someone to preside over baptism and the Lord's Table. They understood that Christ authorized the church and that the church could authorize those to oversee the ordinances. The doctrine of the priesthood of all believers led many Baptists to allow for all to participate in laying hands on those they ordain to ministry.

The earliest Baptists understood that any authority vested in the pastor by ordination was derivative. As early as 1609, John Smyth and other Baptists affirmed that Christ had empowered the church to select its pastors.[9] Pastoral authority flows from Christ to the church and then, by ordination and calling, to the pastor.[10] Andrew Fuller made this same argument in the late eighteenth century.[11]

In the late nineteenth century, except for the Landmark movement, Baptists rejected the notion that the pastor "ruled" the church. They believed that ordination granted the authority to lead and serve but not to coerce.

9. R. L. Child cites John Smyth's "Paralleles, Censures, Observations": "For when the Church chooseth the minister, doth not the Church in effect say: 'We give thee, A.B., powre to administer the Word, seales of the Covenant, and censures in the behalf of the whole Church'? . . . The Minister-elect doth then actually possess and assume that powre delegated unto him by the Church." "Baptists and Ordination," *Baptist Quarterly* 14, no. 6 (1952): 249.

10. Isaac Watts wrote to the Marks Lane Church in 1702, "Though the pastor be named and chosen for this office by the people, yet his commission and power to administer all divine ordinances is not derived from the people, for they had not this power in themselves; but it proceeds from our Lord Jesus Christ who is the only King of this Church and the principal of all power; and he has appointed his Word that the call of his Church and solemn ordination shall be the means whereby his ministers are invested with this authority." Cited in Child, "Baptists and Ordination," 248–49.

11. Keith S. Grant, *Andrew Fuller and the Evangelical Renewal of Pastoral Theology*, Studies in Baptist History and Thought 36 (Milton Keynes, UK: Paternoster, 2013), 72.

The church body functioned as a democracy, and pastors were not free to arbitrarily impose their will on the congregation. Obedience to the pastor was entirely voluntary. Pastors, Baptists affirmed, had no authority "to lord it over God's heritage."[12] In what became a standard handbook for Baptist church life, Edward T. Hiscox wrote in 1894, "The pastor is to be loved, honored and obeyed, in the Lord. He is placed over the Church by both the Head of the body, and by the free and voluntary act of the body itself. Though he professes no magisterial authority, and has no power, either spiritual or temporal, to enforce mandates or inflict penalties, yet the very position he occupies as teacher and leader supposes authority vested in him."[13] These words capture the tension of power and servanthood that a biblically founded pastoral ministry embraces.

B. H. Carroll recognized the need for a pastor both to exercise leadership in the church and to represent the servanthood that Christ commanded. He wrote,

> What the general is to the army the pastor is to the church. As the oriental shepherd goes before his sheep and leads them into green pastures, so the pastor goes before the people to lead them into green pastures of spiritual development. In Hebrews 13:7, 17, and 24, three times pastors are said to "have the rule over" the individual Christian, or over the church, the word "rule over" literally means "go before," then comes to mean "rule, command, have authority over"; also "control in counsel, lead in influence." In Hebrews 13:17, the apostle counsels, "Obey them that have the rule over you and submit yourselves." This is a plain statement declaring the pastor's authority over the church.[14]

Carroll tempered this strong expression of pastoral authority in the church with a warning against the pastor becoming a dictator. He said, "Not even ancient Rome would tolerate dictators, or modern Russians. The Czar has to live under guard much of his time. The pastor is not the head of a monarchy but a spiritual republic." Carroll encouraged pastors to "rule in love" and to "lead in service."[15]

In the last half of the twentieth century, the tension between pastor as leader and pastor as servant grew as church leadership increasingly reflected

12. G. Thomas Halbrooks, "The Meaning and Significance of Ordination among Southern Baptists, 1845–1945," *Baptist History and Heritage* 23, no. 3 (July 1988): 28–29.

13. Edward T. Hiscox, *The New Directory for Baptist Churches* (Philadelphia: Judson, 1894), 100–101.

14. B. H. Carroll, "The Twentieth-Century Pastor; or, Lectures on Pastoral Theology," *Southwestern Journal of Theology* 58, no. 2 (2016): 216.

15. Carroll, "Twentieth-Century Pastor," 218.

business models. Baptists writing about pastoral ministry struggled to keep a biblical balance. Franklin M. Segler averred, "The essential nature of the ministry is service (*diakonia*)."[16] He emphasized that "the idea of an authoritarian ministry is foreign to the principles of evangelical Christianity."[17] Yet Segler acknowledged the "necessity" of leadership that the pastor must exercise. The authority behind such leadership is primarily that of influence, not raw power.[18] Returning to the arguments of the earliest Baptists about the derivative nature of pastoral authority, Segler wrote,

> Authority of office grows out of the responsibility of office. It is not an ecclesiastical authority or an assumed authority, but a given authority. Acknowledged as necessary, it is given by the congregation. The pastor's divine call to the ministry, the gifts he has received from God, and the church's call to the pastor to serve in a specific office of leadership all combine to imply that certain prerogatives and acknowledged authority go with the office. But this is not a personal authority. Christ is the authority, and the ministry is performed in his name. The ministry is entirely a ministry of Christ performed by his servants.[19]

Baptist pastoral theologians urged that an affirmation of the priesthood of all believers and the servanthood of Christ temper the pastor's authority.

The tension between the poles of servanthood and authority or pastoral authority and believers' priesthood can result in either a disempowered, anemic pastoral leadership or a religious dictatorship. Loren Johns addresses the danger of surrendering legitimate pastoral leadership authority by adopting a purely functional view of the ordained ministry. He says that such an argument results in "a disempowered pastorate, ineffective leadership, and the prospect of a church adrift without authority vested in designated leaders." He asks, "How many times has the church, in the name of the priesthood of all believers or of the diverse giftedness of the Spirit, actually succeeded in disempowering its leadership?"[20] On the other hand, religious dictatorships have become a familiar aspect of the twenty-first-century Baptist landscape.

The tension manifested itself in 1988 among Southern Baptists meeting for their annual convention in San Antonio, Texas, at the height of a

---

16. Franklin M. Segler, *A Theology of Church and Ministry: The Christian Pastor; His Call, His Life, His Work in and through the Church* (Nashville: Broadman, 1960), 57.

17. Segler, *Theology of Church and Ministry*, 59.

18. C. W. Brister, *Pastoral Care in the Church* (New York: Harper & Row, 1964), 61–62.

19. Segler, *Theology of Church and Ministry*, 73.

20. Loren L. Johns, introduction to Sawatzky, *Heart of the Matter*, 3.

denominational controversy between fundamentalist and moderate Baptists. That body approved a controversial resolution on the priesthood of the believer. Moderate Baptists had been making much of that doctrine to affirm the freedom to read Scripture apart from prescribed interpretations. Some left the impression that the principle meant one could believe whatever one wanted as a Baptist. The resolution was a conservative reaction to such a claim and offered in its place a strong statement on pastoral authority.[21] The resolution expressed the position of only those messengers who affirmed it at that specific convention and was binding on no one. Nevertheless, it demonstrated the tension that Baptists have felt over pastoral authority almost from the beginning of the movement, a tension that continues to exercise an influence over our practice and thought.

The following year (1989), American Baptist Churches USA issued a policy on the ordained ministry, addressing pastoral leadership and authority. The American Baptist Churches USA represents a more moderate expression of Baptist life, and its approach to religious authority displays a more nuanced view of the polar tension than the Southern Baptist Convention resolution. This statement leaned toward the servanthood aspects of pastoral leadership. In part it reads, "In recognizing and calling men and women to ordained ministry, the church exercises its authority to order its life and mission under God. It then recognizes in those it ordains an entrusted authority to instruct, guide, comfort, and challenge in the name of the gospel. The authority ascribed to ordained ministers is not to be exercised as power over others. It is not authority over the church but in the church."[22]

Baptist opinions on pastoral authority have ranged all along the spectrum, from full authoritarian leadership to a merely functional role among equals. However, above the sometimes noisy discussion, we can hear overtones of the Baptist vision: "this is that." Stanley Grenz writes, "Baptist responses to what they perceive as significant questions of polity are the result of an attempt to hear and be obedient to the voice of the Lord of the church as he speaks in the New Testament."[23] Baptists are unlikely to unanimously resolve this dilemma, but the tension will continue to drive them to the Scriptures for their answers.

21. For the text of the resolution, see chap. 3 above, note 58.

22. American Baptist Churches USA, "American Baptist Policy Statement on Ordained Ministry," adopted December 1989, modified September 1992, 1997, 2002, https://www.abc-usa.org/wp-content/uploads/2019/02/ordain.pdf.

23. Stanley J. Grenz, *The Baptist Congregation: A Guide to Baptist Belief and Practice* (Valley Forge, PA: Judson, 1985), 10.

Theological Reflection

What Is Pastoral Authority?

The issue of authority touches at least three dimensions of pastoral ministry. First, it raises the question of the authority that ordination confers to preside over the celebration of baptism and the Lord's Table and to participate in the laying on of hands in an ordination service. Early on, Baptists differentiated their congregational polity from the hierarchical model of Roman Catholicism, Anglicanism, and Lutheranism. As they worked on defining their governance, they faced the question of the extent of pastoral authority.

Second, pastoral authority addresses the issue of the representational nature of the ministry. Ordination authorizes pastors to a ministry in which we represent Jesus Christ and his church, not ourselves.[24] Such authority shows up in acts of ministry: in the pulpit, in weddings, in hospital rooms, in pastoral conversations. These are acts performed in the name of Jesus, to whom God has given all authority in heaven and earth (Matt. 28:18–20; Acts 3:6–7; 4:8–10). In this sense, acting with pastoral authority refers to accepting the authorization that Christ and the church have given us as their representatives in the world. When we enter a hospital room where death is near and a family huddles in fear and grief, we do so not in our own name, representing ourselves, but in Jesus's name. Regardless of how young or old we are, how experienced or inexperienced in ministry, we step into those moments as pastors with authority that is not our own. Accepting this sense of pastoral authority is necessary if we are to serve effectively. Baptist pastoral theologians such as Franklin Segler, C. W. Brister, and Wayne Oates have addressed this dimension of our authority.

The third aspect of pastoral authority came to the fore during the latter half of the twentieth century: What power and authority do pastors hold in leadership roles and responsibilities? Baptists had not paid much attention to this question in the past. In our culture, we associate this kind of authority with power, the ability to have one's way as a leader. Perhaps the church growth movement, which demonstrated an openness to learn management and leadership techniques from the business world, "plundering the Egyptians,"

---

24. Wayne E. Oates writes, "The symbolic strength of your role gives a weight far beyond that of your own personal appeal to people. Paul described it well when he said, 'We are ambassadors for Christ, God making his appeal through us' (II Cor. 5:20). You represent and symbolize far more than yourself. You represent God the Father; you serve as a reminder of Jesus Christ; you follow the leading of the Holy Spirit; you are an emissary of a specific church; and you activate the caricatures of the Christian faith to those who are hostile, suspicious, and/or detached from the Christian faith." *The Christian Pastor*, rev. ed. (Philadelphia: Westminster, 1982), 65; see also 69–95.

stirred this approach to pastoral authority. Is the pastor the CEO of the congregation? What areas of control does the pastor exercise when it comes to "ruling" the church or "overseeing" its life? What accountability does the pastor have to the congregation? This understanding of the pastor's authority exists in tension with our confession of the priesthood of all believers and Jesus's clear teaching on servanthood as a model of leadership.

The challenge with this aspect of authority is finding the appropriate balance in one's specific context. How do pastors lead fellow believers who are, in all ways that matter, their equals? How do they move the church forward while honoring the teaching of Jesus regarding servanthood? How do they avoid both the passivity and the authoritarianism that can damage their congregations? How do they take the initiative and yet maintain accountability to their congregations?

The Nature of Pastoral Authority

In Baptist church life, pastors derive three aspects of authority from the congregation: presiding over the ordinances, representing Christ and the church, and leading the church. Christ authorized the church to serve in his name, and the church chooses and ordains its pastors to act on its behalf. God grants the pastor no autonomous power. Instead, pastors receive authority as a stewardship from the church and from Christ who called them to serve. Authority to lead accrues to the pastor in several practical ways, which blend differently with a given pastor and congregation.

Positional authority is present simply because of the office one occupies. The leaders may or may not possess the competence, character, or abilities to fill the office, but they nevertheless have the power to impose their will on the organization they lead. Increasingly for clergy, the respect, trust, and authority once accorded their position has eroded in our culture.[25] Consequently, positional authority alone will seldom produce effective pastoral leadership. More is required.

Authority can accrue because of the respect others hold for one's expertise in an area. To be "an authority" in a field means that reasonable people listen to what one has to say. Seminary training and ministry experience lend a degree of authority to pastors as they address biblical interpretation, theological issues, and church life. Wise pastors are aware of where their expertise ends and when it is necessary to yield to others in the congregation whose expert authority may supersede their own.

25. Brister, *Pastoral Care in the Church*, 60.

Charismatic authority refers not to the Holy Spirit's gifts but to the sociological category of leadership delineated by Max Weber. Charismatic leaders are frequently highly skilled communicators who are capable of stirring people emotionally. Their magnetic personalities attract people to their vision and often elicit deep devotion. Like those who exercise positional authority, charismatic leaders may or may not possess the character and competence required to lead, but their emotional influence over people can make it possible for them to realize their own will in the organization's life. Pastoral leaders who possess such charismatic charm must carefully cultivate their characters and develop the competencies required to lead effectively. Charismatic pastors will often be tempted to depend on their personalities alone, which is not sustainable.

A final aspect of pastoral authority is relational. Pastors accrue this power as they come to be trusted and respected over time. Relational authority contains a moral component. It assumes that the pastor possesses a depth of Christian character that is worthy of trust. As the pastor offers genuine care during crises, faithful preaching week by week, and genuine affection for God and the church, relational power increases. This kind of authority is not manipulative, but it is influential.

In rural Texas, it is common to see a rancher driving a truck through the pasture. Often a long line of cattle follows the vehicle because they are accustomed to being fed when the pickup appears in the field. Jesus's words about the Good Shepherd come to mind: "My sheep hear my voice. I know them, and they follow me" (John 10:27). Pastors who work faithfully among their flock, feeding and caring for them, will find that flock more willing to follow as they lead. Brister observes,

> If a minister cannot claim special power and privilege above any other Christian, wherein does his authority of office lie? Acknowledging God's ultimate authority, the minister offers to men, not simply a set of authoritative spiritual facts, but himself in a relationship which embodies both spirit and intent of the Christian gospel. The minister's authority, humanly speaking, is acknowledged as he demonstrates his authenticity as a Christian person and pastor. He is accepted as a Christian minister to the extent that he both perceives man's spiritual plight and makes God known to him in his situation (Rom. 10:14–15). Those who bear in their bodies *the marks of the Lord Jesus* serve as living images of his love for men. The authentic minister, who can put others in touch with the living God, has authority both *in* and *beyond* himself.[26]

Relational authority works like that.

---

26. Brister, *Pastoral Care in the Church*, 61–62.

Servant Leadership

Jesus's teaching on servant leadership provides a model that merges these notions of power and authority into a consistent approach to pastoral ministry. To speak of Jesus's leadership approach as "servant leadership" does not imply that he was a mere doormat. Jesus humbly washed his disciples' feet once, but nothing indicates that he did so on any other occasion. At times, servant leadership required Jesus to harshly rebuke his disciple's behavior or words (Mark 8:14–21, 31–33). Such reprimands functioned in the same way as the foot washing: Jesus, the servant, was teaching and forming his disciples so that they might follow him more faithfully. Jesus did not diminish his authority over them as "Teacher and Lord" (John 13:13) by holding a towel and a basin.

Robert Greenleaf popularized the notion of servant leadership in the corporate world in the 1970s, implicitly drawing on Jesus's teaching. He defined the servant leader as one whose first inclination is to serve, not to lead.[27] Servant leaders offer themselves to something higher than themselves, and they devote their gifts, abilities, time, and effort to advancing that cause. If the congregation needs someone with leadership skills, then stepping up to take charge is an act of service. During a moment of crisis, that leadership may take on a more directive and authoritarian appearance. In calmer, more reflective times, the leader may spend more time listening than speaking. Regardless, the servant leader's commitment is to serve the church's needs, not to satisfy the pastor's ego. Max DePree asserts, "The first responsibility of a leader is to define reality. The last is to say thank you. In between the two, the leader must become a servant and a debtor. That sums up the progress of an artful leader."[28] In a faithful partnership between clergy leaders and congregational members, ministers owe their church a debt of service.

Servant leaders provide two vital elements necessary for congregational life: a missional focus and a clear vision.[29] The missional focus will manifest some concrete engagement with the Great Commission (Matt. 28:18–20) and the Great Commandments (Matt. 22:34–40). Servant leaders thoughtfully engage the entire congregation of believer-priests in exploring Scripture and thinking through their understanding of what it means to be the church. They keep that mission before the church as they worship weekly or perform the quotidian tasks of conducting church business.

27. Robert K. Greenleaf, *Servant Leadership: A Journey into the Nature of Legitimate Power and Greatness*, 25th anniv. ed. (New York: Paulist Press, 2002), 27.

28. Max DePree, *Leadership Is an Art* (New York: Crown Business, 2004), 11.

29. C. Gene Wilkes, "Servant Leadership: The Place to Begin," in *Pastor, Staff, and Congregational Relationships: Through Servant Leadership and Quality Administration*, ed. Bernard M. Spooner (Coppell, TX: CreateSpace, 2014), 23–26.

Such a missional focus creates a more faithful ministry because it keeps both the pastor and the congregation from diverting their attention away from the church's central calling. Although the pastor may not be the only one who defines the mission, the pastor as a servant leader is responsible for seeing that the church identifies its missional focus and keeps it at the center of the church's life.

Similarly, the servant leader assumes responsibility for engaging the congregation in conversation about its future. Leadership is inherently about the future, and a leader, like a midwife, assists the church in giving birth to it. "Vision" may be understood as the preferred future that the congregation comes to believe God is offering them. Such a vision is not usually given to the pastor on a mountain, to be brought down to the church waiting passively in the valley. Instead, the pastor leads the congregation to discern a shared vision under the Holy Spirit's leadership. Such a dream, as it becomes clear, provides direction, guidance, and hope.

In the absence of a clear vision, a church's life can erode into conflicting agendas, stale traditionalism, or mere religious shopkeeping (Prov. 29:18). Clear vision supplies the hope and future orientation that sustainable, faithful ministry requires. Achieving clarity of vision and keeping that vision before the congregation is part of the debt that the servant leader owes.

Servant leadership can balance the equation between pastoral authority and the priesthood of all believers. It can offer a way of traversing the dangerous territory of seductions to abuse power or people while pursuing one's agenda. The servant leader faces and overcomes the wilderness temptations to be powerful, relevant, or spectacular.

CONCLUSIONS

Authority rooted in power to impose one's will on others without accountability is inherently dangerous and destructive. British historian Lord Acton famously said, "Power tends to corrupt; absolute power corrupts absolutely." The observation seems to be as accurate in ministry as it is in politics. Jesus understood that the unredeemed human heart is inherently idolatrous. Therefore he warned against power just as he cautioned against riches. The antidote to power's capacity to corrupt is the kind of leadership authority that Jesus himself demonstrated as a servant. "Let the same mind be in you that was in Christ Jesus," Paul says (Phil. 2:5).

Focusing on serving a purpose higher than a private agenda can mitigate the intoxicating effect of a leader's power. Although Baptists have understood that leaders require the authority to carry out responsibilities, we have also recognized that they derive such power from the church and Christ. The pastor does not inherently possess authority due to a divine call or the laying on of hands. We have also understood that pastors must exercise their power with appropriate accountability. Churches that neglect or forget these guardrails often suffer at the hands of spiritual dictators. They also often become clergy dependent. If they have not learned to take responsibility for the church's vision or mission, a pastor's departure may hinder them. They wander or become paralyzed, like sheep without a shepherd.

However, either out of fear or out of their desire for power, individual church members, deacon boards, or committees sometimes disempower their pastors so that they find it impossible to lead. The biblical model, the "that" corresponding to the "this" of contemporary church life, is servant leadership marked by affection for God and for the church that is affirmed by congregational respect and trust. Such leadership is nearly always a work in progress in a congregation as flawed pastors authentically seek to lead flawed church members in their mutual desire to be the faithful people of God.

FOR FURTHER REFLECTION

1. What biblical material would you include in seeking to understand the role of pastoral authority in addition to that contained in this chapter?

2. How have you balanced the equation of pastoral authority and the priesthood of all believers in your thinking? Which do you think is most being neglected in Baptist churches these days?

3. What part do church members play in allowing extreme power to accrue to the pastor or church staff? What benefit do church members gain from this exchange? How would you explain the relationship between a high degree of pastoral power and a low degree of congregational responsibility?

4. How would you define servant leadership? Where have you seen that lived out by pastors?

5. Which areas of church life would you say require a pastor to have a high degree of authority? In which areas do you think the pastor's power should be more circumscribed? Why?

11

The Equipping Leader

Sharing Ministry

The call to salvation and the call to the ministry is one and the same call.

—Findley Edge, *The Greening of the Church*

I therefore, the prisoner in the Lord, beg you to lead a life worthy of the calling to which you have been called.

—Paul (Eph. 4:1)

The title "pastor" as a reference to a church leader occurs in only one passage in the New Testament, in which Paul explicitly assigns the task of "equip[ping] the saints for the work of ministry" (Eph. 4:11–12). This pastoral responsibility involves sharing the ministry with the congregation and preparing them to serve Christ in the world and the church. How have Baptists understood and practiced this specified pastoral leadership role over time? How have we articulated our understanding of the role of the laity in the church and the world? This chapter focuses on a distinctively Baptist perspective on this aspect of pastoral ministry: how Baptist pastors have described and fulfilled their role of equipping the saints for ministry in Jesus's name.[1]

Biblical Foundations

The ministry of the laity is a doctrine rooted in ecclesiology and the priesthood of all believers. Biblically, 1 Peter 2:9–10 is the foundational text:

> But you are a chosen race, a royal priesthood, a holy nation, God's own people, in order that you may proclaim the mighty acts of him who called you out of darkness into his marvelous light.
>
>> Once you were not a people,
>>> but now you are God's people;
>> once you had not received mercy,
>>> but now you have received mercy.

Peter's words echo crucial Old Testament texts: Exodus 19:5–6 and Hosea 1:6–8 and 2:23.

In Exodus 19:5–6 the Lord tells Moses to announce to his people: "Now therefore, if you obey my voice and keep my covenant, you shall be my treasured possession out of all the peoples. Indeed, the whole earth is mine, but you shall be for me a priestly kingdom and a holy nation." These words form a covenant in which God will say of Israel from this point on, "My people"; and Israel will say, "My God." That language recurs throughout the Hebrew Scriptures.[2]

For Peter to cite this text and apply its language to gentile believers is scandalous. He had struggled to accept the reality that God was welcoming gentiles into the church (Acts 10–11, 15). However, here he boldly claims that the people of God, true Israel, comprise both Jew and gentile. His readers are part of God's people, a royal priesthood, a holy nation. Those who once were, like Israel in the eighth century BC, not a people (Hosea 1:9) are now

---

1. Findley Bartow Edge did more to establish a biblical and theological foundation for the doctrine of the laity and equipping ministry than any other Baptist during the lay renewal movement of the 1960s and 1970s. See his books *The Greening of the Church* (Waco: Word, 1971) and *The Doctrine of the Laity* (Nashville: Convention, 1993).

2. These expressions occur hundreds of times in the Old Testament. God speaks of "my people," and Israel refers to God as "my God" or "our God." Israel identifies itself in worship as "your people," and God says "your God." This is the essence of covenant language. So, when in Hosea 1:9 God says, "You are not my people and I am not your God," the covenant forged at Sinai between Yahweh and Israel is called into question.

the people of God (Hosea 2:23), having received the mercy of God (Hosea 2:1, 23).[3] Peter dubs the church of Jesus Christ "the people [*laos*] of God," assigning to it the cherished identity of Israel in the Old Testament.[4]

The "laity" are the people of God, occupying a privileged position that comes with a task. Peter calls the church to "proclaim the mighty acts of him who called you out of darkness into his marvelous light" (1 Pet. 2:9). He declares the entire church to be a company of royal priests. He charges the whole church with bearing witness in the world to God's power and goodness. The priesthood of all believers implies the gospel ministry of all believers. To be baptized into the people of God is to be ordained to that ministry. What, then, is the role of those who lead the people of God in this work? How do pastors fit into the picture?

In Ephesians 4:11–12 Paul defines church leaders' work with the "saints," God's holy people. Apostles, prophets, evangelists, and pastor-teachers are to "*equip* the saints for the work of ministry." The word "equipping" (*katartismos*) derives from the verb *katartizō*, which means "to cause to be in a condition to function well."[5] This act can involve restoring something to its former condition, as the mending of torn nets after a night of fishing (Mark 1:19), the changing of one's behavior (2 Cor. 13:11), the rehabilitating of a brother or sister who has gone astray (Gal. 6:1), or the healing of a church ravaged by persecution (1 Pet. 5:10). The word can also mean to prepare something for service by putting it into proper condition, as a trainer might prepare the body of an athlete. The faith of the believers may need shoring up (1 Thess. 3:10), as may their commitment to what is right and good (Heb. 13:21) or their sense of community (1 Cor 1:10). Outside the New Testament, the noun (*katartismos*) appears as a medical term describing the setting of a broken bone.[6] In Ephesians 4:12 the meaning is specified: saints need to be prepared for ministry in the world (*ergon diakonias*).

The punctuation of Ephesians 4:11–12 seriously affects the meaning of Paul's words. The King James Version understands 4:11–12 as a series of

---

3. This is one of many parallels between 1 Peter and Ephesians. See Eph. 2:11–3:6.

4. Our word "laity" derives from the Greek *laos*. Unfortunately, so does our word "lay," as in a layperson in the church. "Layperson" has come to denote someone untrained in some field, a nonprofessional, reinforcing the clergy-laity divide in the church. The clergy are the trained professional ministers, and laypersons are the untrained and, therefore, less qualified and less responsible ones who serve as "volunteers." This is not the intent of the use of "laity" and "lay" in this chapter, however. The laity *are* the people of God, the church.

5. Frederick W. Danker, Walter Bauer, William F. Arndt, and F. Wilbur Gingrich, *A Greek-English Lexicon of the New Testament and Other Early Christian Literature*, 3rd ed. (Chicago: University of Chicago Press, 2000), 526.

6. Danker et al., *Greek-English Lexicon*, 526.

parallel phrases and inserts a comma between them: "And he gave some, apostles; and some, prophets; and some, evangelists; and some, pastors and teachers; For the perfecting of the saints, for the work of the ministry, for the edifying of the body of Christ." By this interpretation, the offices listed in verse 11 (apostles, prophets, evangelists, pastors and teachers) serve three purposes: (1) perfecting the saints, (2) performing the work of ministry, and (3) edifying the body of Christ. Punctuation, however, was not part of the ancient Greek texts but is always supplied by translators. When the Anglican translators of the Authorized Version punctuated this text, they possibly reflected the clergy-laity distinction that still obtained in the Church of England in the early seventeenth century.

Contemporary translations remedy the issue.[7] The Greek text itself does not contain the simple parallelism implied by the KJV, describing three purposes of the offices listed. Instead, Paul offers a series of prepositional phrases that point toward the goal of these leaders. Christ gave these leaders to the church "for the equipping of the saints" (*pros ton katartismon tōn hagiōn*). The equipping takes place so that the saints, not merely the pastors, might engage "the work of ministry" (*eis ergon diakonias*). The saints' ministry "builds up" the church, "the body of Christ" (*eis oikodomēn tou sōmatos tou Christou*). In Ephesians 4:13–16 the fully developed body of Christ exhibits unity of faith, knowledge of Christ, spiritual maturity, Christlikeness, faithfulness to the truth, and love for one another. To this end, pastors equip believers. They do it to bring disciples of Jesus to a level of competence and maturity so that they may effectively serve the church and the world in the name of Jesus, contributing to the building up of the body of Christ.

An Old Testament precedent to the work of equipping occurs in the life of Moses. After God delivers Israel from Egypt, Moses brings them to camp before Mount Sinai. Exodus describes Moses's overwhelming task of serving

7. The NRSV and ESV translate Eph. 4:12 "to equip the saints for the work of ministry, for building up the body of Christ." The NASB (1995) translators render the verse "for the equipping of the saints for the work of service, to the building up of the body of Christ." The NIV reads "to equip his people for works of service, so that the body of Christ may be built up." Even the New King James Version makes that correction: "for the equipping of the saints for the work of ministry, for the edifying of the body of Christ." However, Andrew T. Lincoln argues *for* the comma in his commentary on Ephesians: "'for bringing the saints to completion, for the work of service, for the building up of the body of Christ.' Why does the exalted Christ give the apostles, the prophets, the evangelists, the pastors and teachers? Three reasons follow, each of which has a slightly different focus." *Ephesians*, Word Biblical Commentary 42 (Grand Rapids: Zondervan Academic, 2017), 252. Lincoln asserts his suspicion that the popular exegesis reflected in contemporary translations is "too often motivated by a zeal to avoid clericalism and to support a 'democratic' model of the Church" (253). He is in the minority with his reading of the text.

as a judge for the people, inquiring of God for them, or settling their disputes (Exod. 18:13, 15–16). Jethro, Moses's father-in-law, observes the situation and offers Moses wise advice: this work needs to be shared. He says, "What is this that you are doing for the people? Why do you sit alone, while all the people stand around you from morning until evening? . . . What you are doing is not good. You will surely wear yourself out, both you and these people with you. For the task is too heavy for you; you cannot do it alone" (Exod. 18:14, 17–18). Jethro advises Moses to distribute the work among competent people, leaving Moses to teach the people the ways of God and arbitrate only the most challenging cases (Exod. 18:19–23). Moses accepts Jethro's advice in the matter (Exod. 18:24–27). Later in the story, when Moses faces the monumental task of building the tabernacle in the wilderness, he follows a similar strategy. He finds artisans, such as Bezalel and Oholiab, who have skills he does not possess to take on many construction tasks (Exod. 31:1–10; 38:21–23).

In the New Testament, Jesus engages the work of equipping in his ministry to his disciples. Although crowds follow him around Galilee listening to his teaching, he selects only twelve "to be with him, and to be sent out to proclaim the message, and to have authority to cast out demons" (Mark 3:14–15). Jesus proceeds to "equip them for the work of ministry." They accompany him as he serves (Mark 3:16–6:6), and he sends them out to replicate the works they saw him do (Mark 6:7–13), debriefing them when they return (Mark 6:30–31). His relationship with the Twelve focuses on preparing them for future service, so he directs much of his teaching not to people in general but to the Twelve. Even when he teaches in a public setting, he sometimes takes the Twelve aside to be sure they understand (Mark 4:33; 7:17–23; 8:14–21; 10:23–31). His ministry often serves a dual purpose, simultaneously meeting human needs and making the truth about the kingdom or himself more apparent to his disciples (Mark 6:30–44; 8:1–10; 9:28–29; John 2:11).

Jesus eventually leaves them, confidently entrusting the ministry of the kingdom into their hand, for he has equipped them to handle the responsibility. The book of Acts opens with the line, "In my former book, Theophilus, I wrote about all that Jesus *began* to do and to teach" (Acts 1:1 NIV). Luke implies that the following story narrates a ministry of Jesus Christ through the church, his body.[8] This ministry is by no means an extension of the incarnation, which remains a unique event. However, Jesus is acting in his people

---

8. Jason Ripley, "'Those Things That Jesus Had Begun to Do and Teach': Narrative Christology and Incarnational Ecclesiology in Acts," *Biblical Theology Bulletin* 44, no. 2 (May 2014): 87–99.

through the Holy Spirit.[9] Through the equipping of the Twelve, the messianic mission that Jesus initiated expanded exponentially.[10]

The Twelve continue the practice of equipping others to do the work of ministry. As the church grows in Jerusalem, part of the community feels neglected. Widows among the Greek-speaking Jewish Christians complain that the church is overlooking them in the distribution of food. When the Twelve hear of it, they wisely delegate the work rather than taking it on themselves. Echoing Jethro's advice to Moses, they urge the Hellenistic Jewish Christian community to select seven men of good character whom they trust to attend to the matter (Acts 6:1–3). The apostles will devote themselves to the work of prayer and teaching (Acts 6:4). This decision pleases the community, and they choose men to take charge of the ministry. This multiplication of leadership increases the effectiveness of the church's witness: "The word of God continued to spread; the number of the disciples increased greatly in Jerusalem, and a great many of the priests became obedient to the faith" (Acts 6:7).

Paul speaks of a similar process as he further equips Timothy for the work of ministry. He tells him, "You then, my child, be strong in the grace that is in Christ Jesus; and what you have heard from me through many witnesses entrust to faithful people who will be able to teach others as well" (2 Tim. 2:1–2). The Pastoral Epistles themselves provide examples of Paul equipping leaders to equip others. As the pastor broadens the church's leadership base so that all the parts work together, the ministry expands and the church flourishes.

A biblical foundation for pastoral ministry as equipping ministry draws on Paul's teaching regarding the role of "spiritual gifts" (*pneumatika* or *charismata*) in the church's life. The Holy Spirit distributes these abilities among the congregation. These gifts allow the church to function as the body of Christ as the various parts work together (Rom. 12:3–8; 1 Cor. 12:1–14:39; Eph. 4:7–16). The Spirit has parceled out the ministry of the body of Christ among its "members." Equipping, then, involves helping people understand their giftedness, providing them opportunities to exercise their gifts, and training them to exercise such gifts in humility and love for the body's sake (1 Cor. 13:1–14:1). Like the skills of Bezalel and Oholiab in constructing the tabernacle, the gifts of God's people must be called on and refined to serve the work of building the church, the body of Christ.

9. See chap. 3 above, note 11, on the distinction between Christ's ministry and his work through the church.

10. Two older studies trace Jesus's work in equipping the Twelve. See Alexander Balmain Bruce, *The Training of the Twelve: Or, Passages out of the Gospels, Exhibiting the Twelve Disciples of Jesus under Discipline for the Apostleship*, 5th ed. (Edinburgh: T&T Clark, 1898); and Robert E. Coleman, *The Master Plan of Evangelism* (Old Tappan, NJ: Revell, 1970).

Peter describes the church as Christ's royal priesthood, a holy nation (saints), God's own people. The people of God bear witness in this world to the mighty act of deliverance in Jesus Christ; their testimony is that they were called out of darkness into God's marvelous light. Christ has given gifted leaders to the church, such as apostles, prophets, evangelists, and pastor-teachers responsible for equipping God's people to accomplish that assignment effectively.

Historical Bypaths

From their beginnings, Baptists have focused on the importance of all believers following Christ in discipleship and ministry. Historian Franklin H. Littell, writing about the Radical Reformers, claims, "It has sometimes wrongly been said that the Anabaptists, Baptists, Quakers, Mennonites, Brethren and like groups have no true doctrine of ordination and frequently no clergy at all. A more perceptive oversimplification would be to say not that they have no *clergy* but that they have no *laity*."[11] Attempting to live into the Baptist vision, our ancestors saw the New Testament church as a movement with no clergy and laity classes. All believers are priests; all receive a call from Christ; all are saints. Desiring to follow the pattern they perceived in the New Testament, they often downplayed the clergy's role in the earliest days. They wanted the believers' church to express the first-century church's life: "this is that."

Baptist historian Bill J. Leonard has thoroughly traced the history of the tension between pastoral authority and the believers' priesthood.[12] Beginning with the early church, moving through the patristic and medieval periods and on through the Reformation into the modern era, he describes the ebb and flow of Baptist attention to the ministry of the laity. Leonard offers this overall summary:

> A general study of the role of the laity reflects the following developments: (1) The sense of unified ministry for the whole people of God in the New Testament and post-apostolic period; (2) The growing distinction between clergy and laity in the patristic era; (3) The rise of clerical authority and status in the Middle Ages; (4) Monastic and sectarian reassertion of lay ministry in the church; (5) The Reformation emphasis on vocation and the priesthood of the believer; (6) The rise of the Free Church tradition, democratic polity, and voluntary church

11. Franklin H. Littell, "The Radical Reformation," in *The Layman in Christian History*, ed. Hans-Reudi Weber and Stephen Neill (Philadelphia: Westminster, 1963), 263.

12. Bill J. Leonard, "Southern Baptists and the Laity," *Review & Expositor* 84, no. 4 (1987): 633–47. Notes document direct citations from Leonard's excellent article, but I will summarize the story he tells without further notes for that summary.

membership; (7) The growing trend toward ministerial professionalism in the modern church; (8) The reassertion of the role of the laity through lay renewal; (9) The growth of clerical authoritarianism among evangelical Protestants.[13]

This story includes other denominational traditions, of course, but we Baptists have been in the thick of it. Eileen Campbell-Reed observes the complexity of that tension between clergy (who have historically been male) and the laity (the majority of whom are often female), which is nearly always "overlaid and complexified by gendered struggles for power."[14]

We experience the tension between two necessary affirmations. On the one hand, we understand the church as the *laos tou theou*, the people of God, in which Christ calls everyone to obedience and service. On the other hand, we recognize that the church needs an official, ordained clergy authorized to carry out certain representational and ministerial functions. As late as the patristic period, the recognition of the laity as ministers still remained. Leonard says, "Clement acknowledged that all Christians have a priestly function in the church's worship. This 'ordination' to a royal priesthood was given to every believer by virtue of baptism. It was symbolized in the apostolic era (and later among seventeenth-century Baptists) by the laying on of hands. The rite was administered to all Christians at baptism and was a sign of the coming of the Holy Spirit."[15]

By the fifth and sixth centuries, the clergy-laity distinction was emerging more clearly. Controversies over heresies, authority, and church order arose in the rapidly expanding church, composed increasingly of believers of purely pagan backgrounds. In this context, the church evolved a complex hierarchy that culminated with the medieval papacy, making the clergy-laity split complete. The Reformers tried to undo the separation by emphasizing that all believers are priests who have access to Scripture and a duty to spread the gospel. Luther affirmed the equality of the calling of every Christian, whether a cobbler or a theology professor.

Anabaptists, the Radical Reformers, went further than Luther and emphasized the equality of all believers. Leonard reports, "The radicals sought to restore the New Testament church as a community of adult believers bound by covenant in faith, witness, and discipline. All believers were called to minister to the people of God. The radicals suggested that the distinction between

---

13. Leonard, "Southern Baptists and the Laity," 633, adapting and updating Howard Grimes's summary in *The Rebirth of the Laity* (Nashville: Abingdon, 1962), 42.

14. Eileen R. Campbell-Reed, "New Intersections in Baptist Studies," *Perspectives in Religious Studies* 44, no. 3 (2017): 285.

15. Leonard, "Southern Baptists and the Laity," 634.

clergy and laity undermined the nature of the church itself. It created a church organized around religious professionals. . . . This 'free church' tradition significantly influenced Baptist understanding of the church and the laity."[16] A focus on the laity's importance continued in early Baptist life, influenced by German Pietism in the seventeenth century. Early British Baptists shared the religious culture of the time with other groups that rejected "priestcraft," such as Quakers, Levellers, Seekers, and others. The atmosphere of egalitarianism among these groups was the air that early Baptists breathed as well.

Although Baptists ordained their leaders, they nevertheless continued to emphasize that God calls all believers to ministry. They understood that any authority held by the ordained derived from the church. Congregational rule found fertile soil in the New World, as democratic ideas were plentiful and an emphasis on the freedom of the individual conscience was growing. Baptists in America understood the church to be a voluntary community of believers that operated on democratic principles. A clergy class no longer dominated the laity. This perspective continued to flourish as Baptists moved across the frontier, where churches often did not have a resident pastor.

Southern Baptists experienced the tension between pastoral authority and the ministry of the laity throughout the twentieth century. Although lay leaders regularly played significant roles in local congregations, clergy filled most posts at the denominational level. In 1907 some Baptist laymen began the Layman's Missionary Movement to engage Baptist men in missionary efforts. They especially reached out to wealthy businessmen to provide financial support for missionaries. The laymen submitted a report to the Southern Baptist Convention meeting in 1909, revealing a deference to pastoral authority. The document affirmed that "the pastor is the divinely ordained leader of the church, and we would not seek to supplant him, but to supplement him."[17] This organization eventually became the Baptist Brotherhood and served as a defining feature of Southern Baptist churches.

Lacking a broader influence in denominational leadership, Baptist women invested themselves in the Women's Missionary Union (WMU). They were not allowed to vote or speak at Southern Baptist Convention meetings, and for the first twenty years of the Convention meetings, women who attended were seated in balconies. Nevertheless, the WMU provided missionary leadership in local churches and the denomination. They raised funds and offered missionary education to the entire church, especially women and girls. However, Leonard notes that creating such a sphere of influence for women in the

16. Leonard, "Southern Baptists and the Laity," 635.
17. Leonard, "Southern Baptists and the Laity," 641.

churches and denomination was one way of excluding them from full access to other leadership positions, both lay and clerical.[18]

In the 1960s and 1970s, a lay renewal movement arose among evangelicals and some mainline denominations. Many Baptists joined the chorus, calling for a rediscovery of the laity as partners with pastors in ministry work in the world. The laity was encouraged to reaffirm its calling as priests and ministers. The Baptist pastor Carlyle Marney called the effort "an *anti-preacher* movement" and warned that the clergy were unlikely to surrender their powers. He wrote at the time, "Our answer is not a 'servanthood of the laity' as a nice addition to round out a hired professional staff; instead, what we are trying to say here is that the lay people must become *the ministry of the church in the world*. It *is* yours! This forces us to re-define everything! It is not that you as laymen are to pitch in and help out; it's that you are the only hope we have, and this forces us to re-define everything! This is ministry."[19] The movement's goal was to equip the laity to be more than good church members and faithful attendees. Laypeople were learning to practice their faith in the world where they lived and worked.

The expected equal and opposite reaction to emphasizing the laity's importance emerged among Southern Baptists in the mid-1970s as the Conservative Resurgence movement. Leonard refers to it as the "clergification" of the Southern Baptist Convention.[20] Ordained professionals dominated roles in the churches and denomination. Additionally, churches began to ordain ministers to multiple ministries once led primarily by laypeople. Clergy in large churches with numerous programs designed by "professionals" increasingly treated laypeople as clients or customers. "Church shopping" became a reality as people compared congregations in their area, looking for the right fit, worship style, or programs to satisfy their preferences. The laity began to view clergy as hired professional ministers. American consumerism infected church culture, eroding any sense the laity might have once had of being the people of God ordained to serve the world.

Beginning in the mid-1970s, a model for pastoral ministry surfaced among Baptists that emphasizes the authority of the pastoral office.[21] The pastor is the one authority in congregational life, representing Christ to the congregation

18. Leonard, "Southern Baptists and the Laity," 642.

19. Carlyle Marney, *Priests to Each Other* (Macon, GA: Smyth & Helwys, 2014), xv. This book was originally published in 1974 during the lay renewal movement.

20. Leonard, "Southern Baptists and the Laity," 644.

21. In 1988 Southern Baptists passed a resolution on the priesthood of the believer, downplaying an emphasis on that doctrine as "a recent historical development" that was "undermining . . . pastoral authority in the local church." See chap. 3 above, note 58.

and accountable only to God. Finances, personnel, programs, and spiritual matters all fall under the pastor's authority. This more autocratic model proved more efficient in producing numerical growth in congregations. Borrowed from the business world, the CEO model has taken a firm hold in many Baptist churches. In this model, the congregation submits to the guidance, spiritual and otherwise, of the authoritative pastor. Leonard opines that, despite the apparent "success" of the model, "the phenomenon requires serious evaluation in light of historic Baptist understanding of the ministerial vocation of all Christians, the priesthood of believers, and the ultimate authority of the congregation."[22]

Theological Reflection

The Doctrine of the Laity

Attending to almost any dimension of pastoral ministry leads us back to the critical Baptist principle of the believers' priesthood. The reason is apparent: pastoral ministry is essentially relational, and the laity are the ones on the other side of that relationship. We cannot be clear about who pastors are and what God has called us to be and to do without insight into what God has called the church we serve to be and to do. The biblical testimony points to a distinctive role for followers of Jesus as part of his church. We are together, clergy and laity, "the people [*laos*] of God." God's call to ancient Israel was an invitation to bear witness in the world to God's goodness. God designated them to be a "treasured possession" out of all the nations, who also belonged to God and who were the objects of divine love (Exod. 19:5). Israel was to be a "priestly kingdom," mediating the truth of God to the other nations. Like their ancestor Abraham, God blessed them to make them a blessing to the nations of the earth (Gen. 12:1–3). Later, Isaiah would designate them as "witnesses" to God's power, goodness, and truth (Isa. 43:10, 12; 44:8). Israel's faithlessness in carrying out this redemptive mission became their downfall (Jon. 1–4; Mark 12:1–12).

The New Testament makes clear that the appearance of the Messiah and the inauguration of the kingdom of God redefined "the people of God." All who place their faith in Jesus the Christ are part of God's kingdom and the people who proclaim the redemptive message (2 Cor. 5:17–20; 1 Pet. 2:9–10). The "Israel of God" is no longer composed of those with Abraham's blood in their veins but of those with Abraham's faith in their hearts (Rom. 4:1–24;

22. Leonard, "Southern Baptists and the Laity," 645.

Gal. 3:6–9; 6:16). God has grafted gentiles into the olive tree of God's people on the basis of their faith, not starting over but continuing the redemptive mission begun with Abraham and continued with the covenant at Sinai (Rom. 11:13–24).

Moses sprinkled sacrificial blood over the people of Israel at Sinai and ratified God's covenant with Israel, saying, "See the blood of the covenant that the LORD has made with you in accordance with all these words" (Exod. 24:8). Similarly, Jesus shared a cup with his disciples in the upper room and said, "This is my blood of the covenant, which is poured out for many" (Mark 14:24). This moment echoed Exodus 24:1–8 and was foreshadowed in Jeremiah 31:31–34, in which God promised a "new covenant" to replace the one Israel had broken:

> The days are surely coming, says the LORD, when I will make a new covenant with the house of Israel and the house of Judah. It will not be like the covenant that I made with their ancestors when I took them by the hand to bring them out of the land of Egypt—a covenant that they broke, though I was their husband, says the LORD. But this is the covenant that I will make with the house of Israel after those days, says the LORD: I will put my law within them, and I will write it on their hearts; and I will be their God, and they shall be my people. No longer shall they teach one another, or say to each other, "Know the LORD," for they shall all know me, from the least of them to the greatest, says the LORD; for I will forgive their iniquity, and remember their sin no more.

The writer of Hebrews connects the "this" of Jesus's sacrifice to the "that" of Jeremiah's promise (Heb. 8:6–13; 9:15; 10:16–17; 12:24; 13:20).

This renewed people of God, inclusive of all who place their faith in Jesus the Messiah, both Jew and gentile, continues the mission God assigned to ancient Israel at Mount Sinai. They are "a chosen race, a royal priesthood, a holy nation, God's own people" (1 Pet. 2:9). Their task is to "proclaim the mighty acts of him who called you out of darkness into his marvelous light" (1 Pet. 2:9). As with ancient Israel, God subpoenas them as "witnesses" to the divine grace, goodness, and power (Acts 1:8; Isa. 43:10, 12; 44:8).

God's plan is just this: the ministry does not belong to a handful of professional ordained church leaders but belongs to all God's people, the *laos*, the laity. This concept is widely ignored in a church increasingly characterized by consumer Christianity. As consumers, we are interested in having our needs met. Evangelical Christians have adapted the message of the gospel to that perspective over the past century or more: "You have a need. You are a sinner. You will perish eternally. Jesus died to meet that need. Pray this prayer and accept Jesus, and you'll go to heaven when you die." When people accept that message, we must then convince them to be baptized and become part of a church. We tell them how it will meet their needs. When some join a church, we try to motivate them to invest their time, talents, and treasures sacrificially in God's work in the world. We need to persuade them that it is in their interest to do so. This is exhausting.

The gospel that Jesus preached said nothing about accepting him into one's heart. Instead, it was an announcement that the kingdom of God was dawning. He called for people to change their hearts and minds and align their lives with that reality (Mark 1:14). He invited people not just to pray a prayer but to follow him (Mark 1:17; 2:14; 10:21). Jesus enjoined those who followed him to take up a cross, to live sacrificially for the sake of the kingdom (Mark 8:34). This gospel reverses the order of the consumer gospel, beginning with God's purposes, not human need. It declares that God is doing something globally: "the kingdom of God is at hand." Jesus invites us into that kingdom to participate with him in this new people through whom God is working in the world toward full reconciliation (2 Cor. 5:17–20). When we say yes to that invitation, we also receive the forgiveness that is part of the new covenant (Jer. 31:34) and the promise of eternal life (Jer. 31:34; John 3:15–17; 17:1–3). This gospel starts not with our needs but with God's work. God invites us not simply to have our own needs met but to enter the kingdom of God, to submit to God's reign through Christ, and to participate in God's work in the world.[23] This calling belongs to all God's people. The pastors' task is to make that truth clear as we "equip the saints for the work of ministry."

The Ministry of All Believers

Greg Ogden has argued that although the first Reformation returned the Word of God to the people of God, a second Reformation is needed to restore the work of God to them.[24] Ogden is not the first to make such an argument. Theologians and pastors have raised their voices since the 1960s and 1970s.[25]

23. See Donald B. Kraybill, *The Upside-Down Kingdom*, 5th ed. (Harrisonburg, VA: Herald Press, 2011); Scot McKnight, *The King Jesus Gospel: The Original Good News Revisited* (Grand Rapids: Zondervan, 2011); Dallas Willard, *The Divine Conspiracy: Rediscovering Our Hidden Life in God* (San Francisco: HarperSanFrancisco, 1998); N. T. Wright, *How God Became King: The Forgotten Story of the Gospels* (New York: HarperOne, 2012).

24. Greg Ogden, *Unfinished Business: Returning the Ministry to the People of God*, rev. ed. (Grand Rapids: Zondervan, 2003).

25. Keith Miller, *The Taste of New Wine* (Waco: Word, 1966); Elizabeth O'Conner, *Call to Commitment: The Story of the Church of the Saviour in Washington, D.C.* (New York: Harper & Row, 1963); D. Elton Trueblood, *The Company of the Committed: A Bold and Imaginative Re-thinking of the Strategy of the Church in Contemporary Life* (New York: Harper, 1961).

Some of those voices have been Baptist, such as Carlyle Marney and Findley Edge.[26] Such a call has gone out among evangelicals, and particularly among Baptists, for more than fifty years; yet the task of summoning the laity to effective ministry in the world remains, in Ogden's words, "unfinished business."

The connection between this concept and the Baptist principle of the believers' priesthood is obvious, but we have often ignored it. We have been content to affirm that our "royal priesthood" has given us privileges but have not quickly recognized the priesthood's responsibilities. Edge writes,

> In breaking with the sacramental and ecclesiastical view of the church, Baptists, in general, have interpreted this doctrine to mean only that every believer has free and direct access to God without the necessity of a priest as mediator. While this interpretation is certainly true, it is only half the meaning of this doctrine. What Baptists (and others of the Free Church tradition) have failed to understand adequately is that the priesthood of believers also teaches that every Christian is a priest or minister and thus has a ministry to perform.[27]

Rather than develop disciples who understand their call to ministry, we have produced good church members who support their church and its work. Good church members attend church regularly. They give financially. They accept responsible positions within the church. Many of them support their church faithfully for years. But enlisting believers to serve in one of the hundreds of jobs generated by a busy programmatic church is not necessarily the same as making disciples who exhibit the character of Christ or equipping saints for ministry in the world.

Professional ministers often view the laity as volunteers who support the pastor's ministry by their faithfulness. That understanding is the obverse of an equipping perspective. Equipping pastors view their task as supporting the ministry of the laity.

Some ministries of God's people rightly take place within the church's life, helping build it up. For example, someone who teaches a weekly Bible study for adults, students, or children may perform that role and still not see that as "their ministry." If they accepted the position out of guilt, pressure, or the professional minister's need to "fill a slot" in the organizational chart, their understanding of their service to the church might be flawed. On the other hand, if a pastor helps someone discover that they have a gift for teaching coupled with a heart for, say, children's spiritual formation, then the teacher's

---

26. Edge, *Greening of the Church*; Marney, *Priests to Each Other*.
27. Findley Bartow Edge, "Priesthood of Believers," *Review & Expositor* 60, no. 1 (January 1963): 9.

approach to the assignment begins to look more like their ministry. The pastor's task is not to fill a slot in the chart but to help people discover their gifts and passions, find ways to match people to places of service, and offer resources to enhance their work. The ministry of equipping looks like this.

The laity may decide not to exercise their gifts within the walls of the church building, however. That prospect can make professional pastors nervous. If people find ministry opportunities outside the church's organization, will we have enough volunteers to staff our programs? That is a risk one runs by practicing equipping ministry. Returning the work of the Lord to the people of God can be a messy business. When people hear their pastors call them to ministry in the world, discover that God has given them gifts for service, and open themselves to the Spirit's voice and the world's needs, they may find their ministry in prisons, women's shelters, or hospitals. They may spend their time serving the poor and homeless or participating in international ministries or disaster relief. Equipping pastors offer guidance, resources, prayer, and support as these ministers among us try their wings.

Our Story: Living Out a Theology of the Laity

When I was a Baptist seminary student in 1975, I first encountered the notion of equipping ministry. Since that time, a vision for this kind of pastoral ministry has captivated me.[28] I received no formal training for the task in my theological training, but I read and talked with friends motivated by a similar passion. I finished my theological training unequipped to carry out the work of equipping. However, in time, teachers, colleagues, and other resources crossed my path as I needed them.

After graduate school, I served as the pastor of a small inner-city church in Houston, Texas. I was doing my best as a novice pastor to keep up with weekly sermon preparation and the excessive number of funerals I had to officiate. I had no idea what it would mean to "equip" those dear senior adults for ministry in the world. Three years later, Houston Baptist University invited me to join the faculty as a New Testament professor. I was confident

---

28. My exposure to the concept of equipping ministry did not take place in the seminary classroom, where well-meaning professors were preparing us to run a programmatic Baptist church. Instead, I was introduced to the notion by a fellow student and friend, Randy Butler, who directed me to read Elton Trueblood. Randy left seminary after a year, convinced he could best live out the doctrine of the laity as a layperson. He has done that remarkably well for the past forty years, earning a law degree and developing the Institute for Sustainable Peace, a nonprofit organization that has addressed reconciliation in some of the most difficult settings in the world (https://sustainablepeace.org). Randy has done this as an active Christian layperson, a faithful member of his church who serves in the world in Christ's name.

that academia was where my calling lay, and I supposed I would spend the remainder of my life in a role like that. I was twenty-seven years old. The university setting provided opportunities for me to read, think, and theorize about pastoral ministry. I served as an interim pastor for several congregations and often wondered how I would engage equipping ministry in those places if I were the pastor.

Seven years later, the University Baptist Church in Houston (UBC) asked me to leave the university faculty and become their pastor. I was thirty-four years old and had never served as the pastor of a multi-staff congregation. My head was full of ideas about what congregational life could be like as an equipping pastor. In my interview with the search committee, I affirmed my untried theology of equipping, which they at least did not find objectionable. My first sermon was from 1 Peter 2:9–10, in which I laid out my theology of the laity. I preached my final sermon from that pulpit twenty-two years later, having done my best to put that theology into practice, and returned to the classroom to teach pastoral ministry at Baylor University's Truett Theological Seminary.

The equipping ministry at UBC did not spring to life immediately, but I laid foundations in teaching and preaching. We found resources in an organization called Leadership Network, which offered churches training in "lay mobilization," based on work done by Sue Mallory and her pastor at Brentwood Presbyterian Church in California.[29] We found lay leaders who were excited by the prospect of creating systems in our congregation that would help our members discover their spiritual gifts, explore possible areas of ministry, and connect to places of service in the church or the world. As we put those processes in place, we saw fruit borne in the followers of Christ who found profound fulfillment in their ministries, in the people who received the gospel of Christ and were changed by it, and in the church's reputation in the community as a people who cared.

I recall my first effort as an equipping pastor, which took place before we had developed any systems. Gwen Wolfe, a young Black woman, attended our Wednesday night Bible study for several months. One evening after the meeting, she called me aside and asked if our church had a prison ministry. I told her we did not. "Why not?" she asked. I saw this as an equipping opportunity. "Because," I said, "we don't have any prison ministers. Maybe you are the first."

---

29. Sue Mallory later simplified and published this material. See Sue Mallory, *The Equipping Church: Serving Together to Transform Lives* (Grand Rapids: Zondervan, 2001); and Sue Mallory and Brad Smith, *The Equipping Church Guidebook* (Grand Rapids: Zondervan, 2001).

I learned that Gwen's concern for prisoners grew out of her brother's incarceration at a facility about nine hours away in the Texas Panhandle. I put her in touch with a couple of prison ministries, but neither satisfied her longing. As we talked and prayed about her calling, Gwen reached a point of clarity. She told me that she wanted to organize a bus trip at Thanksgiving to take people from the Houston area to visit family members in that distant prison in Tulia, Texas. Gwen arranged transportation with a bus company and contacted the prison chaplain, who communicated with prisoners, who then passed the word to their families. She soon filled the bus for that trip. A church near the prison received the visitors, providing a meal and childcare, while mothers, fathers, sisters, sons, and daughters spent Thanksgiving together.

Meanwhile, Gwen faithfully bore witness to those she encountered in the project. When she returned, we debriefed. "I want to do that once a month," Gwen told me. For several years, she did. She formed a nonprofit organization, Rebirth America, to support the work. Others from the congregation came alongside her to serve. The church staff provided consultation, prayer, and support. Although we had no prison ministers the night Gwen first asked, we had dozens by the time she was finished.[30]

Such stories like this multiplied over the years. University Baptist Church members developed a ministry to provide transportation for cancer patients to receive their treatment at the Texas Medical Center. Some worked in women's shelters, planted churches in apartment complexes, and formed partnerships with elementary schools in disadvantaged areas. Others created disaster relief units to serve in the aftermath of natural disasters. A faithful group of builders constructed more than twenty church buildings for Navajo congregations in Arizona and New Mexico; other provided sports camps and Vacation Bible School for teens and children during the project. Some had a passion for the needs of the deaf community, and they extended our worship ministry to the deaf population in our area. The complete list of ministries that flourished is quite long. These ministries were not born in a church staff meeting as creative ideas generated by professional ministers. Each ministry germinated in the heart and mind of a layperson who heard us when we told them they had gifts and a call to ministry, and they needed to discover what those were. We told them we would help them discover those gifts and support them in their effort to find a meaningful expression of ministry. They believed us. And we

30. True to Jesus's promise that those who are faithful in little are trusted with more (Matt. 25:21), eventually more than a hundred church members became prison ministers through two other prison ministries, Write-Way Prison Ministries (https://writewaypm.org) and Bill Glass Behind the Walls (https://behindthewalls.com).

took responsibility for equipping them to follow God's leadership in bearing witness as the people of God, the laity.

CONCLUSIONS

It is difficult to think of a truth more closely tied to the Baptist vision than a robust doctrine of the laity. "This," faithful pastors equipping and releasing the laity to ministry in the church and the world, is "that," the early church moving through its world with compassion and courage to proclaim the mighty acts of him who called them out of darkness into his marvelous light. Yet this doctrine runs counter to that cultural understanding of church and ministry in North America that has succumbed to a consumer-focused approach to the gospel and ministries. Pastors must understand that Ephesians 4:11–12 is not a mere suggestion about the goal of their ministry but a statement of God's plan for the work of redemption and reconciliation in the world. Theological seminaries need to equip pastors to equip the saints as a central part of their pastoral calling. As this unfinished business takes effect, we should expect to see the church in the world built up in unity and maturity, increasingly immune to the false teachings that blow in the wind, growing in Christlike character and mutual love (Eph. 4:13–16).

FOR FURTHER REFLECTION

1. What do you believe is the role of the laity in the plan of God? How does your understanding of that help define the part the pastor plays?

2. What is the most robust biblical foundation for your understanding of the doctrine of the laity? Which passages most help you formulate a doctrine of the laity and the role of pastors in equipping?

3. What dangers do you see in contemporary church life that threaten the practice of a robust biblical doctrine of the laity? What evidence do you see of congregations fully living out that doctrine?

4. What would you list as the primary components of an equipping ministry? What is it precisely that pastors do as they equip the saints?

5. What would an equipping ministry look like in a smaller congregation? How might it look different in a larger one? What aspects of that ministry need to be put in place in the church where you now serve?

12

Dreaming of the Future

Offering Hope

I have a dream.

—Martin Luther King Jr., "I Have a Dream" speech

Then he said to me, "Mortal, these bones are the whole house of Israel. They say, 'Our bones are dried up, and our hope is lost; we are cut off completely.'"

—Ezekiel (Ezek. 37:11)

Biblical leaders were dreamers and visionaries. They saw a future for God's people and, through prayer and work, led them into it. Baptists often turn to such leaders as examples of pastoral leadership that teaches the flock to listen to God, dream together about their future, and follow in obedience.

In Romans 15:13, Paul identifies God as "the God of hope." Hope in Christian theology is inherently about the future. It is more than wishful thinking, however. Hope is confidence about the future founded on a trust in God's promises. "Hope," Paul says, "does not disappoint us, because God's love has been poured into our hearts through the Holy Spirit that has been given to us" (Rom. 5:5). Our hope in God grows out of a relationship in which we experience God's love through the Holy Spirit. From this experience in the present, we can confidently anticipate that God will be with us in the future. The God of hope is the God of the future, the God of the exodus, and the God of the resurrection. God stands in the future and speaks to us in promises, inviting us to the new things that lie before us.[1] Consequently, God's people have lived with a focus on the future over the centuries.

Biblical Foundations

The biblical message is itself future-oriented, inherently eschatological. God called Abraham and promised him a future: "Now the LORD said to Abram, 'Go from your country and your kindred and your father's house to the land that I will show you. I will make of you a great nation, and I will bless you, and make your name great, so that you will be a blessing. I will bless those who bless you, and the one who curses you I will curse; and in you all the families of the earth shall be blessed'" (Gen. 12:1–3). God renewed that promise repeatedly in Abraham's life, especially in moments of crisis when the future was called into question (Gen. 13:14–17; 15:1–21; 17:1–22; 22:15–19). Abraham's son Isaac (Gen. 26:1–5, 23–24) and Isaac's son Jacob (28:1–17; 35:9–15) heard God repeat that promise to them as well. Jacob's son Joseph believed the ancient promise that God would give the land of Canaan to Abraham's people and, even in Egyptian exile, requested that his bones be taken there for burial when his descendants returned (Gen. 50:24–25; cf. Josh. 24:32; Acts 7:16; Heb. 11:22). God's promises oriented the patriarchs toward a vision of the future, and they followed that vision in faith (Heb. 11:8–20).

Joseph's dreams comforted him when circumstances were difficult. Believing that he would one day serve in a place of authority (Gen. 37:5–11) sustained him when suffering as a prisoner and a slave (Gen. 37:36; 39:1, 20). His gift for interpreting dreams put him in a position of authority that allowed him to lead Egypt through a period of famine (Gen. 42:25–45), ultimately saving his family in the process and seeing his original dream fulfilled (Gen. 45:1–15). Joseph's dreams were a promise from God that kept him oriented toward hope.

A vision for the future that resumed the theme of the promise made to the patriarchs accompanied Moses's call at the burning bush:

> I have observed the misery of my people who are in Egypt; I have heard their cry on account of their taskmasters. Indeed, I know their sufferings, and I have

---

1. Jürgen Moltmann, *Theology of Hope: On the Ground and the Implications of a Christian Eschatology* (New York: Harper & Row, 1975), 31.

come down to deliver them from the Egyptians, and to bring them up out of that land to a good and broad land, a land flowing with milk and honey, to the country of the Canaanites, the Hittites, the Amorites, the Perizzites, the Hivites, and the Jebusites. The cry of the Israelites has now come to me; I have also seen how the Egyptians oppress them. So come, I will send you to Pharaoh to bring my people, the Israelites, out of Egypt. (Exod. 3:7–10)

This vision of deliverance and a new land guided Moses and Israel in the wilderness for a generation before they entered the place God promised.

Moses passed the vision on to Joshua, but with a new dimension. Joshua would be the one to lead the people of Israel in conquering and settling the land God promised to Abraham, Isaac, Jacob, and Moses (Josh. 1:1–9). This dream saw Joshua and his people through bloody battles and difficult decisions.

The lack of a decisive vision to guide Israel marked the period of the judges, which followed Joshua's conquest of the land. Once Israel settled the land, leaders occasionally arose to deliver them from enemy oppression. However, these leaders held no common dream of how the future might look. The lack of godly leadership meant the absence of a vision, without which people often lose a sense of direction. The Hebrew word *khazon* in Proverbs 29:18 is translated as "prophecy" in the NRSV, "vision" in the NASB, and "revelation" in the NIV. The word denotes prophetic visions such as Daniel's (Dan. 8:15) and Isaiah's (Isa. 1:1) or the purported dreams of false prophets (Jer. 14:14; Ezek. 7:26). The consequence of a failure to provide a revealed vision is that people "cast off restraint" (Prov. 29:18).[2] The book of Judges closes with a sad summary of the times: "In those days there was no king in Israel; all the people did what was right in their own eyes" (Judg. 21:25).

During the period of the monarchy, Israel seldom experienced royal leadership with a divine vision. David envisioned constructing the temple in Jerusalem (2 Sam. 7:1–3) but had to defer the project to his son Solomon (2 Sam. 7:12–13). Solomon carried out the dream, but at a high cost to the people of Israel. Great and godly visions do not characterize Israel under its kings, either in the days of the united monarchy or following its division.

The failure of Israel's kings to hold a common, God-focused vision for the nation contributed to its downfall. Samaria, the Northern Kingdom's capital, fell to the Assyrians in 722 BC; Jerusalem, the capital of Judah in the south, fell to Babylon in 587 BC. The exile (587–539 BC) provided a crucible in which God gave Judah an opportunity to renew their vision as the people

---

2. The Hebrew verb is *para'*, used in the Old Testament to refer to disheveled hair (Lev. 10:6; 13:45; 21:10; Num. 5:18).

of the covenant. Beginning with Jeremiah's and Ezekiel's preaching, a hope for returning to the land took shape even in the most discouraging time.[3] As the exile finally came to a close, leaders like Ezra, Nehemiah, Haggai, and Zechariah offered guiding visions of returning and rebuilding the walls of Jerusalem, the temple, and the nation.

The monarchy's disappointing leadership also made space for a new hope to develop among God's people. The prophets in the eighth and seventh centuries began to share a dream of another king who would come to rule righteously over the nation, a descendent of David who would fulfill God's promise in 1 Samuel 7 (Isa. 9:1–7; 11:1–5; 16:4–5; Jer. 23:5–6; 30:9; Ezek. 37:24–28; Hosea 3:4–5; Amos 9:11–15; Zech. 3:8; 6:12; 9:9–10).[4] This messianic hope endured through the period of the exile and the return, forming the basis for Jesus's vision for the kingdom of God.

Jesus's life and preaching focused on a vision of God's kingdom. That kingdom defined the gospel he preached. Mark writes, "Now after John was arrested, Jesus came to Galilee, proclaiming the good news of God, and saying, 'The time is fulfilled, and the kingdom of God has come near; repent, and believe in the good news'" (1:14–15). The gospel Jesus preached was not about a theory of atonement but about the appearance of God's long-promised kingdom. Jesus's inaugural sermon in Nazareth declared the arrival of the kingdom and explained its nature (Luke 4:16–31). His teaching, from the Sermon on the Mount (Matt. 5–7) to his parables (Mark 4; Matt. 13), focused on life in a kingdom that was invading the present world order. His miraculous works of power were the dawn of God's reign that would one day appear in full noonday brightness (Rev. 21:1–4). He was inaugurating a reign in the present that was starting as small as a mustard seed but would inevitably consummate in the kingdoms of this world becoming the everlasting kingdom of God. Everything he said and did arose from the vision for God's kingdom that he passed on to his followers.[5]

Simon Peter's vision produced his conversion of thought about gentiles in the church (Acts 10:1–16, 27–29) and shaped the early Christian movement (Acts

3. Although Jeremiah and Ezekiel both preached the coming destruction of Judah, they also offered a message of hope beyond destruction. See Ronald E. Clements, "Jeremiah, Prophet of Hope," *Review & Expositor* 78, no. 3 (August 1, 1981): 345–63; and Joel K. T. Biwul, "The Vision of 'Dry Bones' in Ezekiel 37:1–28: Resonating Ezekiel's Message as the African Prophet of Hope," *Hervormde Teologiese Studies* 73, no. 3 (July 2017): 1–10.

4. For the development of this Davidic hope and its fulfillment in the New Testament, see F. F. Bruce, *The New Testament Development of Old Testament Themes* (Grand Rapids: Eerdmans, 1969), 68–82.

5. See the works listed above in chap. 11, note 23.

15:6–11).[6] Paul's vision on the Damascus Road (Acts 9:1–9; 22:6–16; 26:12–18) determined his ministry's focus and the gospel's progress in Asia Minor and Europe. Paul's letters allow us to hear his vision for the church in the world as a community of God's new creation (2 Cor. 5:17). Peter's vision for faithful discipleship supplies his suffering readers with direction during difficult times (1 and 2 Peter). James's vision for Christian living provides practical wisdom for the church in its daily effort to follow Jesus. The writer of Hebrews offers a vision of perseverance that flows out of what God has done in Christ. In the book of Revelation, John's vision extends hope and a way forward to the churches in his community in Asia Minor during intense persecution. The entire New Testament is a hopeful vision for the future of God's people.

Calling a local church to write a vision statement is a modern phenomenon that a pastor may consider optional. Encouraging God's people to live out of a clear, hopeful vision for the future based on God's promises is not an option, however. Baptist pastors may not always have expressed this in terms of a "vision," but where they have exercised effective leadership, the biblical precedent has extended its influence into their ministries. James McClendon's expression of the Baptist vision contains an inherently future dimension. "This is that" means not only that Baptists understand the present church to be one with the ancient church but also that we are one with the church at the close of the age. We live with a vision that encourages perseverance to the end (Matt. 24:13–14).[7]

Historical Bypaths

Baptist leaders have regularly stood before their congregations, or their culture, and described a future they envisioned to bring about change. Pastors have cast a vision to build new facilities to enhance ministry in their community. Good shepherds have raised voices of hope, assuring people whose lives were being torn apart by war, persecution, natural disaster, or financial depression that God has not deserted them. Some Baptist pastors have articulated a vision for world missions, education, or religious liberty that has influenced many beyond their congregation. Dreaming, in this sense, is part

6. Lesslie Newbigin writes, "The story of the meeting of Peter and Cornelius is especially significant in the light that it throws on the sovereign work of the Spirit in mission. It has been rightly said that this is the story not only of the conversion of Cornelius but also of the conversion of Peter and of the church." *The Open Secret: An Introduction to the Theology of Mission* (Grand Rapids: Eerdmans, 1995), 59.

7. James William McClendon Jr., *Systematic Theology*, vol. 1, *Ethics*, 2nd ed. (Nashville: Abingdon, 2002), 30.

of the pastoral task. Leaders work with the future, which requires a willingness to dream and invite others into that future.

George Washington Truett (1867–1944): A Dream of Religious Liberty

On Sunday, May 16, 1920, at the request of the Baptist Churches of Washington, DC, George W. Truett delivered an address from the east steps of the national capital to an audience of fifteen thousand people, including Southern Baptists who had gathered in the city for their annual convention as well as Supreme Court justices, military officials, members of President Wilson's cabinet, US representatives and senators, and foreign ambassadors.[8] Truett began his speech by looking over his shoulder at those Baptist voices who had cried out for liberty in the past, such as Roger Williams, John Clarke, Obadiah Holmes, and Isaac Backus. Then he laid out a vision for religious freedom founded in Baptist teaching—the absolute lordship of Christ, the Bible as the rule of faith and practice, the priesthood of all believers, believer's baptism, the symbolic nature of the ordinances, the democratic nature of the church, and finally, a free church in a free state. He proceeded to call his listeners to a vision of securing religious liberty, not merely toleration, for all people, in the United States and around the world. He declared,

> And now, my fellow Christians, and fellow citizens, what is the present call to us in connection with the priceless principle of religious liberty? That principle, with all the history and heritage accompanying it, imposes upon us obligations to the last degree meaningful and responsible. Let us today and forever be highly resolved that the principle of religious liberty shall, please God, be preserved inviolate through all our days and the days of those who come after us. Liberty has both its perils and its obligations. We are to see to it that our attitude toward liberty, both religious and civil, both as Christians and as citizens, is an attitude consistent and constructive and worthy. We are to "Render therefore unto Caesar the things which are Caesar's and unto God the things that are God's." We are members of the two realms, the civil and the religious, and are faithfully to render unto each all that each should receive at our hands; we are to be alertly watchful day and night, that liberty, both religious and civil, shall be nowhere prostituted and mistreated. Every perversion and misuse of liberty tends by that much to jeopardize both church and state.[9]

8. Keith E. Durso, *Thy Will Be Done: A Biography of George W. Truett* (Macon, GA: Mercer University Press, 2009), 176.

9. George W. Truett, *Baptists and Religious Liberty* (Nashville: Sunday School Board of the Southern Baptist Convention, 1920), 24–25, https://digitalcollections-baylor.quartexcollections.com/Documents/Detail/baptists-and-religious-liberty/820079.

Truett's address, which he delivered extemporaneously and without a public address system, became one of his most memorable. Although he received criticism for the speech from some quarters, even among some Baptists who thought aspects of it too political, it was for the most part widely acclaimed.[10]

Truett communicated his vision for religious liberty beyond this single speech. Religious freedom was a conviction he held deeply and expressed often. Truett's vision for religious liberty continued to shape the Baptist perspective until the late twentieth century, when his own denomination began to engage in partisan national politics in ways he would not have suspected.

Martin Luther King Jr. (1929–1968): A Dream of Racial Equality

No Baptist figure is more closely associated with their dreams than is Martin Luther King Jr. Historians have evaluated and explained King's brief life in various ways. McClendon insists that King cannot be understood apart from the religious vision that motivated his entire life. He writes, "Neglecting the view that his own native religious vision, the religion he had drunk almost with his mother's milk, could possibly provide the organizing principle by which to understand his life, many interpreters have come up with a variety of alternative explanations of his life."[11] McClendon argues that neglecting King's religion would make it impossible to understand his dream of racial equality achieved by nonviolent means.

King's broader vision entailed a social equality between Blacks and Whites in America described in the often-quoted speech delivered at the Lincoln Memorial on August 28, 1963. He spoke to a quarter of a million people gathered on the Washington Mall during the March for Jobs and Freedom. He said,

I have a dream that one day on the red hills of Georgia, the sons of former slaves and the sons of former slave owners will be able to sit down together at the table of brotherhood.

I have a dream that one day even the state of Mississippi, a state sweltering with the heat of injustice, sweltering with the heat of oppression, will be transformed into an oasis of freedom and justice. I have a dream that my four little children will one day live in a nation where they will not be judged by the color of their skin but by the content of their character.

I have a *dream* today![12]

10. Durso, *Thy Will Be Done*, 184.

11. James William McClendon Jr., *Biography as Theology: How Life Stories Can Remake Today's Theology* (Eugene, OR: Wipf & Stock, 2002), 48.

12. "Martin Luther King, Jr.: I Have a Dream," American Rhetoric, August 20, 2020, https://www.americanrhetoric.com/speeches/mlkihaveadream.htm.

McClendon observes that "it would require a high order of cynicism to suppose that the man who so eloquently spoke and so profoundly moved his hearers was not speaking from the deep wells of his own being, was not then truly declaring his own dream, his own faith."[13]

A few years later, on April 3, 1968, King spoke to sanitation workers on strike in Memphis, Tennessee. King's address contained many biblical references, but most famously he echoed the experience of Moses on Mount Horeb while viewing the future home of his people, the promised land of Canaan (Deut. 34:1–5). Keenly aware of the possibility of an untimely death, King said, "Well, I don't know what will happen now. We've got some difficult days ahead. But it doesn't matter with me now. Because I've been to the mountaintop. And I don't mind. Like anybody, I would like to live a long life. Longevity has its place. But I'm not concerned about that now. I just want to do God's will. And He's allowed me to go up to the mountain. And I've looked over. And I've seen the promised land."[14] The next day an assassin's bullet cut King's life short at age thirty-nine. His vision of racial equality clarified the scene for a nation like no one before him, naming the injustice of the present and fostering hope for a better future.

King's dream is yet to be fully realized more than fifty years later. But it continues to portray a future that exposes every present moment's failure to measure up to the possibilities of our life together in this country. King's vision of racial equality in America was itself rooted in an even grander vision cast two thousand years earlier—Jesus's vision of life in the kingdom of God, as enunciated in the Sermon on the Mount (Matt. 5–7). This vision guided King's methodology of nonresistance. Jesus's gospel had gripped King's heart. King truly believed that those who violently opposed his vision were people whom Jesus loved and had died to redeem. They were people God called him to love.

In this sense, King's vision was Baptist at its core. He understood that what was transpiring in the present ("this") was connected directly to those biblical events and teachings ("that") shaping his own vision. He made sense of the events of the present and his place in them by turning to Scripture. The narrative of Israel's slavery in Egypt and God's deliverance in the exodus was not ancient history for King. It was a continuing story, which he believed to be playing out again in his world.

McClendon says of King's vision,

It was a dream which overflowed into a mighty flood of concern for America and beyond America, for all to gain the strength to love. It was a dream which

13. McClendon, *Biography as Theology*, 58.
14. "'I've Been to the Mountaintop' by Dr. Martin Luther King, Jr.," AFSCME, https://www.afscme.org/about/history/mlk/mountaintop.

remembered old stories told long ago, of a God who did not desert his people on the earthly journey, but who went before them night and day. It was a dream whose interpretation required a voice to cry out, and weary feet to march, and many a soul to pray. The dreamer is done, but the interpretation is not ended until we also are free.[15]

Seldom do visionaries expound a dream that remains the standard for understanding the world long after their lives end. Martin Luther King Jr. cast such a vision.

Theological Reflection

Few pastors will cast a vision as grand as Truett's or King's, and few will share their dreams with as vast an audience. Nevertheless, the pastor's task includes helping the congregation see beyond the horizon of the present moment. J. Nelson Kraybill says, "Helping the church articulate and own a vision is perhaps the most empowering task leaders can perform."[16] The work of dreaming about the future is a corporate task, shared by the whole body of Christ. Pastors may not bear responsibility for discerning the vision on our own, but we are responsible for taking the initiative to stir and guide the process. We are also accountable for seeing that the congregation hears, understands, and embodies the vision God gives them.

Without a Vision

To be without vision is to operate blindly, to exist in a leadership fog (Prov. 29:18). Congregations deserve the blessing of a clear vision that can guide their work and their decisions. Part of the leadership debt we pastors owe the church is to ensure that such a vision is in place. Absent a shared vision, the congregation inherently flounders, driven rudderless through a stormy culture. Decisions become difficult and divisive since we have no standard against which to measure our options. The loudest voices tend to prevail.

A congregation that depends too much on the pastor to supply the vision faces its own set of problems. Things may seem to work as long as the pastor is present. But when the leader leaves, so does the vision. Interim periods are often stagnant times if congregations do not possess the self-awareness provided by a shared vision. They await the next leader, who will hopefully

15. McClendon, *Biography as Theology*, 65–66.
16. J. Nelson Kraybill, "Power and Authority," in *The Heart of the Matter: Pastoral Ministry in Anabaptist Perspective*, ed. Erick Sawatzky (Telford, PA: Cascadia, 2004), 225.

have a dream to share. Because they depend too much on the leader to supply that vision, the congregation is jerked right and left as leadership changes, heading first in this direction and then in another direction.

Churches deserve a pastor-initiated and pastor-led process of vision discernment in which they learn to listen for God's voice and to share what they are hearing. Over time, out of prayer and conversation, a vision distills, coming not from a single leader but from the Holy Spirit at work in the hearts of God's people. Such a vision abides even when the pastor leaves. That vision continues to guide as the congregation seeks new leadership, looking for someone who can step into that vision with them and equip them to live more fully into it. The experience of vision discernment calls for the body of Christ to function together and to grow more attentive than ever to the direction of the Holy Spirit. Through this process, we learn to live and serve together with authentic hope.

Visionary Pastors

Some visionary leaders stir grand dreams in others and find people so enthused that they willingly sacrifice time, money, and even their lives to bring the vision into reality. However, tens of thousands of visionary leaders in the kingdom of God work on a smaller and less glamorous scale. They live in hope, trusting the God of hope, and they are catalysts for God's generating hope in others. Their pastoral ministry offers hopeful proclamation, hopeful pastoral care, and hopeful leadership. Believing that the future is God's future, they help others revise their future stories to include God as well. They believe in the future that Scripture declares, in which God "will wipe every tear from their eyes. Death will be no more; mourning and crying and pain will be no more" (Rev. 21:4). These visionary leaders call the church to live already in light of that approaching future. They develop ministries to express that hope, wiping the tears of the sorrowful, assuaging the mourners' grief, staving off disease and famine and violence, and easing the pain of the wounded. They seek to express now, in the present, what God's future promises. Actions like these exemplify hopeful pastoral ministry.

Offering Hope throughout Pastoral Ministry

The tasks of pastoral ministry overlap in ways we often overlook. Leadership calls for pastors to exercise skills in corporate discernment, equipping church members to discern a shared vision or view of the future toward which they can live together. Pastors help churches learn to dream of a future where

God is present. Pastors lead congregations into the green pastures and still waters of hope.

Pastors take on the work of dreaming in their pastoral care as well. People face various crises in their lives in which the future becomes obscured or called into question, leading to despair. The pastor's goal in such ministry is to help people discover the hope that is in Christ. Andrew Lester and Wayne Oates analyzed clinical pastoral research involving people facing extreme crises. They concluded that suffering people often struggle with the dissolution of what Lester calls their "future stories." Lester writes, "These persons were not worried about their past or even their present suffering, but about what would happen in the future. Despair was the major threat, and hope was the central psychological and theological issue with which they were struggling."[17] Hope, then, becomes the primary expression of Christian pastoral care to extend in crucial times. Oates writes, "The pastor represents hope to persons who face the unalterable, the unknown, or the frightening. . . . In an age when despair, discouragement, and disillusionment are the predominant emotional dynamics, it becomes increasingly necessary for the Christian faith to unmask, refurbish, and communicate its belief in hope."[18]

Counselors, Christian or otherwise, sometimes attend to the client's past, exploring the forces that formed or traumatized them. Alternatively, they may focus on the present, offering the client coping practices to deal with the current suffering. What counselors often neglect, Lester contends, is the fact that we tell ourselves "future stories" and then often live into them. Future stories may be "worst-case scenario" narratives, anticipating a future in which our powerlessness, loneliness, or pain only intensifies. We imagine the worst and then seem to do our best to bring it to pass. People need hope when the future is in question. What does our future look like with God as part of it? "Hope, or its absence in despair," says Lester, "is the basic psycho-spiritual dynamic with which the pastoral caregiver must contend, particularly when attending to a crisis."[19]

Pastors, working from a perspective of hope, can accompany those who are despairing over the future as they revise their future stories. When we do so, we lead them in a prayerful discernment process similar to the one we use when we engage church leaders in understanding their congregation's future as one in which God promises to be present. Offering care to individuals in

17. Andrew D. Lester, *Hope in Pastoral Care and Counseling* (Louisville: Westminster John Knox, 1995), 1.

18. Wayne E. Oates and Andrew D. Lester, *Pastoral Care in Crucial Human Situations* (Valley Forge, PA: Judson, 1969), 18.

19. Lester, *Hope in Pastoral Care and Counseling*, 1.

a time of crisis and envisioning a hopeful future with a congregation are pastoral tasks that, though not identical, often resemble each other.

Sometimes congregations need the kind of pastoral care we offer to individuals in crisis. Rather than face a calm and deliberate period of discerning a vision, churches can suddenly and unexpectedly face traumatic situations. Financial problems, a church leader's moral failure, a natural disaster, a pandemic, or an act of violence can pick up a thriving congregation like a tornado and deposit it in the middle of confusion and despair concerning its future. In such times, pastoral leadership looks like pastoral care. The congregation needs to revise its future story to include God's presence as part of the vision of days to come.

Other congregations may have experienced a long and slow diminishment of their health and well-being. The demographics of the community shifted around them, and they failed to adjust their ministries. Dependable, longtime members have aged or died, and the congregation struggles financially. In the minds of remaining members, their best days are receding into the past. Despair defines their future narrative. Such churches need a leader to help them dream again, re-visioning a future story in which God is present with them.[20]

Rethinking the future is part of the preaching task as well. To proclaim the gospel of the cross and the resurrection is to proffer hope. To preach the good news of Jesus Christ's future coming and reign is to extend hope. And to preach to struggling or suffering believers about the love of God and the presence of the Holy Spirit is to give hope. Preaching itself is a call to repent, to change one's mind, in light of the good news of the kingdom of God (Mark 1:14). By preaching the gospel of the kingdom, we tell people that the future is not what they thought, because the God of hope is present there.

Despair is increasingly part of the world in which we serve. In a worshiping congregation on an average week, the odds are that some present have considered taking their own life during the past week.[21] They have once more mustered the energy to attend a worship service, hoping to find a reason or resources to go on. They need hope. For them, preaching may be a life-or-death matter. Hopeful preaching connects the good news of Jesus Christ to the human need for a future story that includes God.

---

20. Baptist church consultant Robert Dale developed an organic model of congregational life cycles that can help a congregation do the work of re-visioning, or dreaming again. Robert D. Dale, *To Dream Again, Again! Growing Healthy Congregations for Changing Futures* (Macon, GA: Nurturing Faith, 2018).

21. For a helpful resource on preaching and the suicide crisis, see Scott M. Gibson and Karen E. Mason, *Preaching Hope in Darkness: Help for Pastors in Addressing Suicide from the Pulpit* (Bellingham, WA: Lexham, 2020).

Once more, the pastoral tasks intersect. The pulpit is a place from which to extend pastoral care. Pastors also lead from the pulpit. As we bring a congregation to attention before God's Word in preaching and allow the Holy Spirit to address our future together, we lay the groundwork for creating the story into which we determine to live. Biblical calls to care for the poor can generate a vision in which the church engages those in their community suffering from a lack of resources or opportunities. Hearing the Word of God address injustice can form believers who determine to work for justice. Preaching God's promise of answered prayer can stir a church to imagine itself as a praying community. Preaching is leadership when it is involved in summoning God's people to consider what their future will look like with God present.

CONCLUSIONS

The Good Shepherd "leads" beside still waters and along righteous paths (Ps. 23:2–3). Leadership is inherently part of shepherding the flock of God. And leadership is intrinsically about the future and change. If we are not going anywhere, if the future looks just like the present, we need no leader. If the pasture where we are grazing has everything we ever need, then we require no shepherd to lead us elsewhere. But that is not the case with God's people. We are a pilgrim people—strangers, aliens, sojourners. We are pursuing a vision of a life that is more than what is offered here, a kingdom that surpasses all earthly kingdoms, a city not built with hands, eternal in the heavens (Heb. 11:10; 13:14). We require leaders who help us envision that future and find ways to live into it in hope. God has given us pastors to shepherd us toward that dream.

FOR FURTHER REFLECTION

1. What is your doctrine of hope? How would you define hope to someone who asked? How would you distinguish the biblical concept of hope from the cultural one? How do you believe one acquires hope and lives in hope?

2. What do you understand by words like "vision," "dream," "imagination"? How are these related to hope? What makes a vision or a dream authentic and therefore worthy of a congregation's pursuit?

3. How would you go about working with a group of congregational leaders to discern a vision? What resources would you need? What practices would you employ? What processes would you follow? How would you know when you had succeeded?

4. How is ministering to individuals during a time of crisis like the work of discerning a congregational vision? What do those situations have in common? What is distinctive about each one?

5. How is leading a congregation during a time of crisis like the pastoral care of an individual? What do they both need?

Conclusion

Young pastors frequently lament, "They didn't teach us this in seminary!" I have probably uttered that frustrated complaint a time or two myself. What seminary did teach me, however, was how to think like a pastor. That capacity to integrate biblical teaching and sound theology makes it possible for someone to find their way through an ecclesiological and cultural landscape that changes, sometimes radically, from one decade of ministry to the next. Pastoral theology can help us adapt to those changes while remaining faithful to the persons we believe pastors are and what we believe God calls pastors to do.

Our ministry in this contemporary context has ancient roots. Hebrew prophets, priests, and scribes have gone before us. So have Jesus and the apostles. Our calling echoes theirs. Our work rhymes with theirs. The same Holy Spirit empowers us as we serve. We proclaim the same good news and call people to the same kingdom. We do not merely imitate them; we participate in a common story. This—who we are and what we do—is that.

Baptist pastors have faithfully served over the centuries in many places and circumstances. Today, in every part of the world, men and women among us respond to a call and offer their lives in ministry. We are now so diverse and scattered that a robust Baptist pastoral theology requires pastoral theologians from every quarter to think and speak about what our work means and why we do it. We especially need to hear those pastoral voices that have been so far from the center that we have ignored them: voices of women, the people of the global South and East, Black Americans, Latinx, Native Americans, and others. As these voices become more prominent and influential, a more complex range of notes will contribute to a richer understanding of the pastoral task. True to Baptist principles, we each need to work out our theology in the context and congregation we serve. We each answer the question "What does it mean to be a Baptist pastor?" Then we share our answers.

In an interview, Eugene Peterson once said that if we want to understand what it means to be a pastor, we should read Wendell Berry. Whenever Berry says "land" or "farm," we should read "parish." And when he speaks of "farmers," we should think "pastors."[1] In the poem that serves as an epigraph to this volume, Berry describes the gardener who finds mystery in the soil and the processes of life and death. The gardener's hands dig into the rich soil and sprout! This "grower of trees" seems to have swallowed some miraculous seed; like a vine, an "unending sentence of his love" flows from his mouth. I have wondered about that line. Is Berry describing those who love what they do so much that they just cannot help talking about it? Or is this love something like a prison sentence, binding the gardener forever to this life? The gardener is one who is "born to farming."

Baptist pastors understand that God has called us to this work. In a sense, we were "born to pastoring" (Jer. 1:4–5). On our best days, we love the work God has given us to do. The list of holy moments that mark the pastor's life is long and rich: study and prayer, preaching and teaching, sitting with the grieving, bringing hope to broken lives, watching disciples grow in Christ. Such moments can feel like digging deep into rich, warm soil where life mysteriously emerges from seeds.

Other days are less glamorous. Unending meetings can consume our weeks. Crises emerge that we have not anticipated. Conflict can erupt over seemingly trivial matters. The gardener's task seems more like yanking up weeds and spreading manure during these days. But these times, too, are holy. They are part of what it means to care for God's people.

The call of God and the ordaining hands of God's people have set us to this task. We preach the gospel and bear witness in the world like gardeners planting seeds (Mark 4:14). Baptizing and serving at the Lord's Table, caring for God's people in their suffering, teaching them to live as Jesus's disciples, and leading them in worship—all these tasks are our holy privileges. Serving God's people, encouraging them to find their giftedness, equipping them for ministry, and teaching them to live in hope—such are our sacred tasks. Paul says, "I planted, Apollos watered, but God gave the growth. So neither the one who plants nor the one who waters is anything, but only God who gives the growth. The one who plants and the one who waters have a common purpose, and each will receive wages according to the labor of each. For we are God's servants, working together; you are God's field" (1 Cor. 3:6–9). The work of care and cultivation of the congregation is the pastoral calling. We are born to this.

---

1. Eugene H. Peterson, *The Contemplative Pastor: Returning to the Art of Spiritual Direction* (Grand Rapids: Eerdmans, 1993), 3–4.

APPENDIX

A Baptist Who's Who

Backus, Isaac (1724–1806): a New England Baptist pastor in colonial America and an outspoken advocate for religious liberty in the early days of the republic.

Baker, Robert Andrew (1910–1992): a leading church historian among Southern Baptists in the twentieth century. He was a professor of church history at Southwestern Baptist Theological Seminary (1942–1981).

Berry, Wendell (1934–): a Kentucky farmer and award-winning essayist, novelist, and poet. He is a member of the Port Royal Baptist Church in Port Royal, Kentucky.

Bixby, Ruby (1818–1877): one of the first women to be licensed to the ministry by Free Will Baptists in the United States. She served as a pastor of a church she and her husband organized in Wisconsin.

Brennan, M. A. (dates unknown): the first woman ordained in a Free Will Baptist church in America when the Belle Vernon Free Will Baptist Church in Pennsylvania recognized her as their minister in 1876.

Brister, C. W. (1926–2008): a Baptist pastor and educator. Brister was professor of pastoral ministry at Southwestern Baptist Theological Seminary from 1957 to 2001 and later named distinguished professor emeritus.

Broadus, John Albert (1827–1895): a Baptist pastor and one of the founders of the Southern Baptist Theological Seminary (1856), where he served as professor of New Testament and later as president (1888–1895).

Campbell, Will D. (1924–2013): a Baptist pastor, civil rights activist, author, and lecturer from Mississippi.

Carey, William (1761–1834): a Particular Baptist pastor who was, along with Andrew Fuller and John Gill, instrumental in igniting the modern mission movement among Baptists. In 1792, Carey and his family moved to India, where he served for forty-two years as the first Baptist missionary.

Carroll, Benajah Harvey (1843–1914): a Baptist pastor who served the First Baptist Church of Waco, Texas, from 1871 to 1899. He was instrumental in founding Southwestern Baptist Theological Seminary in 1908 in Waco. The seminary moved to Fort Worth, Texas, in 1910. Carroll taught at the seminary and served as its president until his death.

Churn, Arlene (1941–): an ordained Baptist minister and grief counseling specialist in Philadelphia, Pennsylvania. She was the first woman ordained by the National Baptist Convention, USA (1962).

Conner, Walter Thomas (1877–1952): professor of theology at Southwestern Baptist Theological Seminary (1910–1949). Conner was a student of A. H. Strong, B. H. Carroll, E. Y. Mullins, and Walter Rauschenbusch and a teacher of James William McClendon Jr.

Dagg, John Leadley (1794–1884): one of the leading Baptist theologians of the nineteenth century. Dagg joined the faculty of Mercer University in 1843 and became president in 1845, serving until 1856.

Davis, Addie Elizabeth (1917–2005): the first woman ordained in a Southern Baptist church. However, Davis served American Baptist congregations.

Dobbins, Gaines Stanley (1886–1978): a Southern Baptist educator who influenced Baptist churches in church administration, pastoral care, missions and evangelism, and Christian education. Dobbins taught at the Southern Baptist Theological Seminary from 1920 to 1956.

Edge, Findley Bartow (1916–2002): a Southern Baptist educator and student of Gaines Dobbins. Edge taught at the Southern Baptist Theological Seminary from 1947 to 1985. He was a leading voice in the lay renewal movement.

Estep, William Roscoe (1920–2000): a leading Baptist historian and an authority on the Anabaptist movement. Estep was professor of church history at Southwestern Baptist Theological Seminary from 1954 until his retirement in 1990; however, he continued to teach until 1994.

Fordham, Druecillar McBarr (1906–1981): the first woman and the first female Black pastor of a Southern Baptist church. An American Baptist congregation ordained Fordham. When the American Baptist congregation where she was pastor aligned with the Metro New York Baptist Association, she became the pastor of a Southern Baptist church.

Fosdick, Harry Emerson (1878–1969): an American Baptist pastor and theologian. Fosdick served as the pastor of the prestigious Riverside Church in New York City from 1930 to 1946.

Fuller, Andrew (1754–1815): a Particular Baptist pastor who developed a vision for world missions. He influenced William Carey, who became the first Baptist missionary in 1792. Fuller is considered the theologian of the modern mission movement.

Garrett, James Leo, Jr. (1925–2020): a Southern Baptist pastor and theologian. Garrett taught at Southwestern Baptist Theological Seminary (1949–1959, 1979–1997), the Southern Baptist Theological Seminary (1959–1973), and Baylor University (1973–1979). He was the distinguished professor of theology at Southwestern when he retired in 1997.

Gates, Edith (1883–1962): the first British woman recognized as pastor of a Baptist church (1922).

Graham, William Franklin, called "Billy" (1918–2018): a Southern Baptist crusade evangelist who preached to live audiences of 210 million people in more than 185 countries and territories. His television audience numbered in the billions. Graham was one of the most respected and influential religious leaders in the twentieth century.

Graves, James Robinson (1820–1893): an American Baptist preacher and publisher recognized as the Landmark Movement's leading voice. The Landmarkers were a divisive party among Baptists that traced Baptist origins in an unbroken chain back to John the Baptist and rejected all non-Baptist church forms and practices.

Grenz, Stanley (1950–2005): an American Baptist theologian, ethicist, and educator. His academic career included teaching at the North American Baptist Seminary, Carey Theological College, Regent College, Baylor University, George W. Truett Theological Seminary, and Mars Hill Graduate School.

Helwys, Thomas (ca. 1550–1615): leader of the group of English separatists that founded the first Baptist congregation on British soil.

Hiscox, Edward Thurston (1814–1901): a New England Baptist pastor and writer most well known for his handbooks for Baptist churches, which many congregations continue to turn to for guidance.

Hobbs, Herschel Harold (1907–1995): a Southern Baptist pastor and denominational leader. Hobbs served as pastor of the First Baptist Church of Oklahoma City, Oklahoma, from 1949 to 1973. While president of the Southern Baptist Convention (1961–1963), he supervised the 1963 revision of the *Baptist Faith and Message*.

Hübmaier, Balthasar (ca. 1480–1528): an early Anabaptist leader, theologian, and martyr.

Judson, Adoniram (1788–1850): an American Baptist missionary to Burma from 1813 to 1850. He served with his wife, Ann.

Judson, Ann (1789–1826): one of the first two American Baptist missionaries along with her husband, Adoniram. She served in Burma from 1813 until she died in 1826.

King, Martin Luther, Jr. (1929–1968): a Baptist pastor and civil rights activist whose leadership was directly influential in the passage of civil rights and voting rights legislation. King emphasized nonviolent protest as a means of bringing about change. He was assassinated in Memphis, Tennessee, on April 4, 1968.

LaRue, Cleophus James, Jr. (1953–): the Francis Landey Patton Associate Professor of Homiletics (National Baptist) at Princeton Theological Seminary. LaRue is one of the world's leading teachers of the art of preaching.

Leonard, Bill J. (1946–): an American Baptist church historian and educator. Leonard taught at the Southern Baptist Theological Seminary, Samford University, Berea College, and the Wake Forest University School of Divinity.

Liele, George (ca. 1750–1828): a freed slave who became the first Black Baptist ordained in America and the first American Baptist missionary. He planted churches in Georgia and Jamaica.

Marney, Carlyle (1916–1978): a Baptist pastor, theologian, and author. Marney served as pastor of the First Baptist Church in Austin, Texas (1948–1958), and Myers Park Church in Charlotte, North Carolina (1958–1967).

McBeth, Harry Leon (1932–2013): a Baptist church historian and professor. McBeth taught at Southwestern Baptist Theological Seminary from 1962 until 2003.

McClendon, James William, Jr. (1924–2000): a Christian theologian and educator in the Anabaptist tradition. McClendon taught at Golden Gate Baptist Theological Seminary, the University of San Francisco, Stanford University, the University of Notre Dame, Fuller Theological Seminary, Baylor University, Temple University, Goucher College, St. Mary's College of California, and Church Divinity School of the Pacific.

McCracken, Robert James (1904–1973): a Baptist pastor who succeeded Harry Emerson Fosdick as pastor at Riverside Church, serving from 1946 to 1967.

Menno Simons (ca. 1496–1561): a prominent leader among Dutch Anabaptists in the early days of the movement. His followers took the name Mennonites.

Miller, Calvin (1937–2012): a Baptist pastor, educator, and prolific writer. Miller served as pastor of the Westside Baptist Church in Omaha, Nebraska (1966–1991), and then taught at Southwestern Baptist Theological Seminary (1991–1998) and the Beeson Divinity School (1999–2007).

Moon, Charlotte Digges "Lottie" (1840–1912): a Southern Baptist missionary who served in China for nearly forty years. She was instrumental in helping raise funds to support Southern Baptist foreign missions. An annual mission offering that provides significant support for Southern Baptist missionaries bears her name.

Mullins, Edgar Young (1860–1928): a Baptist pastor, theologian, and educator. Mullins served as president of the Southern Baptist Theological Seminary from 1889 to 1928.

Oates, Wayne Edward (1917–1999): a Baptist psychologist and educator. Oates was influential in the pastoral care and counseling movement. He taught at the Southern Baptist Theological Seminary from 1947 until 1974.

Olford, Stephen Frederick (1918–2004): a British Baptist pastor and writer. His influence extended into American Christianity, touching such prominent Baptist pastors as Billy Graham, Charles Stanley, and Adrian Rogers.

Proctor, Samuel DeWitt (1921–1997): a Baptist pastor and educator. Proctor served as a mentor to Martin Luther King Jr. and adviser to several US presidents. His career included serving as president of Virginia Union University and North Carolina Agricultural and Technical State University.

Rauschenbusch, Walter (1861–1918): an American Baptist pastor, theologian, and educator influential in the Social Gospel movement in the early twentieth century. He served as pastor of the Second German Baptist Church in Hell's Kitchen in New York City, and from 1897 to 1902 he taught church history at Rochester Theological Seminary in Rochester, New York.

Rice, Luther (1783–1836): an American Baptist pastor who was influential in beginning the Baptist Triennial Convention as the first Baptist missionary-sending body in the United States. Rice also raised funds for the establishment of institutions of higher education among Baptists.

Robertson, Archibald Thomas (1863–1934): a Southern Baptist preacher and educator. Robertson taught Greek and New Testament interpretation at the Southern Baptist Theological Seminary from 1888 until 1934.

Scarborough, Lee Rutland (1870–1945): a Southern Baptist pastor, evangelist, educator, seminary president, and denominational leader. Scarborough taught evangelism at Southwestern Baptist Theological Seminary from 1908 until 1942 and served as its president (1915–1942).

Segler, Franklin Morgan (1907–1988): a Baptist pastor and educator. Segler served as a professor of pastoral ministry at Southwestern Baptist Theological Seminary.

Smyth, John (1554–1612): an Anglican priest who separated from the Church of England, taking a group of followers to Amsterdam. His encounter with Dutch Anabaptists influenced his decision to adopt believer's baptism.

Spurgeon, Charles Haddon (1834–1892): an influential Particular Baptist pastor in London, known as the "prince of preachers." For thirty-eight years, Spurgeon served the New Park Street Chapel, later named the Metropolitan Tabernacle.

Stagg, Frank (1911–2001): a Southern Baptist pastor, theologian, and educator. He taught at the New Orleans Baptist Theological Seminary (1945–1964) and the Southern Baptist Theological Seminary (1964–1978).

Strong, Augustus Hopkins (1836–1921): a Baptist pastor and theologian. Strong served as pastor of First Church in Cleveland, Ohio (1865–1872), and later as president of the Rochester Theological Seminary (1872–1912).

Taylor, Gardner Calvin (1918–2015): an American Baptist pastor dubbed "the dean of American preaching." In 1947 Taylor became pastor of the Concord Baptist Church of Christ in Bedford-Stuyvesant, a neighborhood in Brooklyn, New York.

Tidwell, Josiah Blake (1870–1946): a Southern Baptist biblical scholar and educator. Tidwell founded the modern religion department at Baylor University in 1910.

Townsley, Frances E. (1849–1909): one of the first women ordained by Northern Baptists in America (1885). Townsley served a church in Fairfield, Nebraska, and later preached throughout the state.

Truett, George Washington (1867–1944): a Southern Baptist pastor and denominational leader. Truett served the First Baptist Church of Dallas, Texas, from 1897 until 1944. He held leadership positions among Baptists in Texas, the Southern Baptist Convention, and the Baptist World Alliance.

Willard, Dallas (1935–2013): a Baptist pastor and professor. Willard taught philosophy at the University of Southern California from 1965 until 2013. His religious writings focused on spiritual formation.

Scripture Index

Subject Index